Tolley's Guide to Self-Assessment

Eighth Edition

by Tim Sewell MA (Oxon) Solicitor
from an original text by
Peter Gravestock FCA FTII ATT
with contributions from
William Heard BA (Hons)

Tolley
LexisNexis™

Members of the LexisNexis Group worldwide

United Kingdom	Butterworths Tolley, a Division of Reed Elsevier (UK) Ltd, Halsbury House, 35 Chancery Lane, LONDON, WC2A 1EL, and 4 Hill Street, EDINBURGH EH2 3JZ
Argentina	Abeledo Perrot, Jurisprudencia Argentina and Depalma, BUENOS AIRES
Australia	Butterworths, a Division of Reed International Books Australia Pty Ltd, CHATSWOOD, New South Wales
Austria	ARD Betriebsdienst and Verlag Orac, VIENNA
Canada	Butterworths Canada Ltd, MARKHAM, Ontario
Chile	Publitecsa and Conosur Ltda, SANTIAGO DE CHILE
Czech Republic	Orac sro, PRAGUE
France	Editions du Juris-Classeur SA, PARIS
Hong Kong	Butterworths Asia (Hong Kong), HONG KONG
Hungary	Hvg Orac, BUDAPEST
India	Butterworths India, NEW DELHI
Ireland	Butterworths (Ireland) Ltd, DUBLIN
Italy	Giuffré, MILAN
Malaysia	Malayan Law Journal Sdn Bhd, KUALA LUMPUR
New Zealand	Butterworths of New Zealand, WELLINGTON
Poland	Wydawnictwa Prawnicze PWN, WARSAW
Singapore	Butterworths Asia, SINGAPORE
South Africa	Butterworths Publishers (Pty) Ltd, DURBAN
Switzerland	Stämpfli Verlag AG, BERNE
USA	LexisNexis, DAYTON, Ohio

A CIP Catalogue record for this book is available from the British Library.

ISBN 0 75451 204-5

Typeset by Kerrypress Ltd, Luton, Beds
Printed and bound by Bookcraft (Bath) Ltd, Midsomer Norton, Avon

Visit Butterworths LexisNexis *direct* at www.butterworths.com

Preface to the Seventh Edition

When self-assessment was introduced by the *Finance Act 1994*, this represented the first step in the change in the UK tax system. Increasingly the responsibility for taxation is with the taxpayer rather than the Revenue. The taxpayer must notify, complete a tax return, compute tax liabilities and pay all without Revenue intervention. This has been extended to cover Limited Companies.

In addition to those changes, which gave rise to administrative savings to the Revenue, it has always been the intention that there should be a robust enquiries procedure.

Administratively, the first few years of self-assessment has been more time consuming than anticipated and accordingly the number of full enquiries undertaken by the Revenue reduced. That is now changing and it must be anticipated that there will be significant numbers of full enquiries in coming years.

All taxpayers and advisors must ensure that records are maintained and returns submitted against the relevant time limits. The taxpayer or his advisor must be prepared to justify the decisions taken within the return and figures shown on the return whenever challenged by the Revenue.

To recognise the change in emphasis from understanding computational matters to the increased likelihood of an investigation, I am pleased that Will Heard has brought his experience on enquiries and enforcement powers to the publication.

Peter Gravestock, FCA FTII ATT
Will Heard, BA (Hons)
West Midlands
July 2000

Preface to the Eighth Edition

It is always an intimidating prospect to take over the reins of an established handbook. Since it was first published, the Guide to Self-Assessment under the authorship of Peter Gravestock (latterly with the help of Will Heard) has proved itself a popular yet authoritative text on the self-assessment regime. In this eighth edition, I have retained the structure which made the book so successful and contented myself with updating where necessary. In building on these existing foundations, I obviously owe a great debt to the original authors and I would like to acknowledge that debt here.

In their preface to the seventh edition, Peter Gravestock and Will Heard emphasised the increasing importance of the role of the enquiry in the self-assessment process. This has proved prophetic. October 2000 saw the publication of Income Tax Self Assessment Enquiries, a collaborative research study carried out by the Chartered Institute of Taxation and the Revenue, which looked sometimes critically at the way enquiries worked in practice. As a result of this study, the *Finance Act 2001* has made several major changes to the enquiries procedure. These changes are discussed fully in Chapter 13, although it has to be said that at present their significance remains to be seen.

The other main practical change since the last edition is that the Revenue has completely overhauled some of the self-assessment forms. For instance, in the Self-Employment pages of the tax return, almost all of the box numbers have altered. This may seem trivial, but one of the strengths of the Guide has been its willingness to engage with the mundane yet often complex task of filling in the forms. This process after all is at the heart of the self-assessment concept.

The law is stated as at 1 October 2001.

Tim Sewell,
MA (Oxon) Solicitor
Surrey
October 2001

Contents

Contents

Contents

Contents

Chapter 1

Introduction

1.1   Income tax was originally introduced by Pitt. This was in the Budget speech on 3 December 1798, a speech that lasted an hour. The measure was unpopular and yielded a very small amount of money, under £6 million in the first year. Thus in April 1802 Addington repealed the original income tax.

The abolition lasted as long as the peace with France and when hostilities recommenced in May 1803 the Budget of that year introduced what was called 'a separate tax on property'. Although passed under the title *Property Duty Act*, it was in fact income tax in another form and laid the foundations of the Schedular system. Many of the basic principles established in those early years are still with us today.

1.2   The preceding year basis of assessment for the self-employed was introduced by Winston Churchill in 1926. On many occasions since that time attempts were made to change the basis of assessment applied to the profits of the self-employed and certain other income, from preceding year basis to current year basis, without success.

The increasing numbers of self-employed, rising from under two million in 1979 to over four million in 1994, together with changing work patterns and the anticipated growth in home working, put the preceding year basis of assessment under strain. Although the rules were well known to taxation advisors, they often remained a complete mystery to many clients.

With the growth of the number of self-employed persons, the percentage of those taxpayers using professional advisors declined, such that the Inland Revenue found that it had to compute the assessments in many instances. It is estimated that approximately one half of the self-employed do not have professional advisors.

1.3   Before 1944 the yield from employees was comparatively low. This was due in part to a system that required tax to be paid twice yearly by the employed person. Accordingly, the PAYE system was introduced by the *Income Tax (Employments) Act 1943* with effect from 1944/45. The yield almost doubled following the introduction of PAYE. The system did not require the employee to make direct payments to the Revenue but imposed the obligation upon the employer to deduct tax at source. As a result, for the vast majority of taxpayers it was no longer necessary to file a completed tax return each year.

1.4 *Introduction*

1.4 With the increased pressure upon the government to be more efficient, it had not gone unnoticed that in the US the same number of revenue offices collect many times the amount of tax collected in the UK from three times as many people.

The administrative costs of the Revenue computing and issuing assessments was compounded by the failure of the average taxpayer to submit accounts timeously. As a result many assessments were issued in estimated figures against which the taxpayer had to appeal. Of those appeals, a significant number were listed for hearing before the General Commissioners and were no more than delay hearings.

1.5 Parliament therefore decided to undertake a radical restructuring of the UK taxation system. The onus to compute and notify a liability to tax was moved from the Revenue to the individual or trustee. As with all self-assessment systems, this is backed by an effective penalty regime and is monitored by the Revenue, with powers of random audit known as 'enquiry'.

Because self-assessment requires an understanding of the basis of assessment by the taxpayer, it was felt that the previous system of assessment, based upon profits arising in a preceding year, should be replaced by a simpler system.

The original consultation proposals did offer simple solutions, but unfortunately those proposals would have led to inequity in many instances. After lengthy consultation, the *Finance Act 1994* introduced legislation that is fair, but not necessarily simple.

It is clear that the legislator required a system that significantly reduced the possibility of tax avoidance. This has been done by ensuring that the profits that will be taxed for any business, or for any other source, will exactly equal the amount earned. By contrast, the preceding year basis of assessment for the self-employed could result in greater, or lesser, profits being assessed over the life of the business than those actually earned.

In drafting the new legislation, care was taken to ensure that, within reason, a taxpayer can choose whichever accounting date he wishes, and that he can change that accounting date at any time, giving maximum consideration to commercial requirements.

A final problem was that in the UK, traditionally, not all taxpayers have been required to submit a tax return. To incorporate proposals that every taxpayer must submit a tax return each year would have significantly increased the Revenue's collection costs. The reason that the UK can manage without tax returns from all taxpayers is that a significant proportion of the tax yield is collected by way of PAYE from employed persons and by deduction at source. These provisions continue substantially unaltered. However, under self-assessment it is necessary for the taxpayer to notify new sources of income and liability to higher rate tax at an earlier stage.

1.6 The UK tax system for individuals and trusts changed to a self-assessed basis with effect from 1996/97. If the taxpayer wishes the Revenue to assist with the calculation of the liability they will do so, and, providing the taxpayer submits his or her tax return by 30 September after the end of the tax year, will issue a statement showing the due dates for payment of that liability. The change was accompanied for the self-employed by a move from the preceding year basis of assessment to a current year basis. This applied from 1997/98, with a transitional year in 1996/97.

As a result of the above changes, the previous concept of taxing partnerships, with a joint and several liability to each partner, changed from 1997/98 to self-assessment upon the individual partners. The partnership continues to submit a return, together with a statement dividing income from all sources between the partners. The individual partner is responsible for computing his own self-assessment and for paying his own tax.

The current year basis of assessment applied to all new businesses commencing on or after 6 April 1994.

Although the PAYE system will collect the correct amount of tax from most employees it is the responsibility of each and every taxpayer to ask for a tax return if he has a liability to tax on income that is not taxed at source, or a liability to higher rate tax from income other than employment. In addition, for all taxpayers, new sources of income must be notified to the Revenue against a strict time limit, and for the first time there is a statutory requirement to maintain the records needed for the completion of a tax return. Any taxpayer receiving a tax return is obliged to compute his liability to tax by 31 January following the end of the fiscal year (or three months after receipt of a tax return if later), or to submit the return to the Revenue by 30 September following the end of the tax year (or two months after receipt of tax return if later), in order that the Revenue may compute the tax due on behalf of the taxpayer.

Everyone who gets a tax return will need to enter figures for income, gains, reliefs and deductions. For example, an employed person cannot write 'per PAYE' or 'per P11D' on the return; the actual figure must be included in the return.

1.7   The new regime moved the responsibility for the computation of the correct tax liability from the Inland Revenue to the taxpayer. However, the operation of the PAYE system means that the vast majority of employees will not have noticed a change to the tax system other than when they receive a self assessment tax return for completion. Most employees will, however, receive more documents from their employer relating to their tax affairs which they are obliged to keep, together with coding notices issued by the Inland Revenue.

1.8   With effect for accounting periods ending on or after 1 July 1999 self-assessment for limited companies was introduced. This change built on the previous 'pay and file' regime. The legislation for companies is substantially the same as for individuals, but with a filing requirement of twelve months after the end of the accounting period. The penalty regime of 'Pay and File' was retained. New legislation was also introduced for payments on account for companies paying corporation tax at the full rate. The self-assessment includes tax payable on loans to participators. [*ICTA 1988, s 419*]. There is no provision for the Revenue to compute the liability on the behalf of the taxpayer. [*FA 1998, s 117, Schs 18 and 19; FA 1999*].

1.9   The above measures are considered in detail in the following chapters.

1.10   The introduction of self-assessment has also brought with it fundamental changes in the way that the Inland Revenue examines tax returns. Revenue officers now have the ability to pick cases at random for 'full review' without pre-existing information leading them to believe that the return is incorrect. This means that cases can be selected purely at random or on pre-determined lines laid down at national and local level. For example the self-assessment return has been designed firstly to ensure that the taxpayer determines his own tax bill on completion and secondly to be processed by computer. Consequently all business information has to be put on the return in a uniform manner so enabling the computer to be programmed to select cases for examination based on defined selection criteria.

Revenue officers now have the power to require taxpayers to supply information under a time limit and the threat of a fine if they fail to do so. Consequently the turnover of review cases is expected to increase as well as the average 'take' from each case. However, safeguards have been built into the system to counter the overbearing use of these new powers. Taxpayers now have a right to refer the actions of Revenue officers to the General or Special Commissioners and ask them to justify their actions to the Commissioners. The taxpayer may invoke these powers at any time during the process of review of the return by the Revenue officer. Time will tell whether these safeguards will be as effective in practice as those powers designed to ensure greater compliance with tax law.

Chapter 2

Self-Assessment

The previous procedure

2.1 The UK tax system had been based upon the premise that the Inland Revenue would assess the taxpayer. There was an obligation for the taxpayer to report sources of income to the Revenue, and the Revenue would normally issue a tax return on which the quantum of the income could be declared to the Revenue source by source. Having received such information, the Revenue would assess the taxpayer. It was the duty of the Inspector to raise an assessment based upon the details of income provided to him, but if it appeared to him that the return was incomplete or incorrect, or that a return had not been made, then he would assess income to tax to the best of his judgment.

The present system — Self-assessment

2.2 Under self-assessment, the prime responsibility for assessment (i.e. computation of tax due) was moved to the taxpayer. With that change, the need for the Inland Revenue to issue a notice before the taxpayer had a legal liability to account for tax due was removed. Therefore interest now runs automatically, on the tax eventually quantified as payable, from the normal due date to the actual date of payment.

The Schedular system is retained as the basis for quantifying the income liable to tax, but the taxpayer has one tax reference, and submits all details to only one tax office.

Certainty as to liability is only available after the end of the period in which the Revenue can open an enquiry (subject to any subsequent discovery by the Revenue).

A taxpayer is now required to file his tax return by 31 January following the end of the fiscal year. The return is in many parts. The 'tax return' itself contains a series of questions about income, capital gains, charges and allowances. This is supported by supplementary pages, setting out the detail, and where appropriate by 'Help Sheets' giving specific guidance. Further notes are provided in the 'tax return guide' and a 'tax calculation guide' with a pro forma to calculate the tax payable. All items are shown for the actual fiscal year in question, or on a current year basis. From the information contained in the return, the taxpayer or Revenue can compute the tax liability for the year of assessment, and the amounts payable (or repayable) on 31 January following the end of the fiscal year.

2.3   If the taxpayer wishes the Revenue to compute his tax liability, then he should tick the 'no' box at question 18 ('Do you want to calculate your tax?'). In these circumstances, the return should be filed by 30 September following the year of assessment. Although the Revenue may be requested to compute the tax liability, they are undertaking the task effectively as agents for the taxpayer, and the resultant computation is still known as a 'self-assessment'.

Accordingly, the responsibility for the assessment moves from the Inland Revenue to the taxpayer.

Administration

Payment dates

2.4   Any income tax or Class 4 national insurance liability becomes due by 31 January following the end of the year of assessment, insofar as it has not been paid by deduction, covered by tax credits or met by payments on account.

In the case of capital gains tax, the liability becomes due on 31 January following the end of the year of assessment.

2.5   For income tax and Class 4 national insurance, payments on account will normally be required. The actual liability of the preceding year will be used as the basis of the payments on account. The liability for this purpose is the amount assessed in the preceding year, less amounts deducted at source including notional tax credits, tax credits, subcontractors' tax credits and deductions under PAYE (increased by any amount, to be deducted in subsequent years, and reduced by any amounts for earlier years included in the coding notice). There is no adjustment for changing levels of income or tax rates and allowances.

The payments on account will be 50% of the relevant figure payable on 31 January in the year of assessment, together with 50% of the relevant amount payable on 31 July following the end of the year of assessment.

A payment on account will not be required if:

(a)   the tax deducted at source is more than 80% of the total income tax and Class 4 national insurance payable; or
(b)   the total amount payable in the previous year is less than £500.

There are provisions to enable the taxpayer to reduce the payments on account if he believes that his liability for the current year will be less than in the preceding year.

2.6   When the actual tax liability for the year is computed, the balance of the tax payable, or repayable, will be due on 31 January following the end of the year of assessment.

Interest will be charged on all late payments, and repayment interest will be paid on any overpayments of tax from the actual date of payment.

For further details see Chapter 4 below.

Enforcement

2.7   There will be automatic penalties for failure to file a tax return by the due date. Furthermore, any tax unpaid 28 days after the filing date for the tax return will be subject to a surcharge of 5%. That surcharge increases to 10% if tax is unpaid six months after the relevant filing date. See Chapter 12 below.

Corrections to returns

2.8   Where exceptionally a taxpayer does not have the full information needed to complete his tax return by the relevant filing date, he will be required to enter a provisional figure. Tax will be due on that provisional figure on the normal payment date. When the information is available to complete the return, the taxpayer must correct the assessment. This must be done at the earliest possible date and in any event within twelve months of the latest filing date. Interest will then be charged on the additional tax due from the normal due date to the date of payment, or repayment interest will be paid on the tax repayable, from the date of payment to the date of repayment. Surcharges and penalties will not apply.

A taxpayer will be able to correct his tax return at any time in the period of twelve months from the normal filing date. [*TMA 1970, s 9ZA, 12ABA*]. The Revenue will be able to correct a tax return for obvious errors in a period of nine months from the date on which the return is actually filed. [*TMA 1970, s 9ZB(1), 12ABB(1)*]. The taxpayer may give notice rejecting the correction before the end of the period of 30 days beginning with the date of the issue of the notice of correction. [*TMA 1970, s 9ZB(4), (5), s 12ABB(4), (5)*].

Enquiries into a return

2.9   The Revenue have the power to enquire into any tax return, including partnership returns, estate and trust returns, pension scheme returns and corporation tax returns. If the Revenue wish to exercise this power, they must give a formal notice in writing to the taxpayer within one year of the filing date. This period is extended if the taxpayer is late in filing his tax return. After such a notice has been given, the taxpayer may still make an amendment to his tax return under *TMA 1970, s 9ZA* but the amendment will not take effect until the enquiry is concluded (see 2.41).

If a taxpayer believes that an enquiry should not have been undertaken, or is being continued unreasonably, he can ask the General Commissioners to issue a notice requiring the Revenue to close the enquiries. When the Revenue has completed its enquiries, it must issue a formal closure notice to the taxpayer. After such a notice has been issued, it will not be possible for the Revenue to conduct further enquiries into that tax return, unless there is a 'discovery'. For further details see Chapter 13 below.

Determination of tax where no return delivered

2.10 If a taxpayer does not file his tax return, then the Revenue will have powers to issue a determination. The tax shown on such a determination will be payable without appeal and no postponement of tax will be possible. The determination will be superseded when the tax return and self-assessment are filed. See Chapter 12 below.

Discovery

2.11 The legislation introduced provisions relating to discovery. In simple terms, a discovery assessment is only possible if there has been fraud, negligent conduct or inadequate disclosure by the taxpayer. See Chapter 12 below.

Tax district

2.12 Under the new system, each taxpayer has only one tax district and one tax reference. Having arrived at the quantum of the assessable income by using the Schedular System, all income is aggregated, less charges and allowances, to arrive at one liability. The taxpayer will file his self-assessment at his tax district and pay to the relevant tax accounts office.

Time limits

2.13 Most time limits have been brought into line with the filing date of 31 January following the year of assessment. [*TMA 1970, s 43(1); FA 1996, s 135, 21 Sch*]. The general time limit is five years from the 31 January following the year of assessment, i.e. for 2000/01 the filing date will be 31 January 2002 with the normal time limit for claims being 31 January 2007. Many claims have a time limit of one year after the normal filing date, i.e. 31 January 2003 in the above example. In the case of fraud or negligent conduct, the latest date for assessment will be 20 years from the 31 January following the tax year, i.e. 31 January 2022 for 2000/01. When a taxpayer dies, assessments must be issued within three years of the 31 January following the fiscal year of death, i.e. for a death on 6 May 2000 (2000/01), the latest date is 31 January 2005.

In the case of a company the general time limit is six years from the end of the accounting period. However most claims must be made in a tax return, or an amendment to a return. Normally a return is required within twelve months of the end of the accounting period and amendments within twelve months of the latest filing date. Claims for capital allowances and group relief can only be made in a return, or amendment to a return.

Tax returns for individuals

2.14 The tax return covers one fiscal year. All details shown thereon relate to the same period.

Tax returns will not be issued automatically to all taxpayers. Returns will be issued to all taxpayers who are known to require a tax return, i.e. anyone who is self-employed, who has a higher rate tax liability or who is likely to be a special case, e.g. directors, pensioners, or those likely to receive a tax repayment.

The format of the tax return is that there are eight standard pages, plus supplementary pages added by the Inland Revenue as necessary.

The main return requires a yes/no answer to 21 questions. It is essential that all questions are answered. Question 22 requests additional personal details, e.g. forenames, national insurance number, marital status, telephone number, date of birth. Question 23 gives additional information for specific items and Question 24 is the declaration requiring the taxpayer to tick to show which additional supplementary pages have been added. The return then requires a signature.

Where the Revenue believe that the taxpayer requires supplementary pages, these will be included. However, in many instances a taxpayer will need to request additional sheets by contacting the tax office, or by phoning the order line on 0845 9000 404 (or by fax on 0845 9000 604 or on e-mail saorderline.ir@gtnet.gov.uk or by post from PO Box 37, St Austell, PL25 5YN). A separate set of supplementary pages is required for each employment, each sole trade, and each partnership.

The supplementary pages cover:

(a) employment (Question 1);
(b) share schemes (Question 2);
(c) self-employment (Question 3);
(d) partnership (full) (Question 4);
(e) partnership (short) (Question 4);
(f) land and property (Question 5);
(g) foreign (Question 6);
(h) trusts and estates (Question 7);
(i) capital gains (Question 8); and
(j) non-residence (Question 9).

After completing the necessary supplementary pages, the taxpayer must also add details of the actual amounts received during the fiscal year from:

(a) income from UK savings and investments (Question 10);
(b) UK pensions and social security benefits (Question 11);
(c) gains on UK life insurance policies (Question 12); and
(d) any other income (Question 13).

A claim is required for:

(a)   relief for pension contributions (Question 14);
(b)   reliefs and deductions (Question 15); and
(c)   allowances other than single personal allowance (Question 16).

The return then deals with whether the taxpayer is liable to make student loan repayments (Question 17).

The return will also show:

(a)   tax due and payments on account (Question 18);
(b)   repayment authorities (Question 19);
(c)   any tax refunded relating to the year (Question 20); and
(d)   confirmation of personal details (Question 21).

In addition to the return, a taxpayer will receive a tax return guide and a tax calculation guide. In the case of partnership, a partnership tax return guide will be issued. At the last count there were 64 additional help sheets available for individuals plus special notes for ministers of religion and members of Lloyds.

Also, since April 2000, the Revenue has provided an internet service for self-assessment that allows most individuals to send their self-assessment tax returns electronically. From late August 2001, the service has been extended to allow agents to send certain clients' returns over the Internet. To take advantage of this service, the taxpayer must register at the Government Gateway through the Revenue's website at www.inlandrevenue.gov.uk.

The Revenue is providing only a limited number of forms online for the 2000/01 tax return (the core eight page tax return, employment and self-employment pages) in an application called SA Online. However, there is also a variety of commercial products available which have been tested by the Revenue and can be found at the Revenue's Software and Online forms page. Some of the products are free and some offer supplementary pages beyond those provided by the Revenue. As the SA Online forms are open to a wider audience, the Revenue is not providing software on a CD-ROM as it did for last year's tax return. Neither is the £10 'discount' (offered last year to taxpayers using the Internet service) available for 2000/01.

In addition, a taxpayer may submit his return by using the Revenue's Electronic Lodgement Service (ELS).

Where a taxpayer submitted his return in a previous year by using the Electronic Lodgement Service, or his agent used an approved substitute form, then for subsequent years the Revenue will not issue a full tax return. Instead the taxpayer will receive a one page Notice to Complete a Tax Return. A full paper return is then available from the tax office if required.

Agents will be supplied with a small stock of supplementary pages and spare tax returns on request to the order line (0845 9000 404). Photocopies of supplementary pages are acceptable provided that the taxpayer's name and unique tax reference (UTR) are added to the photocopied page.

Filing dates

2.15 Where a return is issued in the normal way, the taxpayer will be required to file the tax return by 31 January following the end of the tax year. [*TMA 1970, s 8(1A)(a)*]. There will be an automatic penalty for failure to meet that deadline.

Where a return is issued after 31 October, then the normal filing date will be three months from the date on which the return is issued. [*section 8(1A)(b)*].

If a taxpayer does not wish to work out his own tax liability, then the return must be filed by 30 September. If the return is issued after 31 July, then it must be filed within two months of the date of issue, if the Revenue are to compute the self-assessment. [*TMA 1970, s 9(2)*].

If a taxpayer submits a tax return without self-assessment after the dates mentioned above, i.e. 30 September or two months after the date of issue, then the Revenue will attempt to assess the taxpayer by the due date for payment. If they fail to issue a computation by that time, then interest will run from the normal due date of payment, notwithstanding that the taxpayer will not know his liability at that time because the Revenue has been unable to quantify the liability. Furthermore, a surcharge may also apply to any unpaid tax 28 days after the due date for payment even though the taxpayer has not received notification of actual liability by that time.

Taxpayers who are employed will wish to file by 30 September so that, if the tax due is under £2,000, it can be collected by way of amendments to the following year's PAYE code. For returns filed after September, the taxpayer will have to settle any outstanding amount on the following 31 January.

Notification of sources of income

2.16 To ensure that the Revenue issues tax returns to all relevant taxpayers, the period of time for notification of new sources of income is six months from the end of the relevant year of assessment, i.e. for income sources arising in 2001/02, notification will be due by 6 October 2002. [*TMA 1970, s 7*].

The above requirement is not applied where there are no chargeable gains and income is subject to deduction of tax at source to meet the full liability. There is however a liability to notify the Revenue by 5 October following the end of the year if a higher rate liability arises due to the receipt of investment income taxed at source. In the same way a liability to notify arises if a new source of untaxed interest is received.

2.17 If the taxpayer fails to notify the Revenue by 5 October following the end of a fiscal year, then he will be liable to a penalty, not exceeding the net tax unpaid by 31 January, following the year of assessment.

Example

2.18 John commenced self-employment on 1 June 2000. He did not give notice of chargeability for the year 2000/01 by 5 October 2001. His accountant gave notice to the Revenue on 12 December 2001. John paid £2,000 on account of his tax liability on 30 January 2002. His eventual liability for that year was £4,200. John will be liable to a penalty of an amount not exceeding £2,200 plus interest on late paid tax. See also Chapter 11 below.

2.19 It should be noted that it is quite possible that notification of a source will be required before the first accounting date, e.g. Jane commenced trading on 1 January 2001 making her accounts up to 31 December 2001. The source will therefore commence in the fiscal year 2000/01 and notification will be required by 5 October 2001. It is quite possible that the professional advisor will not be asked to act until after the end of the first trading year. By that time, the notification date will have passed and in practice it may be that the date for payment, in the above example 31 January 2002, will also have passed. The new client will therefore commence with a tax liability that is increased by interest, surcharges and penalties.

Records

2.20 The legislation has introduced a requirement to keep records for income tax. This is *TMA 1970, s 12B* (inserted by *FA 1994, 19 Sch 3*) which applies from 1996/97 onwards.

All taxpayers are required to retain all records that have been used to complete their tax returns. Such records must be kept until one year after the normal filing date, or, if the return is filed late, one year after the quarter date following the filing date. [*section 12B(1)(b), (2)(b)*]. For this purpose the quarter dates are 31 January, 30 April, 31 July and 31 October.

Example

2.21 Joyce files her tax return for 2001/02 on 3 January 2003. The normal filing date is 31 January 2003, so that records for that year must be maintained until 31 January 2004.

Example

2.22 Jason files his tax return for 2000/01 on 2 May 2002. The normal filing date was 31 January 2002, so that records must be maintained until one year after the quarter date following the date of filing (i.e. the date of filing is 2 May 2002, the next quarter date is 31 July 2002, and the records for 2000/01 must be maintained until 31 July 2003).

It should be noted that the above dates correspond to the last date that the Revenue can commence enquiries into a tax return. If the Revenue opens an enquiry, then the records must be maintained until the enquiry is completed.

2.23 In the case of a person carrying on a trade, profession or business, or engaged in the letting of property, all tax records must be maintained for five years from 31 January following the year of assessment, e.g. Jacqueline is in business, she must maintain her records for the period of account ending in the fiscal year 2000/01 until five years after 31 January 2002, i.e. until 31 January 2007. [*section 12B(2)(a)*].

The records to be kept by traders include records of all amounts received and expended in the course of trade, including evidence relating to the receipts and expenditure, e.g. all sales and purchase and expense invoices. The records maintained must include supporting documents, i.e. accounts, books, deeds, contract vouchers, receipts, etc. The documents (with certain exceptions) need not be maintained in their original form but they must be in a form that is admissible as evidence. [*section 12B(3)(4)*]. Failure to comply with this section will usually give rise to a penalty not exceeding £3,000. [*section 12B(5)*].

Partnership returns

2.24 From 1997/98, for those partnerships that were existing businesses at 5 April 1994, and from 1994/95 for new partnerships, each partner is personally liable to tax on his share of the profits based upon the allocation in the relevant accounting period.

2.25 However, each partner is not required to agree his own share of the partnership profits with the Revenue. Instead the Revenue will issue a partnership return to a nominated partner. [*TMA 1970, s 12AA*]. That partner will submit details of the partnership profits to the Revenue. If the nominated partner is no longer available, the partners may nominate a successor.

Thus the partnership will only deal with one tax office. Having submitted details of the partnership assessment in respect of income from all sources, and the division of that income between the partners in accordance with the profit-sharing ratio of the accounting period, that information will be passed to the individual partners for inclusion in their own tax returns.

It is not possible for each partner to agree his separate share of partnership profits with the Revenue, but it is possible to have a personal expense claim included within the partnership statement to arrive at the tax payable by the partner personally.

2.26 The Revenue will issue a partnership return, which must be filed and must include details of:

(a) income from land and property (Question 1);
(b) foreign income (Question 2);
(c) trading income (Question 3);
(d) chargeable gains (Question 4);
(e) details of partners who are companies or non-resident (Question 5);
(f) details of European economic interest groupings (Question 6);
(g) any other income including interest (Question 7);
(h) confirmation of personal details (Question 8);
(i) telephone reference (Question 9);
(j) details of provisional figures (Question 10); and

(k)   confirmation of contents of form, of pages used and declaration (Question 11).

If the partnership has not notified the Revenue of the name of the partner to receive the return on behalf of the partnership, then the Revenue may issue a notice to make a return to any or all of the partners individually. [*TMA 1970, s 12AA(3)*].

The time limit for filing the partnership return is 31 January following the year of assessment [*section 12AA(4)*], although in practice it is necessary to file the return before that date, so that the information may be passed to the individual partners for inclusion within their own returns. The normal penalty of £100 for failure to file by the due date (increasing to £200 after six months) applies to the partnership return as well as to the individual returns [*section 93A(2), (4)*], and the Commissioners may impose further penalties not exceeding £60 per day. [*section 93A(3)*]. The penalty will be charged on each individual partner for the failure to file the partnership return. The penalty will not be reduced by reference to any tax liability as the partnership does not have a liability itself.

2.27   If the partnership includes a company, the return date is the later of:

(a)   twelve months from the end of the relevant period of account;
(b)   three months after the date of issue; or
(c)   31 January following the end of the fiscal year (providing at least one partner is an individual). [*section 12AA(4), (5)*].

Partnership statement

2.28   The return must be accompanied by a partnership statement. [*TMA 1970, s 12AB*]. The statement contains up to 30 boxes and is available in two formats. If the partnership only has trading income together with taxed interest, the short version may be used. Otherwise the full version must be completed.

The partnership statement sets out details of:

(a)   name, address, tax reference and national insurance number of each partner; and
(b)   date of commencement, or cessation, of being a partner, if during the fiscal year; and
(c)   a division of each partner's share of income, losses, tax credits, etc.

Box 30 of the full statement sets out the total proceeds from disposals of chargeable assets.

Where the partnership has Schedule D Case I income, then the basis of assessment of all untaxed income is determined by the accounting date of the trading source. The untaxed income is treated as arising in a further deemed trade, and overlap relief is computed as for a trade (see Chapter 7 below).

However the overlap relief is only useable on a change of accounting date or when the individual ceases to be a partner (not on the cessation of the deemed trade). [*ICTA 1988, s 111*].

It should be noted that, in the case of an admission of a new partner, it may be that the assessment on the new partner (as an individual) will be based upon a period of account that ends in the following fiscal year. Details of such amounts relating to periods after the end of the partnership accounting date will appear on the following year's partnership statement. Provisional figures must be included in the individual's partnership supplementary pages at box 4.8 for the current year, and then corrected to the actual figures when known.

Amendments to partnership statement

2.29 The legislation includes a power for the partnership to correct its partnership statement at any time up to twelve months after the normal filing date. [*TMA 1970, s 12ABA*]. In the same way, the Revenue may correct the statement in a period of nine months following the date that it is filed with the Revenue. [*TMA 1970, s 12ABB*].

Enquiries into partnership return

2.30 The Revenue can conduct enquiries into a partnership return in the same way that it can conduct enquiries into the returns of individuals. [*TMA 1970, s 12AC*]. If it opens an enquiry into the partnership return, then it will be deemed to have commenced an enquiry into the return of each partner. By contrast, the Revenue can commence an enquiry into the return of an individual partner without opening an enquiry into the return of the partnership. On completion of an enquiry into a partnership, the Revenue must give notice to each individual partner amending that partner's individual return (*section 28B(4)* and see 2.43 below).

Trustees' returns

2.31 The rules relating to individuals set out above will also apply to trustees. They are required to submit tax returns against the same time limits as individuals, and to self-assess in the same way. [*TMA 1970, s 8A*].

A trustee's return will include a statement showing the amounts in which the beneficiaries or settlor is liable to tax, as well as details of the amount upon which the trustees are liable to tax. As with partnerships, the return may be made by a nominated trustee, or the Revenue may give notice to any or all trustees to make returns. The filing date will be as for individuals. All returns issued must be filed by the due date to avoid penalties.

Corporation tax returns

2.32 Self-assessment legislation similar to that applying to individuals has been introduced for limited companies with effect from accounting periods ending on or after 1 July 1999. The legislation is based upon self-assessment for individuals but retains certain aspects of the corporation tax pay and file system. The rules can be found in *Schedule 18* of the *Finance Act 1998*.

A limited company is required to notify chargeability within twelve months of the end of an accounting period, unless a return is issued. The return must be filed within twelve months of the end of the accounting period. There is a penalty of £100 for late delivery rising to £200 after three months and after 18 months to a tax geared penalty of 10% of the tax due. For returns over 24 months late the penalty will be 20% of the tax due. For third and subsequent failures the penalties of £100 and £200 are increased to £500 and £1,000 respectively. [*FA 1998, 18 Sch 17, 18*].

The company must self-assess its tax liability. There is no option for the Revenue to compute the liability on behalf of the company. The tax to be self-assessed will be the corporation tax due plus tax on company loans to participators [*ICTA 1988, s 419*], and any tax due in respect of profits of controlled foreign companies. [*FA 1998, 18 Sch 8(1)*].

The corporation tax liability is due nine months after the end of the accounting period where the company is liable to starting or small company rates, or is in the marginal banding. [*TMA 1970, s 59D(1)*]. For companies paying at the full rate of corporation tax, payments on account will be due in up to four equal amounts payable:

(a) six months and 14 days beginning with the commencement of the accounting period;
(b) nine months and 14 days beginning with the commencement of the accounting period;
(c) twelve months and 14 days beginning with the commencement of the accounting period;
(d) 15 months and 14 days beginning with the commencement of the accounting period with the last instalment always due three months and 14 days after the end of the accounting period. [*Corporation Tax (Instalment Payments) Regulations 1998, SI 1998/3175*].

It should be noted that the liability is based upon the eventually agreed liability for the year; but paid partly during the year. Interest will be chargeable or credited on any under or over payment.

The new system applies with effect for accounting periods ending on or after 1 July 1999 and is phased in over four years.

(a) In the first year 60% of the anticipated liability will be paid under the quarterly rules.
(b) In the second year 72%.
(c) In the third year 88%.
(d) In the fourth year and subsequent periods 100%.

Where a company was previously not liable to make payments on account then, in the first year that the full rate of corporation tax applies, quarterly payments are not required, unless the profits exceed £10 million.

Example — Large company

Accounting period ended 31 December.

Corporation tax payable re year ended 31 December 2001:

14 July 2001	22%	
1 October 2001		28% (y/e 31/12/2000)
14 October 2001	22%	
14 January 2002	22%	
14 April 2002	22%	
14 July 2002		25% (y/e 31/12/2002)
1 October 2002	12%	
	100%	
14 October 2002		25% (y/e 31/12/2002)

A company is not liable to surcharge.

Where no return is submitted the Revenue can issue a Revenue determination as for individuals. Again there is no right of appeal, the determination only being replaced by the filed self-assessment return.

The enquiry procedures for limited companies are very similar to that for individuals (see 2.33 *et seq* below). The Revenue have twelve months from the filing date of the return in which to open an enquiry. Where a return is filed late the twelve-month period runs from the next quarter day. The quarter dates are as for individuals, i.e. 31 January, 30 April, 31 July and 31 October.

Enquiries into tax returns

2.33 The previous principle of in-depth enquiries for the self-employed has been replaced by statutory provisions to enquire into a tax return. [*TMA 1970, ss 9A–9D*]. Because this power is intended to give the Revenue the right to enquire into any tax return, an officer will not have to give a reason for the commencement of an enquiry. However, statutory procedures will have to be followed to open and to close an enquiry.

An enquiry can be made into the return of an individual, a trustee or a partnership. The legislation extends to limited companies with effect from accounting periods ending on or after 1 July 1999. [*FA 1998, Sch 18 part IV*].

2.34 Enquiry must be distinguished from the Revenue's and taxpayer's rights to amend a tax return. The Revenue can amend a tax return to correct any obvious error or mistake in the return. This can include errors of principle, arithmetical mistakes or other obvious mistakes. In the case of a taxpayer, it is his or her right to amend the return for any reason. This will include the correction of figures where provisional figures have been used. This will occur:

(a) where a business commences and profits are not known by the relevant filing date;

(b) when an individual joins a partnership and the accounting date is such that the following year's accounts are needed to compute the current assessable profits;

(c) where the individual was a member of a partnership, and the date of cessation means that accounts will be required for a period of account ending in the following fiscal year (see Chapter 7 below).

2.35 It should be noted that, if a taxpayer is late filing his tax return, then the Revenue's time limit is still nine months from the date of filing the return, whereas the individual's time limit for amending the return remains at one year after 31 January following the year of assessment.

Example

2.36 Jack files his 2000/01 tax return on 1 June 2002. The due filing date for the return was 31 January 2002. The Revenue may amend the return for a period of nine months, i.e. until 1 March 2003, whereas Jack can only amend the return up to 31 January 2003, i.e. twelve months after the normal filing date.

Notification of an enquiry

2.37 If the Revenue decides to enquire into a return, or into an amendment to the return, then they must give written notice to the taxpayer of their intention. If the return was made by the filing date, then the Revenue have twelve months after that date to give notification, i.e. by 31 January in the following year. If the return was late, then the Revenue have twelve months from the quarter date after the date of filing to give notice. The quarter dates are 31 January, 30 April, 31 July and 31 October. [*TMA 1970, ss 9A(1), (2), 12AC(1), (2)*].

Example

2.38 Jack above filed his tax return on 1 June 2002. The following quarter date is 31 July 2002. The Revenue have until 31 July 2003 to issue a notice of enquiry.

2.39 Where the taxpayer amends his tax return after the normal filing date, the Revenue have a power of enquiry into that amendment as though the return had been filed on the date of the amendment.

Example

2.40 Jack, who filed his tax return on 1 June 2002 for 2000/01, amends· that return on 12 December 2002. The quarter date following the date of amendment is 31 January 2003 and the Revenue can therefore issue a notice of enquiry in respect of the amendment at any time up until 31 January 2004.

2.41 As from 11 May 2001, the issue of a notice of intention to enquire into a tax return does not prevent the taxpayer from making an amendment under

TMA 1970, s 9ZA. The amendment cannot restrict the scope of the enquiry but the enquiry officer may take it into account along with other matters arising during the working of the enquiry. The amendment will not take effect until the officer issues the closure notice in relation to the enquiry and not even then if the officer states that he has taken the amendment into account in his own amendments to the taxpayer's tax return or alternatively that he considers that the amendment is incorrect. [*TMA 1970, s 9B*].

Power to call for documents

2.42 When the Revenue have given notice of their intention to enquire into a tax return, the officer conducting the enquiry may at the same time, or at any subsequent time, require the taxpayer to produce such documents as are needed by the Revenue. [*TMA 1970, s 19A*]. Such a notice must be in writing and must specify a time of not less than 30 days by which the taxpayer must produce the documents. It will be noted from above that the taxpayer is required to keep all such documents that are used to complete his tax return for the period of potential enquiry. The taxpayer may produce photocopies or facsimile copies of documents, unless the notice specifies that original documents must be produced. The Revenue can take copies of documents provided to them.

A taxpayer may appeal within 30 days against the notice requiring production of documents. The Commissioners may confirm the notice if it is reasonable, or set it aside. Where there is an appeal, the time limit for production of the documents is 30 days from the determination by the Commissioners.

Amendments whilst enquiry continues

2.43 Whilst the Revenue are conducting enquiries into a taxpayer's return, they will have the power to amend a self-assessment if they believe that the tax shown therein is too low. This is known as a jeopardy amendment. This power will normally only be used if the Revenue believe that a taxpayer will or may dispose of assets, become non-resident, apply for bankruptcy, or be about to be sent to prison. In these circumstances the Revenue may give notice to the taxpayer to amend the return and thereby require the payment of the tax. [*TMA 1970, s 9C*].

In the same way, if an enquiry is opened on a return which shows a repayment due then the repayment (or part thereof) need not be made until the enquiry is completed. [*TMA 1970, s 59B(4A)*].

Conclusion of enquiry

2.44 An enquiry will be complete when the enquiry officer gives notice (known as a 'closure notice') informing the taxpayer that enquiries are complete and giving the Revenue's conclusions. [*TMA 1970, s 28A(1)*].

The closure notice must either state that, in the enquiry officer's opinion, no amendment of the return is necessary or make the amendments to the return required to give effect to the officer's conclusions. [*TMA 1970, s 28A(2)*].

The taxpayer may appeal in writing against any amendment made by the closure notice within 30 days of the closure notice being issued. [*TMA 1970, s 31(1), s 31A(3)*].

The above procedure for ending an enquiry applies where notice of enquiry is given after 11 May 2001 (the date of the passing of the *Finance Act 2001*) or where the enquiry is in progress immediately before that date. Under the previous procedure, the enquiry officer served a 'completion notice' containing his conclusions and where appropriate inviting the taxpayer to amend his own return. In practice the Revenue often issued a standard 'offer' letter setting out the amended tax liability, and invited the taxpayer to agree to their amendments by signing the enclosed 'pro forma' letter, after inserting the Revenue's revised tax liability into the blank space. A completion notice was then not issued. It was understood that the lack of a completion notice, when making an offer to the Revenue, would not place the taxpayer at a disadvantage as to certainty, provided full disclosure had been made. Presumably a similar offer procedure is likely to apply to the new system and it may be that a closure notice will not be issued in every case.

2.45   If a taxpayer believes that the Revenue have no further grounds for enquiry, and should conclude their enquiries, then he can apply to the Commissioners to ask them to direct the Revenue to issue a closure notice within a specified period. [*TMA 1970, s 28A(4)*]. Such a closure notice must include the Revenue's conclusions. The Commissioners must give such a direction unless they are satisfied that the Revenue has reasonable grounds for not issuing a closure notice within the period specified. Such a hearing will be conducted in the same way as an appeal, with both sides being heard and presenting evidence, but with the Revenue having to make the case for the enquiry to remain open.

2.46   Similar provisions apply to partnerships. The closure notice in this case will be directed to the representative partner. Where the closure notice makes amendments to the partnership return, the enquiry officer must also send a notice to each partner affected, amending his or her personal tax return accordingly. [*TMA 1970, s 28B4*].

2.47   The enquiry legislation also applies to limited companies from accounting periods ending on or after 1 July 1999. For further details on enquiries see Chapter 13 below.

Chapter 3

The Tax Return

3.1 The tax return may be filed in its paper form, or may be filed using the electronic lodgement service (ELS). It is also possible to file using the Internet provided only the main return plus employment and/or self employment supplementary pages are used. In future years it is anticipated that the Internet will be the usual form of filing.

Although a taxpayer has a statutory obligation to notify the Inland Revenue of new sources of income, there is no statutory obligation to file a tax return unless a notice has been issued by the Inland Revenue. [*TMA 1970, ss 8, 8A and 12AA; FA 1998, s 117, 18 Sch 3*]. The notice is normally incorporated within the tax return. Where agents file electronically, or use an approved substitute form, then from 6 April 1998 the notice will be a formal document without a return.

The tax return must be fully completed using figures. Failure to answer all of the questions could result in the rejection of the return by the Revenue computer system and the automatic issue of a penalty demand for £100 where the return is not corrected by 31 January following the end of the fiscal year.

The principle to be used is that the returns will be processed, and then at a later date the return will be checked for content.

Any errors that are apparent on processing will result in the Revenue correcting the tax return. These should be mainly arithmetical errors, and simple errors such as failure to complete all of the boxes of a question.

The Revenue will add to the tax return such supplementary pages as they believe necessary. The taxpayer must obtain any further pages that are required, e.g. by phoning the order line on 0845 9000 404 (or by fax on 0845 9000 604, or e-mail (saorderline.ir@gtnet.gov.uk), or in writing to PO Box 37, St Austell, PL25 5YN). This could be because the taxpayer has more than one employment, more than one self-employment, or requires special pages for capital gains, etc. Photocopies of pages will be acceptable.

The return is colour coded to assist ease of completion. This helps to locate the right supplementary pages and help sheets quickly. The colour is not used in the Revenue system and therefore black and white photocopies do not cause concern.

Before completing a tax return, it is advisable to assemble all information that might reasonably be required. Care must be taken in transposing the figures from the prime documents to the return. In many instances only some figures will be required, e.g. from a P60, only details of the net taxable pay for that employment plus the tax deducted from that employment should be entered.

Except when using approved tax software only round pounds are entered on the tax return. Before and after tax amounts are rounded to the whole pound below whereas tax deductions and credits are rounded up. This may mean that the net plus tax does not equal the gross. If a number of similar items are to be entered as one figure, e.g. six bank/building society accounts, then the exact amounts of interest from the six accounts should be added together and only the totals rounded as set out above.

Question 1 — Employment

3.2   If the taxpayer was an employee, office holder, director or agency worker during the year, then supplementary pages in respect of employment are required. A separate page is required for each employment. Although NIL pages need not be submitted, it is advisable to refer to such employments without income in the additional information box.

For 2000/01 onwards, deemed salary attributed to a taxpayer under the personal service legislation (IR35) should also be entered onto employment supplementary pages together with the PAYE paid by the intermediary on behalf of the taxpayer.

The PAYE employer's reference is required as the link in the computer system. This only applies for UK-based employers.

Income from a foreign employment is included on an employment supplementary page. The foreign tax paid will normally be entered on foreign supplementary pages at F3. The reference will be to page E1, the foreign tax paid is entered in column D and the income from box 1.8 is again entered in column E. If tax credit relief is not available then the foreign tax paid is entered at box 1.38.

Before starting it is necessary to obtain some or all of the following documents and information:

(a)   P60 for all employments held in the year.
(b)   P45 (part 1A) for any employments which ceased during the year.
(c)   P11D or P9D for all employments in which a benefit in kind has arisen (for past employments it will be necessary to request a copy of the form from the former employer).
(d)   A summary of business miles travelled together with a note of amounts received from the employer in respect of motoring expenses or FPCS2.
(e)   Notices of coding for the year and also the following year.
(f)   Copies of any notices received showing tax calculations in respect of the employment (including those showing underpayments brought forward, carried forward and, in particular, any repayment notice).
(g)   Details of amounts received other than from the employer, e.g. tips, benefits from third parties and taxed incentive awards.

(h)   Details of amounts received from the employer other than salary, e.g. compensation for loss of office.

(i)   A note of any expenses incurred in carrying out the employment, e.g. union agreed fixed deductions, professional subscriptions and reimbursed expenses shown on form P11D.

(j)   If a private car has been used for business purposes, a note of total mileage, business mileage and loan interest paid on the purchase of the car. Full details of the car will be required, e.g. make, model, cubic capacity, and, if Inland Revenue authorised mileage rates are not being used, total running costs.

(k)   A note of the employee's permanent workplace or base and of duties undertaken elsewhere to determine any allowable claims for travelling and subsistence not reimbursed by the employer.

Employees should be encouraged to maintain records to complete the tax return and to provide evidence to support the above information.

With all of the required information to hand, the total income from employment including tax deducted, together with benefits and expenses, can be entered on page one. Compensation and other taxable lump sums are shown on page two together with foreign earnings not taxable in the UK.

Deductions for expenses (*sections 198–201A* claims) are claimed in boxes 1.32 to 1.35.

Where entries are made for expense claims, it will be good practice to give details in the additional information box of the method of calculation. In the case of a claim for other expenses these again should be specified in the 'white space' provided.

See also Chapter 5 below, and the twelve Revenue help sheets for further assistance in completion of employment supplementary sheets.

Question 2 — Share schemes

3.3   Where benefits arise from share options or share-related benefit schemes, then a supplementary sheet must be completed and reference should be made to the help sheets IR216 'shares as benefits', IR217 'shares acquired: post acquisition charges', IR218 'shares acquired: operation of PAYE' and IR219 'shares acquired from your employment'.

Page one of the supplementary sheet shows a summary of the taxable amounts. Working sheets are provided within the share scheme notes. Details must be provided of approved and unapproved schemes, and of taxable amounts arising where shares are received from the employer. Disposals under the capital gains tax regime must not be included in the supplementary sheets.

In addition a separate copy of page two or page three must be completed in respect of each share option or share acquisition which gave rise to a taxable event during the tax year.

Page S1 is therefore only completed once whereas page S2 or page S3 is required for each event.

Question 3 — Self-employment (sole traders)

3.4   For each trade or profession, and for each accounting period, separate supplementary sheets will be required. The only exception to this basic rule is that where the accounting period is for internal management purposes only and is not to be used as an accounting period for taxation then only accounts to the agreed accounting date are submitted.

The accounting period covered by the supplementary sheet is shown in boxes 3.4 (start of period) and 3.5 (end of period). Any period of account falling partly or wholly within the fiscal year requires completion of Standard Accounting Information (SAI). If the accounts end after the fiscal year box 3.93 should be ticked and an estimate of taxable profits shown at box 3.92. Box 23.3 should also be ticked and details provided in the additional information box 23.6 on page eight of the main return. When accounts are available, SAI boxes must be completed. For any subsequent return period into which the accounting period falls, box 3.10 is ticked and only the adjustment section of the return completed. The full profit for the accounting period being shown at box 3.76 with a deduction at box 3.77 to reduce the profit to the assessable amount to be shown at box 3.83.

Example

Simon commenced business on 1 March 2000 making his first accounts to 30 April 2001.

Tax return 1999/2000

The accounts will be shown on the standard accounting information self-employment pages.

The return will, of course, have been submitted as provisional and then corrected.

The accounting period will be shown as box 3.4 starts 01/03/2000 and box 3.5 ends 30/04/2001.

The basis period will be box 3.71 (box 3.74 for 2000/01) which begins 01/03/2000 and box 3.72 (box 3.75 for 2000/01) which ends 05/04/2000.

The profit in box 3.73 (box 3.76 for 2000/01) will be for the 14-month period.

The deduction in box 3.74 (box 3.77 for 2000/01) will be for the period 06/04/2000 to 30/04/2001.

Tax return 2000/01

Accounting period will be box 3.4 starts 01/03/2000 and box 3.5 ends 30/04/2001.

Box 3.10 will be ticked, meaning SAI detail is blank.

Box 3.74 basis period begins 06/04/2000 and box 3.75 ends 05/04/2001.

Box 3.76 will show '0'.

Box 3.77 will show the profits for the year ended 5 April 2001 (i.e. 12/14 × profits for the 14-month period).

Tax return 2001/02 (assuming 2000/01 box numbers)

Accounting period is again box 3.4 starts 01/03/2000 and box 3.5 ends 30/04/2001.

Box 3.10 is ticked (SAI details left blank).

Basis period is box 3.74 begins 01/05/2000 and ends 30/04/2001.

Box 3.76 will show '0'.

The profits of the year ended 30 April 2001 are shown in box 3.77 (i.e. 12/14 × profits for the 14-month period).

The overlap profit for the period 01/05/2000 to 05/04/2001 is computed and shown in box 3.80.

If, exceptionally, there is a gap between, or overlap of, accounting periods, then box 3.11 must be ticked and an explanation given in the additional information box.

Any permanent change of accounting date should be notified to the Revenue before 31 January following the end of the fiscal year of change and also noted by ticking box 3.12. A second or further change within five years requires the permission of the Revenue. This is noted by ticking box 3.13. (See also Chapter 10.)

The date of commencement (if after 5 April 1998) is shown at box 3.7 and the date of cessation (if before 6 April 2001) at box 3.8. It should be noted that any change from sole trader to partnership, or partnership to sole trader is *NOT* a commencement or a cessation for this purpose.

Where a business is small, i.e. having an annual turnover below £15,000, then only details of turnover, expenses and adjusted profits need be shown on the supplementary sheets. Where a separate computation of adjusted profits has been prepared, the resulting adjusted profits for the accounting period should be entered in box 3.26. As turnover is entered in box 3.24, all of the other figures will fall to be shown in box 3.25. It should be noted that box 3.25 is inclusive of capital allowances. The adjusted profit is then carried forward to box 3.76.

For all other businesses, the standard accounting information on page two of the supplementary sheets must be completed. It is essential that these boxes are completed whether or not accounts are to be forwarded to the Inland

Revenue. If less than three expense boxes have entries then the Revenue computer will reject the return; therefore always analyse over at least three headings.

If the business is not registered for VAT, boxes 3.27 and 3.28 are ignored. If the business is registered for VAT and accounts are prepared on the basis of excluding VAT in accordance with normal accounting principles, then box 3.28 will be ticked. Where the figures shown in the SAI are inclusive of VAT, then the amount paid to Customs and Excise as VAT is shown as an expense in box 3.63, and box 3.27 should be ticked. If the business has received VAT refunds, then they should be included as other income in box 3.50. Where VAT is not excluded from the figures, care must be taken to adjust the VAT payments or refunds for capital items. The calculation of the adjustment should be shown in the additional information box 3.116 on page four of the supplementary sheets.

If the accounts exclude VAT, but the business is partially exempt, then the relevant input tax not claimed for VAT purposes can be included in the expense boxes even though box 3.28 has been ticked.

Care should be taken to indicate that a business has registered for VAT, if this is the case, where turnover exceeds the registration limit of £54,000 (£52,000 until 1 April 2001). Under the joint working initiative, it must be expected that the Revenue would report cases not registered for VAT to their colleagues at Customs and Excise.

When converting accounts to standard accounting information, it is important to be consistent. This is more important than ensuring that the analysis is precisely in line with that suggested by the Inland Revenue. Reference should be made to the self-employment notes (and to help sheet IR224 for farmers) at SEN 2.

Where expenses relate to both business and private activities, it is possible to show the total expenses and then to show the private proportion in the disallowable expense boxes to the left. Alternatively, only the net business expense need be shown in the total expense boxes. Where the second approach is adopted, it would be advisable to disclose the treatment used in the additional information box 3.116 on page four.

Where exceptional items are shown, typically in other expenses at 3.63, then a full analysis of those expenses should be shown in the additional information box. In the same way, if one item of expenditure is out of line with earlier years, e.g. repairs, then an explanation for the unusual level of expenditure should be given in the additional information box.

Because the SAI is a summary of the accounts prepared for the business, it is advisable to ensure that the profit or loss shown in box 3.65 corresponds to that shown on the business accounts. If those accounts include income that is not chargeable under Schedule D Case I or II, such other income should be shown in box 3.50 and then deducted in box 3.71 in arriving at the net business profit for tax purposes in box 3.73.

Capital allowances are computed separately and summarised on page one of the supplementary sheets, with total capital allowances being transferred to box 3.70 and balancing charges to box 3.68.

Only one adjustment section of page three of the supplementary sheets for self-employment should be completed for the fiscal year. Where more than one set of accounts is used and standard accounting information prepared, the adjustment section of the extra sheets must be left blank.

Box 3.74 shows the commencement of the base period and box 3.75 shows the end of the base period.

Example — separate SAI sheets for each period

Supplementary self-employment pages are prepared for each of the accounting periods, e.g.:

1 May 2000 to 30 April 2001; and
1 May 2001 to 31 March 2002.

On the pages for the period 01/05/2000 to 30/04/2001, the adjustment section is left blank.

On the pages for the period 01/05/2001 to 31/03/2002, the adjustment section will be completed showing at 3.74 (commencement) – 01/05/2000 and at 3.75 (end) – 31/03/2002.

If the business commenced in the year, and the first accounts finish before 5 April, then the profits (after capital allowances) relating to the first accounting period will be increased by an estimate of profits for the balance of the period to 5 April by an addition in box 3.77.

Full details of the later accounting period will be filed as a correction to the return. On the subsequent tax return box 3.10 is ticked, the SAI is not completed, '0' is entered into 3.76 and the assessable profits in box 3.77.

Example

Joanna commenced in business on 6 June 1999. Her first accounts were prepared for the year to 5 June 2000 showing profits of £24,000. She included full SAI details on her 1999/2000 tax return. Her assessment for 1999/2000 being for the period 6 June 1999 to 5 April 2000, was £20,000 (i.e. box 3.76 £24,000 less box 3.77 £4,000).

For 2000/01 she need not repeat the information, just tick 3.10, enter '0' in box 3.76 and £24,000 in box 3.77. Overlap relief is then claimed of £20,000 by entry of that amount in box 3.80.

If the business has shown a loss, then that is shown in box 3.84 and the way it is to be used is shown in the following boxes 3.85 to 3.87.

Losses brought forward are shown at 3.88, with any amount used at 3.89.

Any other business income, e.g. business start-up allowance, is shown at box 3.91 to give the total taxable profits from the business for the year at 3.92.

Where an adjustment is made on a change from 'cash basis' or a transitional adjustment over the nine following years is required the amount chargeable is entered into box 3.82. This mainly applies to barristers and other professionals now required to pay tax on a fees earned basis.

Class 4 national insurance is calculated by using the working sheet on page nine of the notes on self-employment. If the taxpayer has more than one business, then the working sheet in help sheet IR220 must be used. It should be noted that if deferment of Class 4 national insurance applies, then box 3.94 is ticked and no entry made at box 3.96. This has the knock-on effect of reducing the total liability payable for the year, which in turn reduces the payment on account for the following tax year. Where, exceptionally, interest can be deducted from Class 4 profits but not from the trading profits, or, more likely, trading losses have occurred in the business in earlier years which have been set off against non-trading income, then an amount equal to the trading losses utilised against non-trading income may be brought forward and deducted at box 3.95.

Where the taxpayer is a foster carer or adult carer and they have special arrangements with the tax office for calculating profits then only the following boxes on the self-employment pages are completed:

(a)   boxes 3.1 to 3.13;
(b)   box 3.92 (profit for year);
(c)   boxes 3.94 to 3.96 (Class 4 NIC).

Where the taxpayer carries on a trade wholly overseas and is only taxed on a remittance basis then the following boxes are completed:

(a)   boxes 3.1 to 3.13;
(b)   boxes 3.74 and 3.75 (basis period);
(c)   box 3.92 (remittances taxable);
(d)   box 3.94 (tick);

relief for foreign tax paid on such profits is claimed on F3 of the foreign supplementary pages.

If the taxpayer is a subcontractor in the construction industry and has borne tax by deduction under the CIS25 scheme, then the total tax deducted in the fiscal year must be shown at box 3.97. Form CIS25 must be sent to the tax office with the tax return unless it has previously been forwarded with an interim claim for repayment computed using form CIS40 (or CIS41 for partnerships).

If a CIS25 is not provided then in the additional information box the following information is required:

—   name and address of the contractor;

— month payment was made to taxpayer;
— amount of gross payment;
— amount of tax deducted.

Any tax refunded during the year on a claim made (using CIS40 or CIS41) must be shown in box 20.1 on page seven of the main return.

Box 3.97 can also be used to claim credit for any PAYE deducted from income treated as taxable under Schedule DI, e.g. when working through an agency. (See Inland Revenue Manual administrative practice SE1226 and ESC A37.)

If accounts have been prepared that include a balance sheet, and turnover is £15,000 per annum or more, the balance sheet summary must be completed. It should be noted that there is no obligation to complete these boxes if a formal balance sheet has not been prepared or if turnover is below £15,000 per annum.

If the balance on the capital account is overdrawn, the end figures will be shown with brackets. In those circumstances care should be taken to ensure that an add-back of bank or other loan interest has been made to reflect the interest that relates to the overdrawn capital account, or if such a calculation is not appropriate, that the reason why is stated in the additional information box.

If capital is introduced, its source should be shown in the additional information box 3.116. If drawings have altered significantly, or include exceptional items, again an analysis is required in the additional information area.

See also Chapter 6 below in connection with the calculation of the adjusted profits and other issues relating to self-employment. Capital allowances are discussed in Chapter 8 and losses in Chapter 9. The implications of changing accounting dates are discussed in Chapter 10. Further information in respect of the transitional provisions relating to 1996/97 only is given in Appendix C.

Question 4 — Partnerships

3.5 For each partnership for which the taxpayer was a member, and for each trade, a separate partnership supplementary sheet will be required. Where that partnership only had income from trading sources or taxed interest, the short version may be used; otherwise, the full version must be used. Before commencing preparation of the supplementary pages, the taxpayer must have in his possession a partnership statement provided to him by the nominated partner of the partnership. If that statement is marked 'full', then a full supplementary page must be used. In the same way, if the details are marked 'short', only the short page is required. It must be noted that only the figures shown on the partnership statement may be shown on the supplementary pages. No alterations are permitted. If the taxpayer needs to have a figure amended, then he must ensure that the partnership amends its return and provides a revised partnership statement to him.

Where an individual commenced in partnership, or ceased to be a member of a partnership during the year, it is possible that the basis of assessment will require accounts that end after the end of the fiscal year. In those circumstances the individual will not receive a partnership statement in time to complete their personal tax return. Accordingly estimates will be required. If no accounting period for the partnership (during the period that the individual was a partner) ends within the fiscal year then '0' should be entered into box 4.7. An estimate of the net profit taxable for the year should then be entered in box 4.8 and 4.13. A tick should also be put into box 23.3 on page eight of the tax return. Because a provisional figure is used, the reason why should be shown in the additional information box 23.6, together with a note of the date by which it is anticipated the return will be corrected

When the figures are eventually available a revised partnership supplementary page will be required. Box 4.7 will still show '0'. Box 4.8 will then show the taxable amount relating to the current fiscal year from accounts ending in the following fiscal year. The correct assessable amount will be then shown at box 4.13, with a '0' in box 4.14 (allowable loss).

Alternatively, if the accounts show a loss, then '0' will be entered into box 4.13 with the loss shown in box 4.14.

In the case of a cessation, where the date of cessation is between the normal accounting date and the following 5 April, the information to the normal accounting date will be included in the return, with an estimate of profits for the balance of the period shown at box 4.8 (and a corresponding deduction for overlap relief used in box 4.10). Again, box 23.3 should be ticked and details of the provisional figure shown in the additional information box at 23.6. When the partnership statement for the subsequent year is available the return must be amended to reflect the actual figure of income for the balance of the period at box 4.8 (and boxes 4.35, 4.42, 4.50, 4.54 or 4.59 as appropriate if other untaxed income has been received).

For changes between sole tradership and partnership, see 7.16 below.

For further details relating to mergers and successions, see 7.13 below.

Question 5 — Land and property

3.6   When a taxpayer receives income from land and property, the supplementary pages relating to land and property must be completed. This includes taxpayers who only receive income from rent-a-room at or below the limit of £4,250, who are only required to tick the 'yes' box on the front of the supplementary pages.

If the income is from furnished holiday lettings then the first page of the land and property supplementary sheets must be completed, not the self-employment sheets. For furnished holiday letting and other land and property income, the statement must be prepared for the fiscal year ending 5 April. It is not possible to complete pages for other dates.

The statement is set out in a similar manner to the self-employment sheets. Income from furnished holiday lettings must be entered at box 5.1. If that figure is less than £15,000, then total expenses should be entered in box 5.7 and in box 5.8 with the resultant net profit (or loss) in box 5.9. Expenses include interest on loans to purchase the property.

Where expenses include private and personal amounts, then an adjustment must be made in box 5.10. It is of course possible to show only the net business expenses in box 5.7, if preferred.

It should be noted that the 10% wear and tear deduction is not available for furnished holiday lettings. The taxpayer may elect to claim capital allowances (box 5.13), or alternatively not to claim any allowance on the purchase of the original items of furniture or furnishings and then to claim a full deduction for replacement costs (box 5.3).

A loss on furnished holiday lettings is to be shown in box 5.15 (with '0' in box 5.14). Such a loss can be offset against other income for the year (box 5.16), or the previous year (box 5.17). It is also possible to offset against gains by making a claim on the form at box 8.5 of the capital gains pages. This is shown in column K2 on page CG3.

If the result is a profit it must be shown in box 5.14 (with a '0' in box 5.15 — losses). That profit must also be shown on the reverse of the form at box 5.19.

All other rent and other income from land and property should be shown at box 5.20, with the exception of premiums on leases treated as rent which should be shown in box 5.22. Any tax deducted from rents, etc. should be shown in box 5.21. If total property income for the year is less than £15,000, then expenses may be shown as one figure in box 5.29 and box 5.30; otherwise the standard accounting information must be provided.

If the income, including balancing charges, from the rent-a-room property exceeds the limit of £4,250, then the total should be shown as rent in box 5.20. Expenses may then be claimed or, alternatively, a deduction of the exempt amount made in box 5.35.

If property is owned and let jointly, then only the relevant share of income and expenses should be included upon the supplementary pages. If the taxpayer receives a share of rent after expenses, then that amount only is included in box 5.20 with no other claims made. In all circumstances, it is necessary to tick box 5.47 to show that the pages include details of property let jointly, and, if appropriate, to show the name and address of the person nominated to keep records in the additional information box 23.6 on page eight of the tax return.

It is necessary to contrast the treatment of property let jointly with partnerships owning property.

As a general rule, if the partnership has trading income, and shows a property within its balance sheet, then a partnership tax return will be required. Income from property must be computed using the accounting period relating to the trade and a partnership statement must be issued to the individual members. Partnership supplementary sheets are then prepared.

By contrast, if the only income source relating to the joint ownership is from property, then land and property sheets will be used with accounts prepared to 5 April for each fiscal year.

In the case of a husband and wife it will be usual to treat property, and other investments, as being held jointly even if a trading partnership exists between the spouses. The exception would be if the property, etc. was shown in the balance sheet of the partnership, when the return would be that of a partnership using the partnership supplementary pages.

Question 6 — Foreign

3.7   If the taxpayer has any taxable income from overseas pensions, benefits, foreign companies, savings, offshore funds, trusts abroad or land and property abroad, or has any gains on foreign life insurance policies, then the foreign supplementary pages must be completed. The taxpayer must also tick or complete page F3, if he wishes to claim tax credit relief for foreign tax paid on foreign income or gains including tax on income shown elsewhere in the return.

The foreign supplementary pages are divided into sections:

(a)   Page F1 is for foreign savings, which are liable to tax at the savings (20%) rate, and foreign dividends, which are liable at the Schedule F (10%) rate.

(b)   Page F2 is for the following:

    (i)   foreign savings taxable on a remittance basis at non-savings rates;

    (ii)   overseas pensions;

    (iii)   overseas partnership income (include in pensions section);

    (iv)   overseas social security benefits;

    (v)   income from land and property overseas;

    (vi)   disposals of offshore funds;

    (vii)   income from overseas trusts or companies; and

    (viii)   overseas chargeable event gains (foreign life insurance policies).

(c)   Page F3 is for claiming tax credit relief for foreign tax paid on employment, self-employment and other income.

(d)   Page F3 also has provision for claiming tax credit relief for foreign tax on chargeable gains.

(e)   Pages F4 and F5 show income from land and property abroad. A separate set of pages is only required if properties are let in more than one country and foreign tax has been deducted.

(f)   Where tax credit relief has been claimed the Tax Credit Relief Working Sheet (TCRWS) should be completed in the foreign notes and the summarised tax credit relief entered into box 6.9 on page F3.

Where income arises from a foreign pension, only 90% is taxable providing the income is assessed on an arising basis. Such a pension is entered on page two in column B as the full amount without deduction. Column D then shows the full foreign tax without deduction, and column E shows 90% of the taxable figure.

If the taxpayer receives income from offshore funds, or income received by a trust that is resident offshore and the settlor is ordinarily resident and may enjoy the income of the trust, then that income should be shown in the relevant part of the tax return. Accordingly:

— income from offshore funds in foreign savings is shown on page F1 with credit for foreign tax claimed;
— income from UK savings and investments is shown at question 10 of the main return;
— the balance of the income, i.e. that chargeable at full rates without tax credits, is shown at box 6.5.

Income from overseas employments should be shown on the employment supplementary pages. Credit can then be claimed for foreign tax by an entry in the first part of page F3 of the foreign supplementary sheets. The reference is page E1. If tax credit for overseas tax is not claimed then the foreign tax should be shown in box 1.38 on the second page of the employment supplementary sheet. That amount is then deductible from income before the tax is calculated.

Further assistance in the completion of the foreign supplementary pages is given in the notes together with help sheets, e.g. IR260 (overlap relief), IR261 (tax credit relief: capital gains) and IR321 (gains on foreign life insurance policies).

Question 7 — Trusts, etc.

3.8   If the taxpayer received any income from trusts, settlements or estates of deceased persons, or if the taxpayer is a settlor and the income of the settlement is to be treated as his for tax purposes (e.g. income is paid to a child under 18 or the settlor or spouse is entitled to capital or income from the settlement), then care must be taken to enter the income into the correct part of the tax return.

If the taxpayer is a beneficiary of a bare trust (i.e. an absolute right to both income and capital), then the income of that trust is included in his tax return as his own income without reference to the trust.

Beneficiaries with an absolute right to income but not capital from a trust should enter into boxes 7.4 to 7.6 income on which tax has been paid at basic rate, into boxes 7.7 to 7.9 income taxed at 20% and into boxes 7.10 to 7.12 income with a dividend tax credit (10%). The taxpayer should exclude from the trust supplementary sheet the following: scrip dividends, foreign income dividends and income from foreign sources. Such amounts should be shown on the main return in boxes 10.21 to 10.23, or on the foreign supplementary pages as appropriate.

Where beneficiaries do not have an absolute right to income from a trust, and the trustees are resident in the UK for tax purposes, then the income is shown in box 7.1 with the tax at the rate applicable to trusts (34%) deducted in box

7.2, giving the gross figure in box 7.3. Where the trustees are not resident in the UK, all entries are made on the foreign pages.

In certain cases, the settlor himself will be taxable on the income from a settlement. This will happen where:

(a) the settlor or his spouse is able to obtain some benefit from the settlement; or
(b) the beneficiaries of the settlement include one or more of the settlor's unmarried children aged under 18 (unless the aggregate amount of the child's relevant settlement income does not exceed £100 in the tax year).

Such income is included as normal income of the settlor within his own return, not on the trust pages. As no deductions are allowed for trust management expenses in such a case, any such deduction must be entered in boxes 13.1 to 13.3 of the main tax return as additional income.

Only income from estates of deceased persons should be shown on the supplementary page. Capital payments, e.g. legacies, should not be included.

Where there is a specific legacy such that the beneficiary is entitled to income from the date of death, then that income should be included as the normal income of the taxpayer, not on the supplementary page for trusts.

Question 8 — Capital gains

3.9 Any disposal of the taxpayer's only or main residence must be shown by ticking the relevant box. However, supplementary pages will not be required to be completed if the gain is fully exempt.

In other cases where there are disposals of chargeable assets in excess of the *de minimis* limit of £14,400 for 2000/01 (£15,000 for 2001/02) or where the total chargeable gain is more than the exempt amount of £7,200 for 2000/01 (£7,500 for 2001/02) then the supplementary pages must be completed. The capital gains pages should also be completed if a claim is made for a capital loss.

Help is given on how to calculate capital gains by way of the notes, together with 22 help sheets (see Appendix B).

The capital gains pages for 2000/01 use a slightly different format from previous versions. The pages are now split into two sections.

If all of the taxpayer's transactions for 2000/01 involve 'quoted shares and other securities' and no taper or other reliefs are being claimed (other than indexation relief), the simple grid on page CG1 can be used. Securities come within the definition of 'quoted shares and other securities' if they were within one of the following categories throughout the period the taxpayer held them:

(a) shares or securities of a company either quoted on the London Stock Exchange Official List (SEDOL) or listed on the Stock Exchange (or on an overseas recognised stock exchange);
(b) unit trusts in a UK authorised unit trust;
(c) shares in a company which was a UK open-ended investment company (OEIC).

If page CG1 is used, page CG8 must also be filled in.

If the taxpayer's transactions involved assets other than 'quoted shares and other securities' (e.g. unlisted shares, land or buildings), or a combination of quoted shares and other assets, the taxpayer must provide more detailed information using pages CG2 and CG3 (and CG4 to CG7 if appropriate). These pages must also be used if the taxpayer is claiming taper and other reliefs (other than indexation allowance). Again, page CG8 must also be filled in.

A description of each asset disposed of is shown in column A of pages CG2 and CG3. The type of transaction is indicated, i.e.:

Q — quoted shares or other rewrites (as defined above);
U — other shares or securities;
L — land and property;
O — other assets, e.g. goodwill.

Column B should be ticked if an estimate or valuation is used; C if the asset was held at 31 March 1982. Column D shows date of acquisition (or 16/03/98 if later), E date of disposal, F disposal proceeds, G if a relief is claimed, H chargeable gains before taper relief, I shows if a business asset, J taper relief as a percentage, K losses deducted, L gains after losses and M as the gain after taper relief.

To the total chargeable tapered gains (box 8.3) is added attributed gains (box 8.4) to give the total to transfer to page CG8 at box 8.7

Assets disposed of at a loss are separately summarised before being allocated against a gain in the manner that maximises taper relief in column K (K1). Income losses are set off at K2 and losses brought forward in K3 again so as to maximise taper relief.

The last page of the supplementary sheets (CG8) then summarises the capital gains (box 8.7) and gives relief for the exempt amount.

Useage of capital losses is also summarised on page eight. Care must be taken to bring forward losses of earlier years (1995/96 or earlier) separately from later losses. Losses of 1996/97 and later years will be used in preference to earlier year losses.

Further information must be provided for all transactions in other shares and securities, land and property and other assets on pages CG4, CG5 and CG6 respectively. This includes a full description of the asset, any connections with the purchaser, details of estimates and valuations and whether CG34 (post-transaction reporting) has been submitted.

Where gains are taxable because of payments or benefits received from a non-resident or dual resident trust, the amount of additional tax on the payment or benefit is entered into box 8.9. The actual liability, computed by deeming the amount from the non-resident trust as the lowest slice of total gains, is increased by (generally 10% × no. of years since offshore trust realised gain) to a maximum increase of 60%. Only that increase is included in box 8.9. See help sheet IR301.

Question 9 — Non-residents, etc.

3.10   Where the taxpayer is:

(a)   not resident in the UK;

(b)   not ordinarily resident in the UK;

(c)   entitled to split year treatment (i.e. because he came to or left the UK partway through the tax year); or

(d)   not domiciled in the UK;

then the supplementary pages for non-residents must be completed (unless the taxpayer is non-domiciled and that fact does not affect the income tax or capital gains tax liability).

The notes on non-residents include a detailed questionnaire to enable taxpayers to determine their resident, non-resident and domicile status. Guidance is also given in the tables at the rear of the notes, as the liability of income may depend upon the residence and domicile status of the taxpayer.

Where a taxpayer is entitled to a personal allowance in the UK but is non-resident, the taxpayer has the choice of claiming UK personal allowances (tick box 9.7) or paying tax only on income from property in the UK (and investment income connected to a trade in the UK through a branch or agency), all other income being excluded. Tax is, or course, still paid by way of deduction at source. See help sheet IR300 'non-residents and investment income'.

Question 10 — Income from UK savings

3.11   The taxpayer's share of any income from UK savings or investments is shown in boxes 10.1 to 10.26. Only a summary figure is required for each heading.

Where relief for accrued income on gilts, etc. exceeds the charge, then the amount of relief is deducted from the gross interest received on the same security. The net amount is entered into box 10.14. However, the tax deducted in box 10.13 is not adjusted. In the same way where charges exceed relief, the total net amount is included in box 10.14 and box 10.13 is not adjusted.

Question 11 — UK pension or social security benefits

3.12   The taxpayer should show the full annual amount of state retirement or other benefits to which he or she was entitled for the fiscal year, excluding the Christmas bonus and Winter Fuel payment or any amounts relating to a dependent child or attendance allowance.

Incapacity benefit is only taxable when the benefit is paid for more than 28 weeks and that period of incapacity began on or after 12 April 1995. The taxpayer should obtain a form from the Department of Social Security showing the taxable benefit.

Although statutory sick pay and statutory maternity pay is liable to tax and will normally be included in box 1.8 of the employment supplementary pages, any benefits paid by the Department of Social Security should be included in box 11.7. Maternity allowance is not taxable.

All other pensions and retirement annuities paid in the UK are also shown in this section. It must be noted that non-cash benefits are also taxable and should be included in box 11.12 when received from a former employer.

Exempt pensions, e.g. pensions for wounds or disability in military service or for other work related illnesses, should not be included in this section as they are not taxable.

Foreign pensions should be included on the foreign supplementary page F2.

Question 12 — Gains on UK life policies; refunds of surplus AVCs

3.13 Gains from non-qualifying UK life insurance policies (but not withdrawals deemed capital within the 5% allowance) should be included in the following sections. If the policy is with a friendly society, or is a life annuity policy not treated as having been taxed at the basic rate, then the entry from the chargeable events certificate should be in box 12.2 with the number of years in box 12.1. For all other such gains the entries of the chargeable event gain are in 12.5 with notional tax of 22% of the gain in box 12.4. The number of years should be shown in 12.3. If gains relate to more than one policy (other than identical gains from identical policies within a cluster), then they must be shown separately in the additional information box 12.3 on page eight of the tax return with the totals transferred to 12.5 (or 12.2) and 12.4. No entry should then be made in boxes 12.1 or 12.3.

If, exceptionally, amounts have been withdrawn from a policy during its life, such that the amount taxed during the life of the policy exceeds the actual gain on the policy, then corresponding deficiency relief is available. This is explained in help sheet IR320 'gains on UK life insurance policies'.

Where a refund of surplus additional voluntary contributions is received there will be a taxable amount which must be entered in box 12.12, with the actual amount received in box 12.10 and the notional tax in box 12.11.

Question 13 — Other income

3.14 Any amounts of taxable income not included elsewhere within the tax return should be included at this question.

The taxpayer may include casual earnings not included elsewhere, e.g. one-off freelance income or commissions. Profits from isolated literary or artistic activities should also be included under this heading rather than on the self-employment supplementary sheets.

Also shown in this section will be post-cessation receipts if they would not otherwise be taken into account for tax purposes during the lifetime of the business.

Other miscellaneous items such as sale of patent rights and taxable 'cashbacks' are also included.

See help sheet IR325 'other taxable income' where losses arise on other income.

Question 14 — Relief for pension contributions

3.15 Relief for personal pension premiums, retirement annuity contributions and superannuation contributions not otherwise relieved by the net pay scheme must be made in this part of the return.

The taxpayer must show the actual payments made in the tax year, from which must be deducted the amounts claimed in an earlier year, and also the amounts now to be claimed as relating to an earlier year. The amount of relief actually claimed in box 14.5, 14.10 or 14.15 is restricted to the maximum relief claimable under the pensions legislation. Full details and a calculation guide is provided in help sheet IR330 'pension payments'. Where excess personal pensions have been paid, the relevant pension provider must be informed and a refund of the excess contributions claimed.

This section of the tax return can be used to make a claim to bring back payments made before the date of submission of the tax return, but in the following fiscal year, to the current year. Such claims are in lieu of submitting a written claim outside the tax return, and as such are memorandum items which must not be treated as deductions of the current tax year. Therefore items shown in boxes 14.4, 14.9 or 14.14 do not affect the relief claimed for the year shown in boxes 14.5, 14.10 or 14.15 respectively. The tax reduction claimable is a claim for the following tax year, but should be calculated for this year and a tick included in box 18.8, with the amount shown in the additional information box 23.6 on page eight of the tax return.

Where claims are made to treat premium payments as brought back from the following year to the current year within the tax return, then the relief when computed will give rise to a tax credit which will be set against any tax due for an earlier year, or set against any tax due within 35 days of the date of processing the tax return, or repaid as appropriate.

Where employees contribute to a personal pension plan, the figures to be shown in the tax return are the gross equivalent. For 2000/01 and 2001/02 this is found by multiplying by 100/78.

Contributions to an employer's pension scheme are deducted at source from pay before tax is charged. However, it may exceptionally be the case that an additional voluntary contribution paid by way of a lump sum at or near 5 April will not have obtained relief in that way. Such amounts should be included in box 14.16.

A medical or dental practitioner who is self-employed may nevertheless be a member of the National Health Service Superannuation Scheme. Relief for contributions paid to that scheme can be claimed by way of a deduction in box 14.16. However the appropriate net relevant earnings for computing retirement annuity or personal pension premium relief must be reduced by the gross equivalent of such superannuation payments. This is found by multiplying the superannuation payments (excluding amounts relating to Additional Voluntary Contributions (AVC) or added years) by 100/6.

Further help is available in help sheet IR330 'pension payments'. See also 11.14 below.

Question 15 — Reliefs

3.16   Relief for various payments can be made in this section including:
(a)   payments in relation to certain vocational training;
(b)   interest on qualifying loans;
(c)   maintenance or alimony payments made under a court order, Child Support Agency assessment or legally binding order or agreement (but only where the taxpayer was born before 6 April 1935);
(d)   subscriptions for Venture Capital Trust (VCT) shares (up to £100,000) and under the Enterprise Investment Scheme (EIS) (up to £150,000);
(e)   Gift Aid and charitable covenant payments, and gifts of qualifying investments to charities;
(f)   post-cessation expenses, pre-incorporation losses brought forward and losses on relevant discounted securities;
(g)   annuities;
(h)   payments to a trade union or friendly society for death benefits;
(i)   certain payments to an employer's compulsory widow's, widower's or orphan's benefit scheme;
(j)   relief claimed on a qualifying distribution on the redemption of bonus shares and securities.

Relief for general vocational training was withdrawn as from 1 September 2000, so only training payments between 6 April 2000 and 31 August 2000 will qualify for relief in 2000/01. This relief is only available for training that counts towards a National Vocational Qualification (NVQ) or Scottish Vocational Qualification (SVQ) subject to certain conditions.

If all the training takes place within the UK, the taxpayer will obtain basic rate tax relief at source by paying the net amount to the training provider. If the taxpayer has paid the training fees gross, he or she should contact the training provider who should give relief retrospectively. In either case, box 15.1 should be left blank. Where the training payment was made to a non-UK training provider for training which took place outside the UK, the taxpayer will not have received tax relief at source and should enter the gross amount of the payment in box 15.1.

Relief for maintenance or alimony payments was abolished as from 5 April 2000 except for those born before 6 April 1935. Where relief is available, it is limited to the lower of £2,000 and the amount of the payments actually made in the year ending 5 April 2001. The relevant figure should be entered in box 15.3.

In the case of deeds of covenant, Gift Aid and Millennium Gift Aid payment, the net amount paid is shown in the return.

Post-cessation expenses and pre-incorporation losses brought forward are claimed in box 15.8.

For payments to trade unions or friendly societies for death benefits, one half of the payment is shown in box 15.10.

Question 16 — Allowances

3.17 A single personal allowance is granted automatically, and the 'no' box should be ticked if no other claim is made.

Where a claim is made for married couple's allowance, details of the spouse's date of birth (if before 6 April 1935) should be shown. If there are surplus allowances to transfer to the spouse, box 16.15 should be ticked. If the taxpayer is to receive such allowances, box 16.16 should be ticked.

Blind person's allowance and widow's bereavement allowance are also claimed in this section.

Question 17 — Are you liable to make Student Loan Repayments for 2000/01 on an Income Contingent Student Loan?

3.18 Where the new type of student loan is made to a new borrower from August 1998, repayments are collected by the Revenue. The amount of the loan repayment depends on the taxpayer's level of income and these loans are therefore known as 'Income Contingent'. If the taxpayer is calculating his own tax, the Tax Calculation Guide can be used to work out the Student Loan Repayment due and the figure should be entered in box 18.2A.

Question 18 — Do you want to calculate your tax?

3.19 If the tax return is filed before 30 September following the end of the fiscal year, and the 'no' box is ticked, then the Revenue will compute the tax and notify the taxpayer of the amount due before 31 January.

If the return is filed after 30 September, then the Revenue do not guarantee to process it by 31 January following. As tax is due and payable on that date in the correct sum, this would mean that the taxpayer would be liable to interest, and possibly also to a surcharge after 28 February, if the correct amount is not paid. Accordingly, it is essential that the taxpayer computes his own liability if the 30 September deadline is not met.

If the taxpayer is employed and the amount of tax due is less than £2,000 and the return is filed by 30 September, then normally the underpayment will be collected by way of coding adjustment (unless a tick is placed in box 23.2). If the taxpayer settled an underpayment in excess of £500 directly in the previous tax year, then the Revenue will not normally code in an underpayment for the current tax year of more than £500.

Taxpayers who wish to calculate their own tax should use the Tax Calculation Guide.

For those calculating their own tax it is possible to make a claim to reduce payments on account for the following year by ticking box 18.7 on the tax return and stating the reasons why the claim is made in the additional information box 23.6.

Where a claim has been made to carry relief back from 2001/02 to 2000/01 (e.g. pension payments, loss relief, farmers averaging etc.), then the quantified amount of tax credit is shown in the additional information box 23.6 on page eight and a tick is entered in box 18.8.

Relief carried back to earlier years is noted by a tick in box 18.5 and full details provided in the additional information box 23.6 on page eight.

For further details on payment see Chapter 4 below.

Question 19 — Do you want to claim a repayment?

3.20 If a repayment is known to be due, then the taxpayer has the choice of obtaining a repayment by cheque by ticking the 'yes' box or of offsetting the amount against a future tax bill by ticking the 'no' box.

If the overpaid tax is less than £10 it will not be repaid, but carried forward against the next tax bill unless a special claim is made to the tax office.

If it is not known whether a repayment may be due, it may be sensible to tick the 'yes' box to ensure that, if such a repayment arises, it will be returned to the taxpayer. Otherwise on becoming aware that a repayment has arisen the taxpayer would need to correct his return to obtain a repayment.

Where a repayment relates to tax paid, rather than to tax deducted at source (PAYE, CIS25 tax or tax credits, etc.), interest will be paid on the repayment from date of payment to the date of repayment.

Where a repayment relates to payments on account, it will be spread equally between the first and second payment on account.

If the taxpayer wishes to authorise a repayment to be made to a third party, then boxes 19.8 to 19.12 must be completed.

Question 20 — Tax repayments relating to the year

3.21   Care should be taken only to show tax refunded directly by the tax office or the unemployment benefits office relating to the current fiscal year in this section. This will include any repayments of tax deducted under the CIS25 scheme, or where current year CIS25 tax has been used to cover the liabilities of earlier years.

Question 21 — Is the name or address on the front of the form wrong?

3.22   If any of the details are incorrectly shown, they should be amended upon the front of the form and the 'yes' box ticked.

Question 22 — Additional personal details

3.23   The taxpayer is requested to give his or her first two forenames, national insurance number and a telephone number or an agent's telephone number. The taxpayer should also state if he or she is single, married, widowed, divorced or separated, and give his or her date of birth.

Question 23 — Additional information

3.24   This section should only be completed if relevant.

Box 23.1 should be ticked if it is expected that a new pension or social security benefit will be received in the following tax year, with details provided in the additional information box 23.6.

Box 23.2 relates to taxpayers who do not want tax to be collected through their tax code.

Box 23.3 is ticked if a figure which is provisional has been used within the return. Such figures will need to be amended as soon as possible and in any event within one year of the normal filing date or else the Revenue will review the return with the view to opening an enquiry into the return. In addition the taxpayer should note in box 23.6 which figures are provisional, why final figures were not available, and when the taxpayer expects to file such figures.

A tax return will not be regarded as incomplete simply because, despite the taxpayer's best efforts, it contains provisional figures. However if a taxpayer negligently submits a provisional figure which is either inaccurate or unnecessary, he may be liable to a penalty. This will include circumstances where the taxpayer has made little or no effort to obtain the relevant information by the filing deadline or the figure is still provisional because of general pressure of work or the complexity of the taxpayer's affairs. Where an estimated figure or valuation is used for capital gains tax, column B in CG1 or CG2 is ticked. Accordingly, it will not be necessary to tick box 23.3.

In the same way, if a figure has been produced on a judgmental basis, e.g. a taxpayer estimates his business proportion of total motoring, then it will not normally be necessary to make any reference to that figure in the additional information box and it will not be necessary to tick box 23.3. This applies when the estimate, whilst not a precise figure, is sufficiently reliable to enable the taxpayer to declare that he has made an accurate return.

By comparison, if an estimate has been used without adequate information, e.g. where records have been lost or destroyed, then reference should be made to the amount in the additional information box 23.6 on page eight, or elsewhere within the return.

It may prove to be good practice to give the Revenue details of the basis upon which estimated figures have been computed. In subsequent years, if the estimate has not changed, it should not be necessary to repeat the information. If, however, the underlying evidence changes, then that must be reflected in the tax return.

Box 23.4 should be ticked if relief is claimed for trading losses of the following year in the current return. Box 23.5 should be ticked if relief is claimed for post-cessation or other business receipts taxed as income of an earlier year or for backwards or carry-forward spreading of literary or artistic income. Again, additional information should be provided.

Question 24 — Declaration

3.25 To complete the return, the taxpayer must tick to show which supplementary pages have been submitted, and must sign the tax return at box 24.1. If the taxpayer is unable to sign himself, then the capacity of the person signing should be shown in box 24.2. A signature by a power of attorney will not normally be acceptable to the Revenue, unless it can be shown that the taxpayer is incapable of signing because of a physical or mental incapacity.

Time limits

3.26 The signed and completed tax return should then be filed with the Revenue before the due date to avoid penalty.

If the Revenue are to calculate the tax payable, the return must be filed by 30 September (or two months after the date of issue if later). The return should also be filed by 30 September to code in underpayments of less than £2,000 for employed persons.

The latest due date to avoid a penalty is 31 January following the year of the tax year (or three months after the date of issue if later). A penalty of £100 will automatically be added to the taxpayer's tax account if this time limit is not met. This rises by a further £100 after six months. In addition, interest is charged on any tax not paid by 31 January (or the due date of payment if later) and a surcharge of 5% will be added if payment is not made within 28 days of the due date, rising to 10% where payment is not made by 31 July following the due date.

Chapter 4

Payment of Tax and Interest

Payment of tax

4.1   The self-assessment regime simplified the payment dates for income tax and capital gains tax. Capital gains tax is due on 31 January following the year of assessment. Income tax is due on 31 January following the year of assessment, but there is a requirement in many circumstances to make payments on account. [*TMA 1970, s 59A*].

The payment on account is based upon the income tax and Class 4 NIC liability of the previous year, net of payments at source, including tax credits, notional tax credits, subcontractors tax credits and deductions under PAYE increased by any amount to be deducted in subsequent years and reduced by any amounts for earlier years included in the 'previous year' coding notices. One half of the previous year's tax liability is due on 31 January in the fiscal year of assessment, with a further payment of the same amount due on 31 July following the end of the year of assessment. [*TMA 1970, s 59A*].

4.2   Small payments on account are not required. The Revenue have made regulations setting out de minimis limits. Payments on account will not be required in the following circumstances:

(a)   if the tax deducted at source as set out above is more than 80% of the total income tax plus Class 4 NIC; or

(b)   if the total tax due net of payment at source is less than £500.

These calculations are based on the income tax and Class 4 NIC due for the preceding year but are used to form the basis of the payments on account for the current year.

Example

4.3   Georgina submits her tax return for 2000/01 on 30 January 2002. Her taxation liability for that year is:

	£
Income tax	9,420
Capital gains tax	3,000
Class 4 NIC	1,030
	13,450

	£	£
Less deducted at source	1,800	
payments on account	6,400	8,200
Due 31 January 2002		5,250

With her return, she submits a cheque for the above liability together with a payment on account for 2001/02 calculated in the following way (based upon 2000/01 return figures):

	£
Income tax	9,420
Class 4 NIC	1,030
	10,450
Less deducted at source	1,800
Relevant amount	8,650

Note: The liability is NOT recalculated using 2001/02 rates or allowances.

Due 31 January 2002 50% × 8,650	£4,325
31 July 2002 50% × 8,650	£4,325

Her tax return for 2001/02, submitted on 30 November 2002, shows taxation liabilities of:

	£	£
Income tax		10,575
Capital gains tax		NIL
Class 4 NIC		1,075
		11,650
Less deducted at source	1,750	
payments on account	8,650	10,400
Due 31 January 2003		1,250

Her payment will also include a payment on account for 2002/03 of:

	£
Income tax and Class 4	
(as above)	11,650
Less deducted at source	1,750
	9,900

50% thereof = £4,950

If the payments on account exceed the liability then repayment will be made by the Revenue, with interest, as soon as the return has been processed, except where the Revenue open an enquiry into the tax return.

4.4   Where a taxpayer believes that the amount due for the current tax year will be less than in the previous tax year, an application may be made at any time before 31 January following the year of assessment for the payments on account to be reduced. The claim may be included in the tax return by ticking box 18.7 and setting out in the additional information box 23.6 the reason for the reduction and showing the amount to be paid per half year in box 18.6.

Alternatively a claim may be made on form SA 303. The payment may be reduced to nil by a *TMA 1970, s 59A(3)* claim, or reduced to a specified amount by a *TMA 1970, s 59A(4)* claim. The claim must set out the reason for the application to reduce the payment on account. If appropriate, repayment of tax already paid will be made to the taxpayer at that time. However, if a taxpayer fraudulently or negligently makes an incorrect statement in connection with such a claim he will be liable to a penalty not exceeding the excess of the correct tax over the actual tax paid on account. [*section 59A(6)*].

It is understood that, in practice, the Revenue will accept all reasonable claims under this section without query. They have also indicated that they will pay an interest supplement where appropriate.

Example

4.5   Georgina ceases trading on 1 December 2002 due to poor profitability. She estimates that after overlap relief she will have no liability to income tax or Class 4 NIC for 2002/03 on trading income. She makes a claim under *TMA 1970, s 59A(3)* on 1 March 2003 indicating that no payments on account are due.

The Revenue will repay the £4,950 paid on 31 January 2003 together with interest and no amount will be due on 31 July 2003.

Her tax return for 2002/03 was submitted on 20 December 2003 and the tax due paid on 30 January 2004. The return shows taxation liabilities of:

	£
Income tax	4,100
Capital gains	1,800
Class 4 NIC	700
	6,600
Less deducted at source	1,400
Payable 31 January 2004	5,200

If the Revenue believed that her claim had been made fraudulently or negligently then the maximum penalty would be:

	£
Income tax	4,100
Class 4 NIC	700
	4,800
Less deducted at source	1,400
Maximum penalty	3,400

Interest would be charged on the payment on account now shown to be due but not paid because of the claim, i.e. total income tax and Class 4 NIC (as above) £3,400, therefore payment on account due 31 January 2003 is £1,700. Interest is due for the following period:

	£
1st payment on account	
1 February 2003 to 30 January 2004 on	1,700
2nd payment on account	
1 August 2003 to 30 January 2004 on	1,700
Balancing payment—due 31 January 2004	
(nil — paid by that date)	1,800
	5,200

(See also 4.10 to 4.19 below).

The taxpayer can make a claim under *TMA 1970, s 59A(4)* to reduce payments on account by a stated amount. In those circumstances the maximum penalty for negligent claims would be reduced further by the amounts paid on account. It is expected that the Revenue will only take penalties where the amounts involved are material.

Interest

4.6   Interest is charged on late-paid tax and on any surcharges added to the tax. [*TMA 1970, s 86*]. Interest is also charged on penalties, from the due date to the payment date. [*TMA 1970, s 103A*].

Interest is charged at the normal rate set by regulations (7.5% from 6 May 2001) on income tax, Class 4 NIC, capital gains tax and on payments on account from the due date until the payment date. Interest payable on repayments is currently 3.5% (from 6 May 2001).

In the case of a cheque, the payment date is the date it is received by the Revenue, providing it is honoured on presentation. [*TMA 1970, s 70A*]. Bank giro payments are treated as made three working days before the value is received and BACS/CHAPS payments one working day before the value is received.

Amendments to tax returns

4.7   If a tax return is amended, interest applies from the normal final payment date. However, an amendment to a tax return will also amend the payment on account due for the following year, which in itself will give rise to an additional interest charge from the normal payment date to the actual date of payment.

Appeals

4.8   Where, exceptionally, an appeal is made with postponement of tax (e.g. a Revenue amendment to a self-assessment) then interest is still chargeable from the normal payment date to the actual date of payment.

Interest on overdue tax

4.9   Interest is charged from the due date for payment to the actual date for payment. This applies to payments on account under *TMA 1970, s 59A* and to the settlement payment of income tax plus capital gains tax under *TMA 1970, s 59B*.

Interest on payments on account where eventual liability exceeds preceding year liability

4.10   If a taxpayer pays a payment on account based upon 50% of the previous year's liability less tax deducted at source, on or before the due date, then no liability for interest arises until the nominal payment date whatever the eventual liability for the current year.

If a taxpayer believes that the payments on account to be made are too high then he may make application to reduce those payments under *TMA 1970, s 59A(3)* or *(4)*. Where a claim has been made under *section 59A(3)* to reduce the payments on account to nil, or under *section 59A(4)* to reduce the payment on account, special rules apply to calculate the interest payable.

Interest will then be charged on the basis that the amount collectable on account is the lower of:

(a)   the original interim payment (50% of preceding year liability); and
(b)   one half of the final liability (50% of current year liability).

The interest due will be calculated on the difference between the actual payment and the deemed payments on account due under the above rule. [*TMA 1970, s 86(4)–(6)*].

If the reduced payment on account proves to be too low, then interest will be payable from the normal due date for the payment on account to the actual date of payment of tax, which will normally be the date of the payment of the final liability.

This means that interest will be charged on an amount up to the difference between the amount paid and the normal payment on account had a claim for reduction not been made, restricted to one half of the eventual final income tax liability.

Example

4.11   Donna has an income tax liability for 1999/2000 of £10,000. Accordingly, £5,000 is payable on 31 January 2001 and 31 July 2001 as payments on account of 2000/01.

She is aware that her income for the current year will be reduced because of falling profits and she makes a claim under *TMA 1970, s 59A(4)* to reduce her payments on account to £3,500 on each occasion, which she pays on time.

Her eventual income tax liability for 2000/01 amounts to £8,200, which she settles with a final payment of £1,200 on 30 January 2002.

Interest will be due on the payments on account as follows:

	£
	£
Original payment on account	5,000
One half of collectible liability	
(50% × £8,200)	4,100
Actual payment	3,500
Lower of the above	4,100
Difference	600

Interest is due on:

	£
Period 1 February 2001 to 31 July 2001	600
1 August 2001 to 30 January 2002	1,200

Example

4.12 Continuing the above example for 2001/02, Donna has a liability to make payments on account of £4,100 on 31 January 2002 and on 31 July 2002. She again makes a *TMA 1970, s 59A(4)* claim to reduce her payments on account to £3,900 on each date. However, her eventual liability for the year 2001/02 amounts to £9,100, which she settles with a final payment on 20 February 2003.

Interest will be due on the payments on account as follows:

	£
	£
Original payment on account	4,100
One half of collectible liability	
(50% × £9,100)	4,550
Actual payment	3,900
Lower of above	4,100
Difference	200

Thus, although the final payment for 2001/02 will amount to £9,100 – (£3,900 + £3,900) = £1,300, interest will only be charged on late payments of £200 from 31 January 2002 and a further £200 from 31 July 2002 giving interest due on:

	£
Period: 1 February 2002 to 31 July 2002	200
1 August 2002 to 31 January 2003	400
1 February 2003 to 20 February 2003	1,300

together with interest on the late paid 2002/03 payment on account:

1 February 2003 to 20 February 2003   4,550

Interest remitted where eventual liability is lower than payment on account

4.13 Similar calculations are to be made where interest is charged on late payments on account where there is an eventual repayment of tax.

If interest has been charged on late payments on account and eventually there is no liability whatsoever for the year, then all interest charged on late payments will be remitted. [*TMA 1970, s 86(7)*].

If the payments on account exceed the eventual total liability for the year, and one or both of the interim payments have been paid late, then the payments on account are deemed to have been reduced to one half of the eventual total liability. Insofar as any interest charged relates to the excess of payments on account over the revised liability, it will be remitted.

Example (assuming the interest rate is 7.5% and repayment rate is 3.5% throughout)

4.14 Ann has a liability to make payments on account for 2000/01 of £2,100 on each occasion. She makes the payments on 31 March 2001 and 28 October 2001 with interest being charged on late payment of:

First instalment	£30
Second instalment	£45

Her liability for that year is self-assessed at £2,800 with repayment made to her on 28 February 2002 of £1,400.

Interest will be remitted on one half of the repayment (£700) in respect of each payment on account, i.e. she would receive a repayment of £1,400 plus repayment interest plus remitted interest on late payment of:

		£
Repayment		1,400
Repayment Interest		
£700 × 3.5% × 31/3/2001 to 28/2/2002	23	
£700 × 3.5% × 28/10/2001 to 28/2/2002	8	31
Remitted Interest		
£700 × 7.5% × 31/1/2001 to 31/3/2001	9	
£700 × 7.5% × 31/7/2001 to 28/10/2001	13	22
		1,460

Repayment supplement

4.15 The repayment interest supplement under self assessment is due for the period from the actual date of payment to the actual date of repayment. [*ICTA 1988, s 824*]. Thus interest will be paid from the actual date the original tax was paid even if that date is before the statutory due date for the tax. The deemed date of payment for cheques and bank giro payments is set out at 4.6 above.

Repayment interest is not paid on any amount in excess of the statutory required amount. This means that if a taxpayer makes a payment on account in excess of 50% of the preceding year liability and it subsequently is determined that the actual liability for the current year is lower than the amount paid (but higher than the previous year's liability), then no interest will be paid with the repayment.

Example

4.16 John has a tax liability for 2000/01 of £2,000. None of that amount is covered by tax deducted at source, etc. On 31 January 2002 John pays £1,800, making a further payment of £1,800 on 31 July 2002. Both payments are payments on account for 2001/02. On 1 October 2002 he submits his 2001/02 tax return which shows a total liability for the year of £3,100. John is repaid £500 on 28 November 2002. There is no repayment interest because the amount paid on each occasion (£1,800) exceeded the statutory required payment of account of £1,000, and the total liability for the year (£3,100) exceeds the amounts of those payments on account.

If the agreed liability had been £1,100 and all other facts were as above, then interest would be paid on £900, being the difference between the statutory payments on account (£2,000) and the eventual liability (£1,100). Interest would be paid as to one half (£450), in respect of 31 January 2002 to the date of repayment and the other half (£450) from 31 July to date of repayment.

4.17 Interest is only paid from the date of payment to the date of repayment where the amount is actually paid to the Revenue. The rule does not apply to income tax deducted at source, where the deemed date of payment of that tax is 31 January following the end of the tax year.

For the purpose of identifying the payment which is now being repaid, any tax repaid is to be identified with tax payments in the following way:

- to the final payment made for the tax year;
- equally to the payments on account made for the year;
- to income tax deducted at source, tax credits, PAYE or CIS25 tax; and
- insofar as attributable to tax paid by instalments, to later instalments in priority to earlier instalments.

In the same way, interest is only due on payments or repayments arising from a Schedule 1B claim (claims for relief involving two or more years, e.g. carry-back of losses, pension payments or farmers averaging) from 31 January following the end of the year of claim.

Example

4.18 Julia claims to carry back a £10,000 retirement annuity contribution paid in 2001/02 to 2000/01. She is entitled to a repayment of £4,000 which is paid on 18 September 2001 computed by using her 2000/01 tax return which was filed on 2 August 2001. She receives no interest on the repayment as the relevant date for interest is 31 January 2003 (i.e. 31 January following 2001/02 being the fiscal year in which the actual payment (and therefore claim) was made).

4.19 A repayment supplement will also be paid on overpaid capital gains tax. The interest will accrue from the date on which the tax is actually paid to the date of repayment. [*TCGA 1992, s 283*].

4.20 Interest is payable and repayment supplements are added to Class 4 NIC liabilities whether these are paid or deferred. However, the due date for a deferred liability is 28 days after the demand for payment is issued, and a deferred liability is not included within the calculation of the payment on account due for the following tax year.

4.21 From 6 April 2001 a claim to carry back a personal pension premium must be made by 31 January following the fiscal year to which it is carried back and payment of the premium must also be made by that date. Accordingly interest will not be paid on any such claim. However where the relief is given by being offset against existing tax liabilities then interest will cease on the existing liability from the date that the claim is notified to the Revenue to the extent that the liability is covered by the claim.

Chapter 5

Employers and Employees

5.1 The introduction of the self-assessment tax returns means that employers have to provide detailed information relating to amounts earned in cash and in kind from employment to employees at an early stage. Failure to provide such information timeously means that the employee cannot complete his personal tax return and as such will be liable to a penalty.

The Inland Revenue has conducted extensive consultation to ensure that sufficient information is provided to employees in time for them to complete their personal tax returns whilst at the same time minimising the impact upon employers.

5.2 It must be remembered that the term 'employer' includes anyone who pays a wage, fee, salary or other benefits to someone working for them under a contract of service, and also includes anyone who pays a pension to a pensioner. An intermediary will also have to provide similar information to a worker in respect of deemed salary under the personal services legislation (IR35).

Provision of information to employees

P60 — year-end summary of pay and deductions

5.3 The employer is currently required to deduct PAYE and national insurance contributions (NIC) at source before making payments to an employee, etc. A summary of gross pay and tax (and NIC) deducted at source is prepared at the end of each year. This is in three parts. The top two parts, form P14, are sent to the Inland Revenue and the third part, form P60, is given to the employee. The P60 has to be given to the employee by 31 May after the end of the tax year, i.e. for 2000/01 the deadline is 31 May 2001.

5.4 The employer is free to provide the P60 in the way that is most convenient. This could be by post, by hand, with payslips, etc. Although many small employers will provide the information on the three-part Revenue form P14 (OCR), others will produce the information on an agreed computerised system.

5.5 Employers are required to give form P60 to employees who are working for them at 5 April. Failure to provide a copy to the employee will give rise to the same penalty as failure to supply forms P14 or equivalent to the Inland

Revenue by 19 May following the end of the fiscal year. The initial penalty is up to £300 per form. If an employer does not provide information then it can be required to do so by the General or Special Commissioners, with a further penalty of up to £60 per form for each day that the failure continues.

Former employees

5.6 An employer is also required to prepare a form P14 for anyone who had worked with them during the fiscal year, or for whom deductions were required (e.g. a Class 1A national insurance charge on a car provided in the previous fiscal year). An employer may give a copy of that form to past employees if it so wishes but is not under a statutory obligation to do so.

P45 — details of employee leaving

5.7 When an employee leaves, a form P45 must be used. This will show the gross pay and tax deducted by the employer during the period of employment in the current fiscal year. The information on P45 part 1A will be needed by the employee to complete his personal tax return. Accordingly employees must keep such forms safely.

As previously, part 1 of the form P45 must be sent by the old employer to the tax office. Parts 1A, 2 and 3 are handed to the employee. The employee must detach and keep part 1A and give parts 2 and 3 to the new employer. The new employer must complete part 3 forwarding the same to its PAYE district and retaining part 2 for its own records.

The information provided on form P45 includes details of pay and tax from the current employment as well as the cumulative pay and tax to date. This additional information will not be required to be completed where it is the same as the cumulative pay and tax.

5.8 Where an employee moves jobs within a group of companies, it is often agreed that form P45 is not given to the employee but dealt with internally. From 6 April 1996 employers moving employees within their organisation are required to provide the relevant employees with pay and tax details in respect of each job. Therefore, although they need not give them a form P45, they must provide the information shown on part 1A of the form at the time that the employee changes his position within the organisation. This is so that the employee can show on his tax return the amount of pay received and tax deducted in respect of each separate employment on separate employment supplementary pages.

P9D/P11D — return of benefits in kind

5.9 In addition to providing details of pay and tax deducted, an employer is required to make a return of expense payments and benefits. In the case of employees earning at a rate of £8,500 or more per annum, the form is P11D. In the case of other employees it is form P9D.

5.10 In determining which form to use, an employer must look at the rate at which an employee is earning, rather than the amount earned in a fiscal year. To the actual pay must be added all expense payments and benefits. Allowable expenses are not deducted in ascertaining whether the £8,500 threshold is exceeded. However, ordinary annual contributions to an approved superannuation fund — including additional voluntary contributions (AVCs) — and any contributions under an approved payroll giving scheme may be deducted. Among the benefits and expenses which need to be included in determining whether the employee has exceeded the £8,500 threshold are:

(a)   the higher of the car benefit and car fuel benefit charges and the cash alternative of a salary sacrifice;

(b)   the amounts chargeable under all of the other benefits sections including reimbursed car expenses, vouchers or credit cards provided by the employer; and

(c)   the settling by the employer of a debt incurred personally by the individual in respect of motoring expenses. [*ICTA 1988, s 167*].

Form P11D is also required for each director, whatever his or her rate of remuneration, except those earning at a rate of less than £8,500 per annum who are full-time working directors or directors of a non-profit-making concern or charity and in either case have no material interest in the company.

Where an employee holds a number of employments with connected companies, all remuneration must be aggregated for the purpose of deciding whether the individual is paid at a rate of £8,500 per annum or more.

5.11 For those employees not caught by the P11D legislation, form P9D is used. This requires a return of the amount of expenses not included in the pay records, together with amounts paid in respect of vouchers, credit cards, accommodation and gifts in kind. It also requires details of pecuniary liabilities of employees met by the employer including personal telephone bills, national insurance, etc. A reference number by each entry refers to the space on the tax return to be used by the employee in reporting the same information to the Inland Revenue.

5.12 The deadline for sending forms P9D or P11D to the Inland Revenue is 6 July. The penalty for failure to file is an initial penalty of up to £300 per form imposed by the General or Special Commissioners. Failure to file can then result in a further penalty of up to £60 per form per day that the failure continues. Under the legislation, a copy of forms P9D or P11D is to be given to the employee. Failure to provide the form to the employee by the same deadline of 6 July can give rise to similar penalties.

5.13 An employer will be required to give a copy of forms P9D/P11D to each employee in his employment on 5 April. This can be provided to the employee in the way most convenient to the employer. For employees who have left employment between 5 April and the date of providing the form, the employer can satisfy the legislation by posting the form to the last known address of the employee.

5.14 An employer will not automatically have to give a copy of forms P9D/P11D to employees who have left during the tax year. However, such employees will require the information shown upon the form if they receive a tax return for completion. Accordingly, it is provided that such an ex-employee may request a copy of the form from his previous employer. The employee must make a written request to the employer within three years of the end of the tax year. He can make only one request. An employer is then obliged to provide the information shown on forms P9D/P11D. The employer must provide the information within 30 days of the written request, or 6 July following the end of the relevant tax year if later.

In practice employers may find that it is more convenient to provide copies of forms P9D/P11D automatically to all employees and ex-employees at the same time.

5.15 The format of the provision of the information to employees will be at the discretion of the employer. Small employers may prefer to photocopy the Revenue form, whereas those providing information on computer spreadsheets to the Revenue will need to set up a system which provides individual output for each of the employees. There will be no set format, although it would be helpful if such spreadsheets provided the information in the same order as that shown on the individual's tax return. The official forms P9D/P11D will have a reference by each box indicating the equivalent reference on the tax return where the amount should be entered. Employers producing computer spread-sheet information should include the same references and, to assist the completion of the employee's tax return, the information should be provided in the same order as that used on the tax return.

5.16 The forms P9D/P11D require the provision of details of the gross cost of benefits and expenses to the employer including VAT. The form provides for the deduction of amounts made good by the employee, and of amounts on which tax has been paid to arrive at the cash equivalent. The employee will still be required to make his or her own *section 198* claim for expenses on his personal tax return. This will include a claim for reimbursed expenses incurred wholly, exclusively and necessarily in the performance of the duties of the employment and qualifying travelling and subsistence expenses. This requirement together with the reporting requirement on form P9D/P11D may be avoided where the employer has a dispensation in force (see 5.26 below). To enable an employee to determine whether a deduction is possible in respect of entertaining costs borne by the employer, the employer is required to indicate on form P11D whether the business is a trade, profession or vocation and to confirm that the amounts shown as entertaining have been disallowed in the employer's tax computations. A tick will indicate that the employee may make an expenses claim against the item, whereas a cross will indicate that no such claim will be possible.

Third party benefits

5.17 In addition to the requirement to report expenses and benefits provided by the employer to the employee, there are reporting requirements in respect of benefits provided by a third party to an employer's employees, where the employer has arranged for that other person to provide the benefit. The term 'arranged' will include the guaranteeing of the provision of benefits by a third party, and the facilitation of the provision by a third party. In all cases, the employer will only be required to report benefits on form P11D if he is actively involved in their provision.

5.18 An employing company is regarded as having arranged benefits or expenses to its employees where another group company has provided the benefit or expense payment. In the same way, where one employer agrees with another non-connected employer to provide reciprocal benefits or expenses including the provision of goods or services to each other's employees free or at a discount, then each employer would be regarded as having arranged the provision to its own employees.

Where an employer is deemed to have arranged a benefit, then the employer will be responsible for reporting the cash equivalent on form P11D.

5.19 An employer is not deemed to have arranged a benefit where he has not been actively involved in the provision of that expense payment or benefit. Mere contact between an employer and a third party would not be 'arrangements' for this purpose. Therefore, if the employer had merely provided a list of employees to a third party, there would be no reporting requirement. In the same way, where a business, as a matter of custom or practice of the particular industry, provides free or cheap goods or services to employees of another employer without the employer's involvement, there would be no reporting requirement on the main employer.

5.20 Where employers agree with retailers for the retailer to offer a small discount on goods to their employees there may be an 'arrangement'. However, no amount would have to be declared on form P11D as long as the retailer charges an amount which is not less than cost of the items concerned. Using the principle established in the case of *Pepper v Hart*, the declarable amount is the marginal additional cost. In this instance there would be no marginal additional cost and therefore no declarable amount, even though the arrangements in principle give the employer the duty to declare such benefits on the employee's form P11D.

As will be seen, the only time that there is a reporting requirement on the employer is where it has had an active involvement with the third party. In those circumstances, full details of the costs involved of providing the expenses or benefits should be readily available to the employer. If, however, such information is not available, e.g. where the third party refuses to disclose the costs involved, the employer must complete form P11D with a best estimate, marking the amount accordingly.

5.21 Where an employer has not actively facilitated a third party benefit, then the responsibility for the provision of information passes to the third party.

From 1996/97 onwards, where a third party makes an expense payment or provides benefits in kind to employees of another employer, then the third party will have to provide to the recipients the same details as would be required from the employer. In other words, the third party must provide the recipient in writing with details of the cash equivalent of any benefit in kind. The information must be given to the recipient by 6 July following the end of the tax year.

Although third parties have to provide the information to employees, they do not have to provide the information directly to the Inland Revenue unless the Revenue has issued a return under *section 15* of the *Taxes Management Act 1970*.

5.22 There will be no set format in which the third party must provide information. It can choose a method that is most convenient to itself. Accordingly, it will be possible to provide details of the payments each time a payment is made or a benefit is provided; alternatively it will be possible to make a yearly return to the recipient. The information may be provided by hand, by post or via the employer.

Although third parties are required to provide details of the cash equivalent of benefits and expenses, there will be no reporting requirements in respect of goodwill, entertainment or small gifts costing (in total) £150 or less to the provider, subject to the proviso that the provider is not the employer nor a person connected with the employer, and that the employer has not directly or indirectly procured the provision of the benefit. The benefit must not be made either in recognition of the performance of particular services in the course of employment or in anticipation of services which are to be performed. The third party will not have to report tips or items included within a taxed awards scheme, although these items are still taxable receipts in the hands of the employee.

Taxed awards

5.23 Where an employer or a third party provides a benefit under the taxed awards scheme, the provider meets the tax liability on the non-cash incentive prices. The provider then gives the recipient a certificate showing the amounts to be included on the individual's tax return.

Motor vehicles

5.24 Where an employer provides a motor vehicle for an employee, it will be required to compute the car benefit charge arising and if appropriate the car fuel benefit charge. Optional P11D working sheet 2 will be available to supplement the P11D in respect of cars. As for national insurance contributions, the employer will be required to state the business mileage undertaken in each car. If mileage records are not available, then the employer must base the cash equivalent on the assumption that the employee had travelled fewer than 2,500 business miles per annum.

The case of *Henwood v Clarke* (1997 STC 789) confirms the Revenue view that if an employee changes his motor vehicle during a tax year, then the relevant proportion of the annual business mileage must be achieved in each motor car.

In this case, Mr Clarke had travelled 1,425 business miles in the period 6 April to 5 August (equivalent to 4,275 miles per annum), and therefore attracted a discount on the 35% benefit charge for the car. (At the relevant time there was a one-third discount, so that the charge was 23.333%, but with effect from 6 April 1999 the charge in such cases has been increased to 25%.) In the second car he covered 1,452 business miles between 6 August and 5 April (equivalent to 2,178 miles per annum) and did not get a discount, even though he had travelled 2,877 business miles in the fiscal year.

If an employee uses his own motor vehicle for business, then details must be provided on form P11D (at point E) of the car or mileage allowance paid in respect of the employee's car. This includes payments made using the rates published by the Revenue known as the Inland Revenue authorised mileage rates, unless the employer has formally joined the fixed profit car scheme (FPCS). Alternatively, to avoid the need to make a return of mileage payments, the employer may obtain a dispensation from the Revenue to make such payments.

Fixed profit car schemes (FPCS) and Inland Revenue authorised mileage rates

5.25 Where an employer has joined the fixed profit car scheme, it will have to complete form FPCS2 showing the gross amount paid to the employee and the business miles travelled. The employer must then compute the profit element of the payment over the scale allowances which is included on form P11D at E. This amount must be included by the employee upon his personal tax return at box 1.15. To enable the employee to have the information, a copy of form FPCS2 together with form P11D should be given to the employee by 6 July following the end of the tax year.

If an employer has not formally joined the FPCS, it is still advisable to provide an employee with a note of business miles travelled in the year as well as providing form P11D. This will give the employee evidence of business miles travelled to enable him to make an expense claim, based upon the Inland Revenue authorised mileage rates, in his personal tax return.

The FPCS rates are the same as the Inland Revenue authorised mileage rates. These rates (up to and including 2000/01) are:

Car engine size	*Up to 4,000 business miles*	*Over 4,000 business miles*
Up to 1,000 cc	28p	17p
1,001–1,500 cc	35p	20p
1,501–2,000 cc	45p	25p
Over 2,000 cc	63p	36p

If the employer does not wish to differentiate between employees a mid-point rate may be used:

i.e.	40p	22.5p

The rate for motorcycles is 24p per business mile and for pedal cycles is 12p per business mile.

For 2001/02, the authorised mileage rates are:

Car engine size	*Up to 4,000* *business miles*	*Over 4,000* *business miles*
Up to 1,500 cc	40p	25p
1,501–2,000 cc	45p	25p
Over 2,000 cc	63p	36p

The motorcycle and pedal cycle rates are the same as for 2000/01.

From 6 April 2002, a new statutory system of free mileage rates is being introduced. The car engine size will no longer be relevant. For all cars and vans, the tax-free rates will be 40p per mile on the first 10,000 business miles and 25p per mile thereafter. The pedal cycle rate goes up to 20p per mile, whereas the motorcycle rate remains at 24p per mile.

See 5.35 onwards as to a note of the basis on which an employee may make a claim for travelling expenses.

Dispensations

5.26 Dispensations are available to reduce the reporting requirements of employers and employees. Where the Inland Revenue grants a formal dispensation, the employer does not have to include details of such expenses on forms P11D, P9D or supplementary forms. The employee is not required to declare the expenses received on his personal tax return and is not required to make an expenses claim under *ICTA 1988, s 198*.

The Inland Revenue will consider a dispensation for expense payments or benefits in kind where no tax will be payable by the employee because he can claim a matching tax deduction. Dispensations will be given for payments of travelling and subsistence on an approved scale for business journeys provided that motoring costs do not exceed the authorised scale (set out in 5.25 above). It is also possible to get dispensations for other expenses incurred. These include reimbursed expenditure, professional subscriptions, business telephone calls and entertainment expenses. It is not the practice of the Revenue to grant dispensations where the person making the claim is also the individual responsible for checking the claim. Dispensations will not be granted for round sum allowances. However it is possible to obtain clearance to pay small fixed allowances, e.g. lunch allowance. Advanced written clearance from the Inspector handling the PAYE affairs of the taxpayer is required to avoid the requirement to pay PAYE and NI on such amounts.

5.27 The Inland Revenue is currently encouraging employers to make dispensation applications in respect of normal expenses and benefits not giving rise to a taxable amount. Employers should seriously consider making application for dispensations for such expenses by completing form 490(DIS) for travelling expenses and P11DX for other expenses. This should minimise the information to be provided on forms P11D and also reduce the number of forms to be completed. Application should be made to the Inspector dealing with the company's PAYE. More details can be obtained from any tax office, or in leaflets IR69 'Expenses: payments and benefits in kind' and booklet 490 'Employee travel'.

Where a dispensation is obtained, it must be noted that any change will invalidate the dispensation. Care should therefore be taken to obtain the dispensation in general terms, e.g. mileage allowances paid in accordance with the current authorised mileage rates.

PAYE settlement agreements (PSAs)

5.28 A PAYE settlement agreement (PSA) — formerly known as an Annual Voluntary Settlement (AVS) — is an arrangement between an employer and the Inland Revenue by which the employer pays tax directly on certain expense payments or benefits. Where a PSA is in force, then no further entries will be required on form P11D. It should be noted that under the PSA arrangements the tax is computed by grossing up the benefits. Although there is no requirement for employers to tell the employees details of such settlements, or dispensations, it is likely to be in the best interests of the employer to provide the employees with information. This should reduce the number of queries from employees in respect of benefit payments. Information could be provided to employees at the time that employment commences, when dispensations or PSAs are agreed with the Revenue, with form P11D each year, or via company magazines or information sheets.

Regulations have been introduced that enable employers to settle voluntarily the income tax liabilities of employees on minor benefits, on benefits provided irregularly, or on benefits which it is impractical to allocate to individual employees.

PSAs could cover such items as:

(a)   working lunches/late night meals;
(b)   Christmas gifts;
(c)   prizes not included in the Taxed Incentive Awards Scheme (see 5.23 above);
(d)   staff parties (where total costs exceed £75 per head and therefore are not covered by extra-statutory concession A70 – Annual Staff Parties);
(e)   home to office travel, e.g. provision of taxis, etc.;
(f)   private use of company assets.

To calculate the tax liability, it is necessary to estimate the number of employees receiving such benefits and their tax rates.

Example

An employer provides each of his 100 employees with a turkey. The total cost is £1,000. Of the employees 10% pay higher rate tax, and 10% are only liable at the starting rate. The PSA tax due will be:

$$£1,000 \times 10\% = 100 \times \frac{100}{60} = 166 \ @ \ 40\% = \quad 66$$

$$£1,000 \times 80\% = 800 \times \frac{100}{78} = 1,026 \ @ \ 22\% = \quad 226$$

$$£1,000 \times 10\% = 100 \times \frac{100}{90} = 111 \ @ \ 10\% = \quad \underline{11}$$

$$£303$$

The tax due of £303 is payable by the employer to the Revenue by 19 October following the end of the fiscal year. Because the amount is a statutory liability of the employer, no national insurance liability arises. However, from 6 April 1999 Class 1B NIC will apply to the tax payable. This will be at the Class 1 employer's rate (11.9% as from 6 April 2001, i.e. £36 – 12.2% until that date), and is payable at the same time as the tax on the PSA, i.e. 19 October 2002 for 2001/02. Class 1B will also be levied on items included within a PSA which would have been liable to Class 1 NIC without the settlement agreement.

The advantages of a PSA to an employer include the following:

(a) there is no need to compute the value of the individual benefit (e.g. the price of the individual turkeys in the above example);

(b) there are no entries on form P11D/P9D (saving 100 entries and possibly as many forms if there are no other benefits);

(c) increased goodwill from the benefit.

The disadvantage is that the employer pays the tax and NIC as well as the benefit.

The Revenue and employees also benefit from PSA by reduced paperwork, i.e. no entries on individual P11Ds or tax returns; no small code number adjustments; no small underpayments of tax to be dealt with.

Major benefits such as cars, beneficial loans or round sum allowances cannot be included in PSAs. PSA schemes commenced from 6 April 1996 and are reviewed by the Revenue annually (by 6 July following the end of the fiscal year).

Filing dates

5.29 Forms P9D/P11D and form P11D(b) have to be filed with the Inland Revenue by 6 July following the end of the tax year, e.g. for 2001/02 by 6 July 2002. Under the provisions, a copy of such information must be provided to the employee by the same date. Information must be provided to ex-employees on request and must be provided to recipients of benefits by third parties, again by 6 July. Working sheets and FPCS2 may be given to employees to help them complete their personal tax returns, but do not have to be filed with the tax office.

Penalties

5.30 Where the information provided is incorrect or incomplete, the legislation provides for a maximum penalty of £3,000 for each incorrect or incomplete form. [*TMA 1970, s 98(2)*]. However, the Revenue will usually invite the employer to give an explanation as to why the form is incorrect before any penalty action is taken. If the error or omission is entirely innocent no penalty will arise. The maximum penalty would only be imposed in the most exceptional of circumstances.

The information has to be provided to the employees. Failure to file the forms with the Inland Revenue or to provide information to the employees would give rise to an initial penalty imposed by the General or Special Commissioners of up to £300 per form plus a further penalty of up to £60 per form for each day that failure continues. [*TMA 1970, s 98(1)*]. It is likely that the Revenue will only pursue penalties where the amounts of tax involved are significant or the employer persists in failing to comply. However, as failure to give the information to the employee could result in the employee not being able to complete his own tax return, and thereby suffering a penalty in his own name, the Revenue will take action where an employee tells it of an employer's failure to comply with its obligations.

Similar rules apply in respect of form P60 where the time limit for provision to the employee is 31 May.

5.31 Table of important dates for employers

Before start of tax year	— Apply for a dispensation for all expenses not giving rise to a tax liability.
	— Agree benefits to be included in a PSA.
	— Apply to use a FPCS.
	— Agree with the PAYE Inspector small round sum allowances that do no more than re-imburse the costs incurred, e.g. overnight allowances, lunch allowances.
	2001/02
2 August 2001	— Notify changes in car/fuel benefit for quarter to 5 July 2001 on form P46 (Car).
2 November 2001	— As above for quarter to 5 October 2001.
2 February 2002	— As above for quarter to 5 January 2002.
19 April 2002	Pay all outstanding PAYE/NI liabilities for 2001/02.
19 May 2002	— File completed P35 together with forms P14 for each employee and supplementary forms, e.g. P38A.

31 May 2002	— Provide all employees (as at 5 April 2002) with form P60.
6 July 2002	— File forms P9D/P11D with Revenue. Provide a copy of such forms to relevant employees. Review PSA with Revenue for 2002/03. Elect for all loans by a close company to one director/employee to be treated as a single loan. Provide details of value of benefits provided to a non-employee to that non-employee.
19 July 2002	— Pay Class 1A national insurance on taxable benefits.
19 October 2002	— Pay tax and Class 1B national insurance due on a PSA.

5.32   The operation of the PAYE system for employees means that many employed persons do not receive a tax return. In the past this has not been important because most employees do not have untaxed sources of income. Furthermore after establishing claims for professional subscriptions and fixed deductions for expenses there are no material alterations year on year.

Under self-assessment the Revenue have continued to obtain the same economies by not issuing tax returns to most employees. Where the employee is known to have a claim for expenses, or small amounts on non-taxed income then the Revenue issue a non-statutory form to request that information to alter the code number.

Where small underpayments arise, these continue to be collected under the PAYE system. Where a formal tax return is issued it must be returned by 30 September to take advantage of this procedure. The time limits do not apply to the non-statutory request for information.

Notwithstanding the lack of a tax return an employee is obliged by law to maintain all documents that are required for the completion of a tax return. This includes form P60, P11D or P9D, form P45 part 1A and vouchers relating to investment income. The documents must be retained until twelve months after 31 January following the end of the fiscal year to which they relate.

Employee expenses

5.33   An employee is entitled to make a claim for expenditure incurred wholly, exclusively and necessarily in the performance of the duties of the employment. This claim must be made on the employee supplementary pages.

5.34   Where an employer has a dispensation for expense payments then the amounts received will not have to be included as income. An expense claim is then not required by the employee. Normally an employer will inform the employee where payments are made under a dispensation.

Notwithstanding the existence of a dispensation, an employee is entitled to treat the amounts received as income and then to make a claim for the actual expenses incurred. This could arise, for example, where the rate of mileage for business travel paid by the employer is lower than the Inland Revenue authorised rates.

An employee is entitled to claim for business motoring by keeping records of actual motoring costs such as maintenance, insurance and road tax. The business proportion is then calculated. In the same way a claim is made for capital allowances. Note that this option will no longer be available as from 6 April 2002, when any claim by the employee will have to be made on the basis of the authorised mileage rates.

As a simpler alternative the employee maintains a record of business mileage and then applies the authorised rates (set out at 5.25 above). For further details see Inland Revenue leaflet IR125 'using your own car for work'.

Employee travel

5.35 The legislation relating to claims for employee travel in *ICTA 1988, s 198* has been completely rewritten from 6 April 1998. The Revenue's views on the revised possibility for claims are set out in booklet 490 — employee travel and also leaflet IR161 — tax relief for employee's business travel.

An employee is now entitled to make a claim as a deduction against emoluments for:

(a)   qualifying travelling expenses; or
(b)   any amount, other than qualifying travelling expenses, expended wholly, exclusively and necessarily in the performance of the duties of the employment.

Qualifying travelling expenses mean:

(a)   necessary travelling in the performance of the duties of the employment; or
(b)   other travelling expenses which:
    (i)   are expenses of travel to or from a place where necessary duties are to be performed, and
    (ii)   are not expenses of ordinary commuting or private or non-business travel.

Ordinary commuting means travel between:

(a)   the employee's home; or
(b)   a place that is not a workplace in relation to the employment; and

a place which is a permanent workplace. [*ICTA 1988, 12A Sch, 2*].

Permanent workplace means a place which the employee regularly attends in the performance of the duties of the employment, i.e. a place which forms the base from which duties are performed, or is a place at which tasks to be carried out in the performance of duties are allocated. [*12A Sch, 6*].

A temporary workplace means a place which the employee attends in the performance of the duties of the employment for the purpose of performing a task of:

(a)   limited duration; or
(b)   temporary purpose. [*12A Sch, 4*].

A place is a temporary workplace if it is not a permanent workplace and duties are performed there:

(a)   for less than 24 months; or
(b)   less than 40% of working time. [*12A Sch, 5* and *Schedule E Manual SE 32080*].

Note that a place where all, or almost all, of the duties are to be carried out will be a permanent workplace, even if the contract for those duties will last for less than 24 months. [*12A Sch, 5*].

A change of workplace is disregarded if it does not have, or would not have, any substantial effect on the employee's journey, or expense of travelling to that place. Travel between any two places that is for practical purposes substantially ordinary commuting or private travel is treated as ordinary commuting or private travel. [*12A Sch, 3*].

The Inland Revenue have indicated that the above are intended to be common sense rules which apply where journeys are broadly the same as the employee's ordinary commuting journey. The application of the provisions will depend on the particular circumstances of any case. However, the Inland Revenue have indicated that they will not normally seek to argue that a journey to or from a temporary workplace is substantially ordinary commuting where the extra distance involved is ten miles or more each way. The Revenue have further indicated that in their view any journey within zone 1 of the London Underground could be considered the same journey and therefore any change of workplace within that area would be disregarded for the above rules.

As a result of the new provisions, a site-based employee, including many one-man company employees, can now claim travelling expenses from home to site. In order to do so the employee must work at more than one site, those sites must be more than ten miles apart (preferably the journey distance must be more than ten miles difference), the time spent at a site must not exceed two years and the employee should not normally return to the previous site within two years. Such employees should keep a note of distances travelled and motor vehicle used to make claim at box 1.32 on the employment supplementary pages. The claim for travelling expenses can be supplemented by a claim for subsistence, e.g. lunch allowance providing receipts are obtained and a record maintained of the date, place and costs involved.

In addition many employees will be able to make claims for tax relief where the amount paid by the employer is less than that allowed by the Inland Revenue. This could be because the employer's rate is less than the actual costs, or the authorised mileage rates. Alternatively the claim could arise because of allowable business miles that are not paid for by the employer. For example Ike lives in Southampton and works in Winchester; he is required to attend a business meeting in Birmingham. The employer pays travel of Winchester to Birmingham 2 × 116 miles = 232 miles at the authorised rates. The employee is entitled to claim from Southampton to Birmingham a distance of 128 miles × 2 = 256 miles. There is therefore an allowable claim of 24 miles at the authorised rates not reimbursed by the employer. It should be noted that the employee can still make the same claim even if he calls into the office en route providing he undertakes no material duties on his visit. In other words, it is in order to call into the office to pick up or deliver files, paperwork, etc., but not to work.

Where an employee uses the Inland Revenue authorised mileage rates then he is not permitted to claim capital allowances or any other expenses except loan interest. Where the motor vehicle has been purchased on finance then a claim for the business proportion of the interest relating to that purchase will be allowable as an additional claim for a period of up to three years from the end of the year of assessment in which the debt was incurred. [*ICTA 1988, s 359*].

The rules relating to personal services provided via an intermediary (limited company, partnership etc.) provide that for the purpose of expense claims the worker is employed by the intermediary, and the relevant engagements are undertaken in the course of performing the duties of that employment. Accordingly the worker can treat the client's premises as a temporary work place, provided that the conditions set out above are satisfied, and claim travelling expenses from home.

Chapter 6

Trades and Professions

Preceding year basis — the reasons for change

6.1   The reforms introduced by the *Finance Act 1994* rank as amongst the most fundamental changes this century in the way in which individuals deal with their tax affairs. When income tax was introduced, the basis of assessment of profits of the self-employed was the average profits of the three accounts years preceding the year of assessment. This was reviewed on a number of occasions, with a Royal Commission in 1920 recommending the adoption of the preceding year basis of assessment. That commission was attracted to the adoption of a current year basis, but concluded that the practical difficulties of assessment and of dealing with the year of change mitigated against its introduction. The commission concluded that the preceding year basis would make the amount of profits assessed correspond more closely to the profits earned and would be 'a very important step in the direction of uniformity and simplicity'. Thus the preceding year (PY) basis of assessment was introduced by Winston Churchill in the *Finance Act 1926*.

6.2   The basis of assessment was considered many times since the introduction of the preceding year basis. These included the report of the committee on 'The Taxation of Trading Profits' in 1951, which concluded as follows: 'we began our consideration of the problem with a strong predilection for a change to some form of current year basis, and with the help of the Board of Inland Revenue we laboured long in an attempt to find a solution. In the end we were driven to the conclusion that, whatever may be the experience of other countries whose size and circumstances differ greatly from those of our own, a current year basis is impractical in this country'.

The 1955 Royal Commission on 'The Taxation of Profits and Income' concluded that unincorporated businesses should remain on a preceding year basis, whereas companies should transfer to a current year basis. Accordingly corporation tax was introduced on a current year basis in 1965. On that change, the time for payment continued to be based upon the length of the previous period between the end of the company's accounting period and the due date for payment. This was finally ended by the *Finance Act 1987*, which reduced the payment time to a standard nine months for all companies.

6.3   Unincorporated businesses, however, continued to be assessed on the preceding year basis, with increasing concern about the complexity and inequities of the system. In the case of partnerships, some of the worst excesses of the exploitation of opening and closing year rules were curbed by the introduction by the *Finance Act 1988* of *ICTA 1988, s 61(4)*, ensuring that partnerships that did not elect for continuation basis would be assessed on an actual basis for at least four years following the change of partners.

6.4 Notwithstanding the generous time provided for between the preparation of accounts and eventual assessment (from nine months for a 5 April year end to 20 months for a 30 April year end), many accounts and computations were submitted late to the Inland Revenue. In 1989/90 the Revenue raised approximately three million assessments on the self-employed for that tax year, two million of those assessments using estimated figures. Approximately 600,000 appeals were listed for hearing.

The preceding year basis of assessment was not only costly in terms of compliance and administration but complex in terms of rules. Thus, many members of the public were unable to relate their profits as shown in their accounts to their tax assessments. The problem was compounded in the case of partnerships by the fact that the assessment was on the partnership, calculated by reference to the allowances and reliefs of the individual partners, insofar as they were used against partnership income.

If the rules posed difficulties for the professional advisors, they posed equal and rising difficulties for the Revenue. In 1990/91 three and a half million taxpayers had Schedule D, Case I or II income and of that total almost one half did not have professional advice, thus relying upon the staff of the Revenue to compute the assessable profits from the returned income.

Dealings with the Revenue under the old system

6.5 The first Inland Revenue consultative document, 'A Simpler System for Taxing the Self-Employed', issued in 1991, used the example of Jim Smith, a grocer, to illustrate how the old system operates.

Jim prepares his financial statements for the year to 31 August and shows profits of £20,000 for the accounting period 1993/94. He also has £400 per month of rental income, and pays gross interest in the tax year 1995/96 on an allowable loan (not his principal private residence). Income tax is assumed to be levied at the 25% rate and his personal allowances are assumed to be £4,200. The following table summarised Jim's dealings with the Inland Revenue for his affairs in the tax year 1995/96:

1 September 1995	The Inspector of Taxes makes an assessment for 1995/96. He estimates profits of £25,000 from Jim's grocery business. With the £4,800 of rent, he calculates that the tax due is £6,400.
15 September 1995	Jim decides to appeal against the estimated assessment. He applies to postpone £2,500 of the tax.

1 October 1995	The Inspector agrees to the postponement application, leaving Jim with a bill for £3,900.
1 January 1996	Jim pays the first instalment of £2,050.
1 July 1996	Jim pays a second instalment of £1,850.
1 August 1996	The Inspector asks Jim for his return and financial statements for the accounting year ending 31 August 1994.
1 September 1996	The Inspector writes again, warning that Jim's return and financial statements are now overdue.
1 October 1996	Jim is summoned to appear before the General Commissioners on 1 November 1996.
1 November 1996	The General Commissioners adjourn the hearing of Jim's appeal for one month to allow time for the return and accounts to be produced.
30 November 1996	Jim submits his return for the tax year 1995/96 to the Inspector, accompanied by his financial statements for the accounting year ended 31 August 1994.
1 March 1997	The Inspector finally agrees Jim's figures. He sends Jim a revised assessment for 1995/96 showing income of £24,800. Mortgage interest paid and personal allowances are deducted to arrive at taxable income. The tax due of £4,400 is above the amount Jim paid in instalments earlier. The assessment therefore includes a demand for the balance of tax due of £500 and interest from 1 July 1996.

6.6 The Revenue consultation papers were taken forward with the issue of a second paper in November 1992, described as 'A Simpler System for Assessing Personal Tax'. This paper pursued various ideas to remove the above complexities. After extensive consultation, the Chancellor announced in March 1993 that a current year basis of assessment would be adopted. The *Finance Act 1994* provided the framework for the current system.

6.7 Any inference from the title and objectives of the consultation papers that the new system would be simple could easily be dispelled by the 70 pages of legislation, together with a second tranche of legislation in the *1995 Finance Act*, and a further 70 pages in the *1996 Finance Act*, and more legislation in subsequent acts.

Current year basis — the concepts

6.8 The system introduced is known as the 'current year basis'. That is to say, the profits shown by the accounts drawn up in each year are taken as those for the year to the following 5 April. [*ICTA 1988, s 60*]. Thus, if Jim

Smith prepares his accounts for the year to 31 August 2000, these will be treated as the basis period for the year 2000/01.

If accounts are drawn up to 5 April or 31 March in each year of assessment, then the actual profits will apply throughout without difficulty or complication. However, if any other accounting date is chosen, then special rules will apply for opening years, on a change of accounting date, and on cessation.

6.9 Some of the complexities of the new legislation arise from the need to allow complete freedom in the choice of accounting date. There is freedom to change the accounting date at any time, subject to certain anti-avoidance provisions. The Revenue have also taken the opportunity to significantly reduce tax planning opportunities, by introducing a system with the stated objective of taxing precisely the profits earned by a business over the lifetime of the business. This is achieved by calculating the profits that are taxed more than once (known as overlap profits) and then by giving a pro-rata credit whenever a change of accounting date results in a period of greater than twelve months being assessed. Any remaining overlap profits will be deducted from the final assessment of the business when it ceases. If inflation is ignored, the result will be that exactly the profits earned by the business will be taxed during the lifetime of the business. As a further simplification, the concept of separate relief for capital allowances is abolished. Under the provisions, capital allowances become trading expenses or trading receipts, as for corporation tax.

6.10 The resultant package for the unincorporated business achieves the objectives of allowing complete freedom in choice of accounting date and taxes profits once and once only, but certainly is not simple, and bears very little resemblance to the proposals in the consultation documents.

The new rules

6.11 The new rules apply to all businesses commencing on or after 6 April 1994.

For businesses in existence on 5 April 1994:

(a)   1995/96 was the last year to which the preceding year basis applies;

(b)   1996/97 was the transitional year (the assessable profits being based upon the twelve-month average of the profits from the end of the preceding basis period for 1995/96 to the commencement of the current year basis period for 1997/98 — see Appendix C);

(c)   1997/98 was the first year in which the assessment was based upon the accounts ending in the fiscal year (current year basis).

6.12 The new legislation relating to cessations applies at all times to businesses which commenced on or after 6 April 1994. The new rules also apply to businesses which commenced before 6 April 1994 and permanently discontinue after 5 April 1999 (see 6.41 *et seq* below).

6.13   For businesses which commenced before 6 April 1994 but ceased before 6 April 1997, the old rules applied. For those ceasing between 6 April 1997 and 5 April 1999, transitional rules apply (see Appendix C).

6.14   With effect from 6 April 1997, partnerships are no longer assessed on the profits of the partnership. Each individual partner's share of profits in a period of account is assessed on him individually.

All partnership expenses and capital allowances are given against the profits of the partnership. The resultant profits are allocated by reference to the profit-sharing ratios for the period of account. Where there is a change in the ownership of the partnership and at least one partner carries on the business before and after the change, then it is not a cessation for tax purposes. The new rules apply to partnerships commencing, or deemed to commence, on or after 6 April 1994. Since 6 April 1997, these rules apply to all partnerships. Partnerships are discussed in detail in Chapter 7 below.

6.15   As a result of the move to a current year basis, a number of changes are made to the provisions granting loss relief. Where relief is claimed against other income, it will be given against the income of the year of loss or of the preceding year. The loss relief will be taken after capital allowances. The previous statutory fiscal year basis of loss relief has been abolished. The new rules apply from 6 April 1997 for existing businesses and from 6 April 1994 for businesses commencing after that date. For examples and further details of loss relief, see Chapter 9 below.

6.16   As well as the introduction of new rules for Schedule D, Case I and II, there were similar provisions to remove the preceding year basis of assessment from Schedule D, Case III, IV and V. The transitional provisions are set out in Appendix C.

Dealings with the Revenue under the new system

6.17   To compare the contacts with the Revenue under the new system, Jim Smith, a grocer making his accounts to 31 August 1997, might have the following dealings with the Revenue:

31 January 1998	Jim pays his first payment on account for 1997/98, being 50% of the 1996/97 assessment excluding capital gains tax (he also makes the balancing payment/obtains repayment in respect of 1996/97).
6 April 1998	Jim receives his tax return for the year ended 5 April 1998.
31 July 1998	Jim makes his second payment on account for 1997/98 (equal to that paid on 31 January 1998).

30 November 1998   Jim submits his tax return for the year 1997/98 to the Inspector of Taxes incorporating his financial statements for the accounting year ended 31 August 1997 and his computation of self-assessment.

31 January 1999   Jim pays the balancing payment in respect of 1997/98. He also pays 50% of the total liability for 1997/98 excluding capital gains as first payment on account for 1998/99.

Note that if Jim wished the Revenue to assess him, rather than to self-assess his liability, then the accounts for the year ended 31 August 1997 would have to be prepared and the tax return for the year ended 5 April 1998 filed with the Revenue by 30 September 1998.

The above table, when compared with the earlier table, shows the reduction of the involvement of the Revenue in the assessing process. If the self-assessment option is chosen, then the onus of computing the correct liability falls upon the taxpayer or his advisors.

6.18 To make the current year basis of assessment work, it is necessary for accounts to be prepared timeously. In the case of a business making its accounts to the fiscal year end of 5 April, there is just under ten months in which to prepare accounts and tax computations together with tax returns. The tax due based upon those figures will then be due as the balancing payment on 31 January following the tax year, with the figures forming the basis of the payments on account for the coming year. In the case of a business making up its accounts to 30 April, the appropriate period of time will be one year and nine months.

Notwithstanding the apparent generous time scale, it must be remembered that where a partnership is involved, the accounts together with the division of profits must be agreed by the partners in sufficient time to enable the individual partner to complete his personal return and self-assessment. In some instances the use of an early accounting date in the fiscal year, e.g. 30 April, will be advisable to give time for proper consideration of all of the issues involved.

6.19 The original proposals in the consultation paper 'A Simpler System for Taxing the Self-Employed' proposed a very rudimentary system whereby there were no adjustments for opening and closing years. Although the proposals had the advantage of simplicity, they could have led to inequity. This would occur where more than one year's income fell into charge in one year of assessment, thus potentially leading to higher rate tax, with another year having nil or limited income and surplus unusable personal allowances.

Overlap relief

6.20 The legislation introduced abandons the object of simplicity in favour of equality. Consequently, it is necessary to compute the assessments in the first and second years of a new business by reference to special rules. As a result of using computational rules for this period, some profits are assessed more than once. The precise amount of profits assessed more than once are calculated together with the number of days of assessment that overlap. This is known as 'overlap relief', with the profits counted twice known as 'overlap profits' and the number of days involved as the 'overlap period'.

When a business ceases, the overlap profits are treated as a trading expense of the final year of assessment and thereby the actual profits assessed over the life of the business are exactly equal to the actual profits earned by that business. However, no account is taken of inflation. Therefore, in times of high inflation, the current year basis of assessment will result in a disadvantage to the self-employed, compared with the preceding year basis which in the same circumstances gave an advantage to the self-employed.

For the interaction of double tax relief and overlap profits, see 11.8 below.

Capital allowances and losses

6.21 The new system does, however, have a number of simplifying features compared with the previous legislation. Capital allowances are treated as a trading expense, with balancing charges treated as trading receipts. All calculations are made on profits or losses adjusted for capital allowances. In the same way, the highly complex rules relating to loss relief in opening and closing years are simplified. In the first instance the losses are dealt with after capital allowances (rather than with the option to add capital allowances). Next, the previous fiscal year basis of loss relief is abolished and is replaced by a current year basis. Thus there is symmetry between profits and losses for the first time.

Finally, partnerships are no longer liable to tax on the profits of the partnership, but each individual partner is assessed on his own share for the relevant period of account. Accordingly, the question of opening and closing years applying on the removal or introduction of partners, and the need for partnership continuation elections, is removed.

Apportionments

6.22 *ICTA 1988, s 72* provides that where apportionment is necessary, such apportionments are to be made on a time basis in proportion to the number of days. Previously, such apportionments were made in months or fractions of months. However, the Revenue will still accept any other reasonable time-based apportionment provided that it is applied consistently. [Inland Revenue SAT 1, 1.17]. Accordingly, it is still permissible to apportion in months.

If a more accurate measure of profits for any period can be found, for example by reference to the transactions which took place during the period, then apportionment by days does not apply. [Inland Revenue SAT 1, 1.18 to 1.20].

Use of 31 March as year end

6.23 Where the taxpayer so requests, the Revenue are prepared to accept accounts drawn up to 31 March as the equivalent of accounts to 5 April. This will have the effect that:

(a) the profits of the accounts to 31 March each year will be taxed as though they were for the year to the following 5 April;

(b) for businesses which commence in the period 1 April to 5 April, the assessment for year 1 will be nil;

(c) there will be no overlap profit and no overlap relief for any later year.

[Inland Revenue SAT 1, 1.99].

However this concession does not appear to apply to partnerships that are intermediaries under the personal service legislation. Accordingly such partnerships are required to prepare accounts to 5 April to obtain a deduction for deemed salary and national insurance for Schedule D in the same fiscal year as the deemed salary is charged to tax under Schedule E.

Opening years

Accounts prepared to 5 April

6.24 To precisely tax the profits of the business over the lifetime of the business without complex opening year rules would have required the compulsory use of 5 April as an accounting date. That date still has much to commend it in terms of simplicity, and for many very small businesses and those not using professional advice it will be the only practicable choice. Where accounts are drawn up for the period to 5 April in each year, depreciation is calculated by using the capital allowance rules, and adjustments have been made on the face of the accounts for private proportions of expenditure, then, providing that there are no disallowable items in the account, the profits shown will be the assessable profit for that fiscal year. There are no opening or closing year adjustments, and overlap relief does not apply.

Example

6.25 Alan Brown commenced trading on 1 May 2001, making up his first accounts to 5 April 2002. His profits as adjusted for income tax purposes are:

	£
1.5.2001 to 5.4.02	22,000
Year ended 5.4.03	30,000
Year ended 5.4.04	18,000

His assessable profits will be:

		£
2001/02	1.5.2001 to 5.4.02	22,000
2002/03	Year ended 5.4.03	30,000
2003/04	Year ended 5.4.04	18,000

Accounts prepared to a date other than 5 April

6.26   Many businesses will not find 5 April to be the most convenient date to which accounts should be drawn up. The new provisions allow any date to be chosen to suit the business needs. However, where a date other than 5 April is used, then the profits assessed in the first fiscal year of the business' life are those earned from the date of commencement to the following 5 April. [*ICTA 1988, s 61(1)*].

6.27   The assessment for the second year will depend upon the accounting date chosen. If the accounts for the first trading period end in the second year of assessment, and the length of that account is less than twelve months, then the basis of assessment for the second year will be the first twelve months of trading. [*ICTA 1988, s 61(2)*].

6.28   In the more normal circumstance of the first period of account being for twelve months or more, with a date ending in the second year of assessment, then the assessment for the second year will be based upon the twelve months ending on the chosen accounting date. [*ICTA 1988, s 60(3)(a)*].

6.29   When a business starts late in a fiscal year, it is quite normal for there to be two fiscal years without any accounting date. In those circumstances the assessment for the second year will be the actual profits of the fiscal year. [*ICTA 1988, s 60(1)*]. The assessment for the third year will then be based upon the twelve months ending on the chosen accounting date. [*ICTA 1988, s 60(3)(a)*].

For subsequent years of assessment, the basis period will be the period ending on the accounting date that falls within the fiscal year. [*ICTA 1988, s 60(2)(3)(b)*].

Short-life businesses

6.30   The new rules apply to all businesses commencing on or after 6 April 1994 and for businesses commencing before that date from 6 April 1997. [*FA 1994, s 218*].

If a business commences and finishes in the same fiscal year, then the profits will be the amounts earned during the life of the business. If the business has a life of less than two fiscal years, then actual basis applies throughout. [*ICTA 1988, s 63(a)*].

To illustrate the possible variations, it is useful to consider a series of examples.

Accounts made up to a date twelve months after the date of commencement

Example

6.31   Brenda Clarke commenced trading on 6 May 2000, making up her accounts to 5 May 2001. Her profits as adjusted for income tax purposes are:

	£
Year ended 5.5.01	24,000
Year ended 5.5.02	30,000
Year ended 5.5.03	18,000

Her assessments are:

	£
2000/01: 6.5.2000 to 5.4.01 (335/365 × 24,000)	22,027
2001/02: 6.5.2000 to 5.5.01	24,000
2002/03: Year ended 5.5.02	30,000
2003/04: Year ended 5.5.03	18,000

Overlap profits of £22,027 will be carried forward for use on a change of accounting date or cessation, based upon an overlap period of 6 May 2000 to 5 April 2001 (335 days). The only accounts taken into aggregation are of the year ended 5 May 2001. The figures are those adjusted for income tax purposes after the claims for capital allowances.

First accounts ending in fiscal year of commencement

6.32 Many businesses commence trading and make up accounts for a short trading period to the chosen accounting date. Where the first accounting period ends in the fiscal year of commencement, then it will be necessary to prepare a second set of accounts before it is possible to compute the first assessment. The assessment for the first trading year is based upon actual profits, and for the second year on the profits to the new accounting date, with the overlap profits being calculated on the second accounts.

Example

6.33 Colin Davies commenced trading on 1 June 2000, making up his accounts to 31 December 2000 and annually to that date thereafter.

His adjusted profits are:

	£
7 months to 31.12.2000	7,000
Year ended 31.12.01	36,500
Year ended 31.12.02	42,000

His assessable profits will be:

		£
2000/01	1.6.2000 to 31.12.2000	7,000
	1.1.01 to 5.4.01 (95/365 × £36,500)	9,500
		16,500
2001/02	Year ended 31.12.01	36,500
2002/03	Year ended 31.12.02	42,000

Overlap profits of £9,500 will be carried forward, the overlap period being from 1 January 2001 to 5 April 2001 (95 days). Capital allowances will be based upon accounting periods, so that for the seven months to 31 December 2000 the claim for writing down allowances will be 7/12ths of the annual amount.

First accounts for more than twelve months ending in second year of assessment

6.34   Where accounts are made up for a first period that exceeds twelve months, but ends in the second year of assessment, then the basis period for that second year will be the twelve months ending with the chosen accounting date.

Example

6.35   Freda Gray commenced trading on 1 June 2000 making her accounts up to 30 September each year, commencing 30 September 2001.

Her adjusted profits are:

	£
16 months to 30.9.01	24,350
Year ended 30.9.02	16,000

Her assessable profits will be:

		£
2000/01	1.6.2000 to 5.4.01	
	(309/487 × £24,350)	15,450
2001/02	1.10.2000 to 30.9.01	
	(365/487 × £24,350)	18,250
2002/03	1.10.01 to 30.9.02	16,000

Overlap profits of £15,450 + £18,250 = £33,700 − £24,350 = £9,350 will be carried forward with an overlap period of 1 October 2000 to 5 April 2001 (187 days).

Capital allowances will be based upon accounting periods, so that for the 16 months to 30 September 2001 the writing-down allowances will be 16/12ths of the annual amount.

First accounts ending in third year of assessment

6.36   If a business chooses an accounting date close to the commencement date, it is often not practicable to prepare accounts for a very short first period. If, for example, a business commences on 1 March and wishes to have a May year-end, it will not wish to prepare accounts for three months but will be more likely to prepare accounts for 15 months. This may cause problems in calculating the tax chargeable for the first two years of assessment (see Chapter 2 on self-assessment and Chapter 4 on interest), as it will be necessary to include a best estimate of assessable profits in the tax return so that it may be filed by the due date, and then it will be necessary to amend the return within twelve months. Therefore, for a commencement on 1 March 2001, an estimate will have to be used in the tax return for the year ended 5 April 2001 and tax will have to be paid on that estimate on 31 January 2002. The accounts for the period to 31 May 2002 must be submitted to the Revenue by 31 January 2003 to avoid the need for a further estimate for the second year, and to be in time to amend the previous return.

It will be noticed that, if accounts are prepared for a first period that ends in the third fiscal year, then the time between the end of the accounting period and the filing date for the second year's accounts can be very short. In the following example only eight months would be available from the end of the accounting period to the last day for filing. Interest would be charged from the due date of payment to the actual date. If the estimate is too high, then the 'repayment' rate of interest will be used to calculate the interest due to the taxpayer. The calculation of the assessments themselves is straightforward. The first year is based upon the appropriate proportion of profits relating to the actual period falling in the first fiscal year. The second assessment is on the twelve months' profits of the first trading period (being the fiscal year), and the third year's assessment will be on the twelve months ending on the new accounting date. Capital allowances will be computed for the period of account unless that period exceeds 18 months (see Chapter 8 below).

Example

6.37   Doreen Ely commenced trading on 1 March 2001 making up her first accounts to 31 May 2002 and annually thereafter.

Her adjusted profits are:

	£
15 months to 31.5.02	45,700
Year ended 31.5.03	30,000

Her assessable profits will be:

	£
2000/01	
1.3.01 to 5.4.01	
(36/457 × £45,700)	3,600
2001/02	
6.4.01 to 5.4.02	
(365/457 × £45,700)	36,500
2002/03	
Year ended 31.5.02	
(365/457 × £45,700)	36,500
2003/04	
Year ended 31.5.03	30,000

Overlap profits of £3,600 + £36,500 + £36,500 = £76,600 − £45,700 = £30,900 will be carried forward, based on an overlap period of 1 June 2001 to 5 April 2002 (309 days). Capital allowances will be based upon the period of account which, being less than 18 months, will give a WDA of 15/12ths.

First accounts for less than twelve months ending in second year of assessment

6.38 The timing of the incurring of expenditure is not the only factor that should be considered in the opening years. The length of the first accounting period, and the number of times in which it falls into aggregation, will also affect the assessments and overlap profits. The following example illustrates an instance where there are two overlap profits to be calculated. The second part shows that different assessments can arise on the same adjusted profits. In total the assessments using separate accounts are £824 lower than combining the accounts, but with a corresponding reduction in overlap relief. It must be remembered, however, that this may not occur in practice, as the capital allowances could be reduced in the second part of the example by virtue of being calculated in two parts. The actual timing of expenditure will determine whether the assessable profits are greater, lesser or the same.

Example

6.39 Eric Fry commences trading on 1 January 2001 making up his first accounts to 30 September 2001 and annually thereafter.

His adjusted profits are:

	£
9 months to 30.9.01	5,460
Year ended 30.9.02	47,450
Year ended 30.9.03	60,000

His assessable profits will be:

		£	£
2000/01	1.1.01 to 5.4.01		1,900
	(95/273 × £5,460)		
2001/02	1.1.01 to 31.12.01		
	273 days to 30.09.01 =	5,460	
	92 days to 31.12.01 =	11,960	17,420
	(92/365 × 47,450)		
2002/03	Year ended 30.9.02		47,450
2003/04	Year ended 30.9.03		60,000

Overlap profits of £1,900 + £17,420 = £19,320 − £5,460 = £13,860 are available to carry forward. Overlap periods of 1 January 2001 to 5 April 2001

(95 days) and 1 October 2001 to 31 December 2001 (92 days) = 187 days. Capital allowances will be based on WDA of 9/12ths in the first period.

Note: If the first accounts are made up to 30 September 2002 with adjusted profits of £52,910, the assessments will be:

		£
2000/01	1.1.01 to 5.4.01 95/638 × £52,910	7,878
2001/02	6.4.01 to 5.4.02 365/638 × £52,910	30,270
2002/03	1.10.01 to 30.9.02 365/638 × £52,910	30,270

Overlap profits of £7,878 + £30,270 + £30,270 = £68,418 − £52,910 = £15,508.

Overlap period of 1 October 2001 to 5 April 2002 (187 days). Revised capital allowances periods of account will be:

Year ended 31.12.01	WDA 12/12ths
1.1.02 to 30.9.02	WDA 9/12ths

The total allowances for the above periods will be deducted from the profits of the 21-month period to 30 September 2002.

Where accounts are divided as to nine months followed by a year, a comparison of the resulting assessments with those resulting from the combining of the first two accounting periods is as follows:

	Separate periods	*Combined accounts*
2000/01	1,900	7,878
2001/02	17,420	30,270
2002/03	47,450	30,270
Overlap profits	(13,860)	(15,508)

6.40 Further factors to consider are the other taxable income and available allowances of the taxpayer. In the above example, if Eric Fry had no other income then he would have unused allowances in 2000/01 if separate accounts were submitted. On the same basis, he could well be a higher rate taxpayer in 2002/03. By combining the accounts, the profit profile is smoother and therefore allowances are not wasted and higher rate tax is not likely to be incurred.

Commencement of the new rules

6.41 For new businesses, the above rules apply to those that commenced trading on or after 6 April 1994. The old rules for the first three years apply to businesses that commenced before that date, even where the second and third years were 1994/95 and 1995/96.

For businesses in existence on 5 April 1994 the new rules apply from 1997/98, with a transitional year of 1996/97. [*FA 1994, s 218*].

Summary of the opening year rules

6.42 Year of Assessment	**Basis of Assessment**
Opening Year	Actual (to 5 April)
Second Year Accounts ending in year: Under twelve months Twelve months or more No accounts ending in second year	 First twelve months of trading Year ending on accounting date Actual (year ended 5 April)
Third Year	Year ending on accounting date

Note: If the accounting date is changed in the second or third year, see 10.15 below for special rules that may apply.

Closing years

Overlap relief

6.43 When a period of account is taken into assessment more than once, the profits that are duplicated are eligible for overlap relief. Such an overlap can arise on commencement, or on a change of accounting date where the new accounting date is earlier in the fiscal year and under the transitional rules. If there is a change of accounting date such that more than twelve months is taken into account, then overlap relief is deducted from profits on a pro-rata basis (see Chapter 10 below). Any relief remaining at cessation is taken into account in computing the profits of the final period. [*ICTA 1988, s 63A(3)*]. There is no provision for indexation of the overlap relief.

Accounting date of 5 April

6.44 If a business makes up its accounts to 5 April in each year, then there will be no overlap profits and the final assessment will be based on the actual profits from 6 April to the date of cessation. [*ICTA 1988, s 63(b)*].

Example

6.45 Alan Brown, who makes up his accounts to 5 April each year, ceases to trade on 30 November 2002. His final assessment will be based upon the period 6 April 2002 to 30 November 2002.

Accounting date of other than 5 April

6.46 When a business ceases and the accounting date is not 5 April, the profits to be taken into account for the final year of assessment will be those arising from the end of the basis period ending in the preceding year to the date of cessation. [*ICTA 1988, s 63(b)*]. This period may be more or less than twelve months. Normally, capital allowances will be computed as a balancing charge or a balancing allowance. However, if the final period of account is for more than 18 months, then capital allowances will be claimed for the twelve-month period, with a balancing charge or allowance for the final period.

Example

6.47 Continuing the example of Brenda Clarke at 6.31 above (a business that commenced on 6 May 2000). On commencement overlap profits of £22,027 were calculated. These are now brought forward and relieved against the final assessment. She makes up her accounts to 5 May each year and ceases to trade on 5 May 2004 with final adjusted profits of £26,000 and overlap profits brought forward of £22,027.

	£
Adjusted profits year ended 5.5.04	26,000
Less overlap profits	22,027
Assessment — 2004/05	3,973

Note: If the final profits had been £6,000 the assessment would be:

	£
2004/05	6,000
Less overlap profits	22,027
	NIL
Loss relief available on	16,027

Relief for the loss may be given by way of normal loss relief or terminal loss relief (see Chapter 9 below).

More than one accounting date in year of cessation

6.48 If the final period of trading is a short period and ends in the same fiscal year as the normal accounting date, then the normal accounting date is ignored and the assessment is based upon the period of the full twelve months from the normal accounting date in the preceding year plus the final period of account, less the overlap profits. [*ICTA 1988, s 60(5)*]. The profits are of course adjusted for capital allowances.

Example

6.49 Take the results of Brenda Clarke shown above and assume that she continued to trade for a further six months, ceasing to trade on 5 November 2004 with adjusted profits of:

	£
Year ended 5.5.04	26,000
6 months to 5.11.04	15,000

Then the assessment will be based upon the period from the accounting date ending in preceding year to the date of cessation:

2004/05	£
6.5.03 to 5.11.04	
(26,000 + 15,000)	41,000
Less overlap profits	22,027
	18,973

In computing the above figures, capital allowances would be deducted for the year ended 5 May 2004 and a balancing allowance (or charge) deducted or added for the final period. Exactly the same assessments would occur if the accounts had been aggregated.

Example

	Profits	*CAs*	*Adjusted profits*
Year ended 5.5.04	36,000	10,000	26,000
6.5.04 to 5.11.04	16,000	1,000	15,000
	52,000	11,000	41,000

based upon a capital allowance computation of:

	Pool £
Brought forward at 6.5.03	40,000
WDA year ended 5.5.04	10,000
	30,000
Sale	29,000
Balancing allowance	1,000

If one set of accounts had been prepared for the 18 months, the adjusted profits before capital allowances would be £52,000, with a capital allowance computation of:

	Pool £
Brought forward at 6.5.03	40,000
Sale	29,000
Balancing allowance	11,000

and adjusted profits after allowances of £52,000 – £11,000 = £41,000 as above.

No accounting date in penultimate year of assessment

6.50   A very common situation will be the closure of a business where accounts are prepared for a final trading period that exceeds twelve months.

There may be no accounts ending in the penultimate tax year so the basis period for that tax year will be prescribed by *ICTA 1988, s 60(3)(b)*, i.e. the period of twelve months beginning immediately after the end of the basis of period for the year before. The rule in *ICTA 1988, s 63(b)* then applies, so that the basis period for the year of cessation is the period commencing immediately after the preceding basis period, i.e. that for the penultimate year, to the date of cessation. The overlap profit relief brought forward is deducted from the final assessment, i.e. that for the year of cessation only. [*ICTA 1988, s 63A(3)*].

By comparison, capital allowances are deducted from the period of account as though they were a trading expense. [*CAA 2001, s 247*]. If the period of account is for more than 18 months, then the period of account is divided, for capital allowances purposes only, into a period of twelve months followed by the balance period. The capital allowances computed for those periods are then aggregated and deducted from the adjusted profits (before capital allowances) for the whole period. [*CAA 2001, s 6*].

Example

6.51 Susan Taylor, who has made up her accounts to 31 December each year for many years, and who has overlap profits for the period 1 January 1997 to 5 April 1997 of £6,500, ceases to trade on 31 July 2002, with adjusted profits before capital allowances for the 19-month period of £28,300.

On 1 January 2001 she had a pool residue of £16,000. On 30 November 2001 she purchased a vehicle (no private use) for £3,200 and on cessation all pool assets were sold for £11,800. Assume no first year allowance is available.

Her capital allowance claims would be:

	Pool £
Forward at 1.1.01	16,000
Additions year ended 31.12.01	3,200
	19,200
Writing-down allowance	4,800
	14,400
Sale period ended 31.7.02	11,800
Balancing allowance	2,600

Adjusted profits before capital allowances:

	£	£
19 months to 31.7.02		28,300
Less CAs — year ended 31.12.01	4,800	
Period ended 31.7.02	2,600	7,400
Profits of period of account		20,900
Assessments:		
2001/02 Year ended 31.12.01		
(365/577 × £20,900)		13,221

2002/03	1.1.02 to 31.7.02		
	(212/577 × £20,900)	7,679	
Less overlap profits		6,500	1,179

The effect of the rules is that any restrictions in the writing-down allowance in the penultimate period will merely be reflected in the balancing adjustment. Therefore, in most instances, it will be possible to take the pool brought forward and deduct the eventual sale proceeds. It will, of course, be necessary to go through the full calculation if, for example, differing private usage occurs in the relevant periods.

It is not possible to increase (or decrease) the assessment of the final period to take into account overlap relief and the need to have sufficient income to cover personal allowances by revision of the capital allowances. In this instance, simplification reduces the ability of the tax advisor to maximise the use of allowances, or minimise the effect of higher rates of taxation in one period against the other.

Existing businesses ceasing

6.52   If a business was trading on 6 April 1994 and ceased to trade before 6 April 1997, then the cessation rules under the old provisions apply. [*FA 1994, 20 Sch 3(1)*].

6.53   If such a business continues to trade beyond 6 April 1997, then the new rules apply (as set out in 6.44 *et seq* above) but with special provisions, enabling the Revenue to amend assessments where cessation occurs in the fiscal year 1997/98 or 1998/99. [*FA 1994, 20 Sch 3(2)(3)*]. (See Appendix C.)

Choice of accounting date

6.54   The new rules limit the opportunities for tax planning. Nevertheless, the actual tax liability can vary even if the total assessable profits are the same. This arises due to bunching of profits, thus giving a charge at higher rates, or very low profits (and loss of personal allowances).

A second consideration will be the time at which the tax is paid. If profits are deferred to a later date then there is a cash flow advantage.

In order to determine precisely the most advantageous accounting date it is necessary to know:

(a)   the date of cessation; and
(b)   the profits of the last 23 months of trading.

Obviously the above information will not be available when the business commences. Accordingly there is an element of chance in the choice in any accounting date.

The use of 5 April eliminates the down side risk. For many small businesses, and those without professional advisers, the simplicity of 5 April (31 March) will mean that it is the obvious choice.

Where a trader makes losses during the overlap period, then there is a very strong argument for using 31 March or 5 April as the accounting date. See Chapter 9 for examples. This prevents a time bomb effect on cessation where overlap relief brought forward is nil and there is a long final period.

In the same way partnerships (other than loss-making businesses) may well find the convenience of the extra time more important than the effect on an individual partner who is joining or leaving the partnership. See Chapter 7 for the problems specific to partnerships.

To many other businesses, the practicalities of stock-taking and other year end procedures will dictate the most practical accounting date. The possibility of a future tax advantage should not be allowed to override the realities of business life.

For any business not covered by one of the above points, the choice of accounting date may be influenced by taxation considerations. If the business is likely to remain a sole tradership, and its cessation profits to be similar to its opening year profits, then overlap relief is not important. Accordingly, the use of an accounting date early in the tax year will give a cash flow advantage if profits rise. Similarly the use of a 5 April year end would be advantageous if profits are likely to fall in the intervening period.

If a business is commencing with low profits and likely to cease (e.g. on formation of a limited company) with high profits then overlap will occur at low rates of tax and only a small amount of relief will be available when the long period is taxed at high rates. In the same way if a business is starting with high profits and likely to finish with low profits then the overlap will be taxed at high rates with relief given at low or nil rates (when profits would otherwise be covered by personal allowances). In those circumstances use of 5 April year end removes the risk of loss.

Use of overlap relief

6.55 For existing businesses consideration should be given to using overlap relief at the highest possible tax rates. This particularly applies to businesses that have transitional overlap profits. If it is likely that the business profits will decline towards cessation then it is possible that the overlap relief will be of minimal value when used. Accordingly consideration should be given to using the relief at 40% rates wherever possible. This can be done by moving the accounting date nearer to 31 March within the fiscal year. Remember that if the resultant period is more than 18 months then two separate sets of accounts and self-employment pages will be required to have a valid change of accounting date. Notice must be given to the Revenue by 31 January following the end of the year of assessment to which the change relates. Care must be taken with the notification date as the date for amending the tax return is twelve months after 31 January following the end of the year of assessment. The date for notification is therefore one year earlier than the latest date for submitting accounting details.

Example

John Smith makes his accounts to 31 August in each year. His profits for the year ended 31 August 2000 being £50,000 after capital allowances. He submits his 2000/01 tax return in July 2001.

When accounts for the year to 31 August 2001 are prepared it is realised that the profits have declined to £12,000. John Smith has overlap profits brought forward of £27,000. In January 2002 accounts are prepared for the period 1 September 2000 to 31 March 2001 which show profits of £8,000. The budgeted profits for the year ended 31 March 2002 being £14,000.

Without change of accounting date

Without change of accounting date, assessments are:

2000/01
Year ended 31/08/2000 — £50,000

2001/02
Year ended 31/08/2001 — £12,000

With change of accounting date

With change of accounting date, assessments are:

2000/01

Year ended 31/08/2000	£50,000
Period ended 31/03/2001	£8,000
	£58,000
Less overlap relief	£27,000
	£31,000

2001/02
Year ended 31/03/2002 (budgeted)   £14,000

Not only has the assessable profits declined from £62,000 to £45,000, but it is likely that the whole of the £45,000 will be liable at rates not exceeding the basic rate.

In the above example the latest date for notification of a change of accounting date is 31 January 2002. The amendment to the 2000/01 tax return can be filed by 31 January 2003. Note the comparatively short time period between becoming aware that profits have declined and the notification of change of accounting date. Early preparation of accounts is still advisable even if the latest date for filing those accounts is some way in the future. This will enable the tax planner to use the information provided to the best advantage.

Chapter 7

Partnerships

Self-assessment with partnership income

7.1   The legislation introduced by the *Finance Act 1994* made fundamental and far-reaching changes to the taxation of partnerships. *ICTA 1988, s 111* previously provided that where two or more people carried on a trade or profession, the income tax was computed for the partnership and they were jointly liable for that tax liability.

7.2   For partnerships commencing on or after 6 April 1994, partnerships changing partners after that date and not making a continuation election, and for existing partnerships from 1997/98, the new *section 111 (as substituted by FA 1994, s 215)* applies, and the partnership is no longer assessed to tax. Instead, each individual partner is responsible for his or her own taxation liability.

7.3   The income of the partnership is still computed in accordance with the schedules to arrive at the taxable amount for the period of account. For partnerships, a 'period of account' basis applies to all sources of untaxed income, not just trading sources. Therefore, if the partnership has Schedule D, Case III or Schedule A income, that amount is computed on a current year basis, rather than an actual fiscal year basis. [*ICTA 1988, s 111(4)*].

Having arrived at the taxable income under each schedule, that amount is divided between the partners in the profit-sharing ratio of the period of account.

7.4   The partnership will be responsible for making a return of its income to the Revenue, showing the division of that income between the partners in the partnership statement. The partnership information will also show the name and address, tax reference number and national insurance number of each partner. The partnership should nominate a partner to provide the above information and to agree the taxation liabilities with the Revenue. A binding agreement between the Revenue and that party will bind all of the partners. If the partnership does not nominate a partner, then the Revenue may issue a tax return to any or all of the partners individually. If the nominated partner ceases to be available (e.g. dies or leaves the partnership), then the remaining partners should nominate a successor.

Any expenditure incurred by a partner on behalf of the partnership must be included in the partnership return. It will not be possible for individual partners to make supplementary claims, whether to expenses or capital allowances, in their own tax returns. (See help sheet IR231.)

7.5   The time limit for filing the partnership return will normally be 31 January following the end of the fiscal year of assessment. However, in practice it will be necessary to complete the detail of the partnership return well before that date, to enable the partnership to provide the individual partners with the detail of income from the relevant sources to include in their own personal tax returns. Each individual partner will then be responsible for filing his or her own tax return and paying his or her own tax.

The Revenue has indicated that, in the case of large partnerships, it would be prepared to accept payment from the partnership, with a schedule of the division of amounts between the individual partners. Note that each partner will have an individual tax reference and possibly a different tax district.

If the individual partner does not receive the detail of his share of income in time to complete his own tax return, there will be a penalty. It will be collected from the individual partner in respect of the partnership's failure to file a tax return. In addition, there will also be a penalty in respect of the individual's own failure to file by the due date. It may therefore be appropriate, in the case of large or difficult partnerships, to have an accounting date early in the fiscal year, so that more time is available to agree the accounts and the division of partnership profits.

New partners

7.6   Under self-assessment, each partner is taxed individually. Therefore, when a person joins a partnership, he must estimate his share of profits from the date of commencement to the following 5 April and include that estimate in his personal tax return. If the partnership makes up its accounts to a date early in the fiscal year, then the actual figures will be available and no estimates will be required.

The new partner will show his income tax basis period on his personal return. In the year of commencement, this will be the date of commencement in box 4.5 and the 5 April following commencement in box 4.6. If no accounting period of the partnership ends in that period then the share of profit to be entered in box 4.7 will be '0'. In those circumstances an estimate of the taxable profit should be entered in box 4.8 with a reference to that being made in the additional information box 4.79. Additionally, a tick should be entered in box 23.3 with a note in box 23.6 of why the figure is provisional and a date by which the correct figure will be filed. If the accounts ending after the 5 April have been prepared then an actual figure can be entered in box 4.8.

Example

7.7   Joan becomes a partner in Books For All on 1 June 2000. Books For All has made up its accounts to 30 April for many years.

First year of assessment (for Joan) — 2000/01

Joan will be assessed on her profits from 1 June 2000 (box 4.5) to 5 April 2001 (box 4.6) (being part of the accounts for the year ended 30 April 2001).

The above amount must be included in her tax return for 2000/01, which must be filed by 31 January 2002. Joan will hopefully have an agreed profit figure for the year ended 30 April 2001 before she needs to file her tax return, entering into box 4.8 the amount relating to the period 1 June 2000 to 5 April 2001.

Second year of assessment (for Joan) — 2001/02

As Joan has only been a partner since 1 June 2000, her period of account is effectively 1 June 2000 to 30 April 2001. As this period is less than twelve months, she will be assessed on the profits of her first twelve months of trading.

Joan is therefore assessed on the period 1 June 2000 (box 4.5) to 31 May 2001 (box 4.6). In order to compute her assessments, she will need the accounts for the year ended 30 April 2002, but as her tax return for 2001/02 does not have to be filed until 31 January 2003, this information should be available by the due date.

Joan will include in box 4.7 her share of the profit or loss for the accounts ending 30 April 2001. This will be for the period 1 June 2000 to 30 April 2001. She will then need to add the period of 1 May 2001 to 31 May 2001 to the return. This is done by adding that relevant share of profit in box 4.8.

Joan will compute overlap profits for the period 1 June 2000 to 5 April 2001 (box 4.11). That overlap relief will be personal to Joan.

Third year of assessment (for Joan) — 2002/03

Joan will now be assessed on the period of account for the year ended 30 April 2002, i.e. in line with all other partners. The accounts for the year ended 30 April 2002 form the basis of assessment for 2002/03, with a latest filing date of 31 January 2004.

Joan will now compute further overlap profits for the period 1 May 2001 to 31 May 2001 (being the amount entered in box 4.8 on the 2001/02 tax return). This is added to the amount brought forward (shown in box 4.9 on the 2002/03 return) to give the increased figure carried forward in box 4.11 of the 2002/03 return.

By comparison, if a partnership makes up its accounts to a date late in the fiscal year, estimates will be needed and time limits will become tight.

Example

7.8   Trevor becomes a member of the partnership of Bookbrowse on 1 June 2000. Bookbrowse has made up its accounts to 28 February for many years.

First year of assessment (for Trevor) — 2000/01

Trevor will be assessed on the profits for the period 1 June 2000 (box 4.5) to 5 April 2001 (box 4.6). This will require the accounts for the year ended 28 February 2001 and also the accounts for the year ended 28 February 2002.

From the partnership statement for the year to 28 February 2001, Trevor will enter his share of profits into box 4.7. He must then estimate his share of profits for the year ended 28 February 2002, putting the proportion relating to the period 1 March 2001 to 5 April 2001 in box 4.8. As this is a provisional figure, he must tick box 23.3 stating when he anticipates filing the corrected figure in the additional information box 23.6.

Trevor is obliged to file his tax return for 2000/01 by 31 January 2002 and yet the accounts needed to compute the assessable profits do not end until 28 February 2002, hence the need for an estimate on which tax must be paid and which, if it is incorrect, will give rise to a charge to interest.

Second year of assessment (for Trevor) — 2001/02

Trevor will have a basis period being the year ended 28 February 2002, i.e. the same period of account as the other partners. The tax return for 2001/02 must be filed by 31 January 2003.

Trevor will compute overlap profits for the period 1 March 2001 to 5 April 2001 to carry forward in box 4.11 for his individual use.

In the second example there are eleven months in which to prepare accounts, agree the division of profits and file any individual returns, whereas in the first example there are 21 months available to prepare the accounting information.

Retirement of a partner

7.9   Similar principles will apply on the retirement of a partner. The final assessment will be based upon the period from the accounting date ending in the preceding fiscal year to the date of cessation in the final year. From that amount will be deducted the overlap profits of that individual.

The first day of the basis period will be entered into box 4.5 and the date of cessation entered into box 4.6 (as well as box 4.4). If more than one accounting period ends in the fiscal year then the share of profit from the most recent set of accounts is entered into box 4.7. If no accounting period ends in the fiscal year then '0' is entered in box 4.7.

The figure in box 4.7 is then changed to the profit for the base period by way of an entry in box 4.8. The overlap relief available is then shown in box 4.10 to arrive at the profit (box 4.13) or loss (box 4.14) for the final period.

If it is not possible to complete box 4.8 accurately because accounts are needed for a later period then an estimate must be used. A tick is required in box 23.3 and an explanation in the additional information box 23.6 as to why a final figure has not been provided. A note of when that information will be provided should also be shown.

Example

7.10   Joan from the above example ceases to be a partner on 31 December 2004. Books For All still makes up its accounts for the year ended 30 April.

Penultimate year (for Joan) — 2003/04

Based upon the year ended 30 April 2003.

Year of cessation (for Joan) — 2004/05

Joan will be assessed on her share of profits for the year ended 30 April 2004 plus her share of profits for the period 1 May 2004 to 31 December 2004, less the overlap profits brought forward. Her basis period will be 1 May 2003 (box 4.5) to 31 December 2004 (box 4.6 and also in box 4.4). She will include her share of profits for the year ended 30 April 2004 in box 4.7 and her share of profits, for the period 1 May 2004 to 31 December 2004, in box 4.8 and her claim for overlap relief in box 4.10, giving the taxable profits (or '0' if a loss) in box 4.13. Any allowable loss should be included in box 4.14.

In order to compute her taxable profits, accounts for the year ended 30 April 2005 will be required. As the filing date for 2004/05 is 31 January 2006, this information should be available by the filing date.

By comparison, if Trevor in example 7.8 above ceases to trade on 31 March 2005, his assessments will be as follows.

Penultimate year (for Trevor) — 2003/04

Trevor will be assessed on his share of profits based upon the year ended 28 February 2004.

Year of cessation (for Trevor) — 2004/05

Trevor will be assessed on his share of profits for the year ended 28 February 2005 plus his share of profits for the period of 1 March 2005 to 31 March 2005. He therefore enters 1 March 2004 in box 4.5 and 31 March 2005 in box 4.6 (and box 4.4). He will include his share of profits for the year ended 28 February 2005 in box 4.7, his estimate of his share of profits for the period 1 March 2005 to 31 March 2005 in box 4.8 and his claim for overlap relief in box 4.10, to give taxable profits (or '0' for a loss) in box 4.13. Any allowable loss should be included in box 4.14.

Accounts for the year ended 28 February 2006 will be required to complete the 2004/05 tax return, which must be filed by 31 January 2006. Because a provisional figure has been required, a tick is required in box 23.3 in the tax return with the usual explanation in the additional information box 23.6, and Trevor is required to provide the actual figure within twelve months from the normal filing date.

The above difficulty will only arise if a partner ceases to trade after the normal accounting date but within the fiscal year, i.e. in the case of Trevor above, he has ceased trading after 28 February 2005 but before 5 April 2005. Where an estimate is required and it proves to be incorrect, interest will be charged on any underpayments or interest paid (at the lower rate) on any overpayment of tax.

The continuing partners

7.11   Because assessments are no longer based upon the partnership profits, but on the individual's own share, there is no longer any possibility of a continuation election under the new rules. Each partner is dealt with as an individual, having opening year rules when he or she joins and applying the closing year provisions with overlap relief on cessation.

Current year basis — a worked example

7.12   The current year basis of assessment rules for a partnership work in exactly the same way as for individuals. That is to say, the profits that will be assessed over the life of the partnership are normally exactly the same as the profits shown in the accounts (adjusted for disallowable items). In addition, the profits of each individual partner over the life of the partnership will normally be the share allocated to the partner in the accounts. The previous adjustments that arose where the partnership made a profit but an individual partner's share was a loss or vice versa are retained. [Inland Revenue Booklet SAT 1, 5.23].

Example

The Quarum partnership commenced trading on 1 August 1994, making up its accounts to 30 June each year. The original partners shared profits in the ratio Kim 50%: Abbie 50%.

On 1 July 1998 Julia joined the firm, which adopted a revised profit share of 40%:40%:20%.

On 30 June 2000 Kim ceased to be a partner, Abbie and Julia then sharing profits 75%:25%. The business ceased on 31 March 2001.

The adjusted profits (no capital allowances) are:

	£
1 August 1994 to 30 June 1995	24,200
Year ended 30 June 1996	18,000
Year ended 30 June 1997	30,000
Year ended 30 June 1998	26,000
Year ended 30 June 1999	48,000
Year ended 30 June 2000	12,000
1 July 2000 to 31 March 2001	8,000
	166,200

The profits assessable on the partners would be:

	Total £	Kim £	Abbie £	Julia £
1994/95				
248/334 × £24,200	17,968	8,984	8,984	
1995/96 (year ended 31.7.95)				
1.8.94 to 30.6.95	24,200			
1.7.95 to 31.7.95				
31/365 × 18,000	1,528			
	25,728	12,864	12,864	
1996/97				
Year ended 30.6.96	18,000	9,000	9,000	
Overlap profits:				
248 days to 5.4.95	17,968	8,984	8,984	
31 days to 31.7.95	1,528	764	764	
279	19,496	9,748	9,748	
1997/98				
Year ended 30.6.97	30,000	15,000	15,000	
1998/99				
Year ended 30.6.98	26,000	13,000	13,000	
1.7.98 to 5.4.99				
279/365 × 9,600	7,338			7,338
	33,338			

(i.e. take Julia's profit share per accounts 48,000 × 20% = 9,600 proportioned to the fiscal year).

	£	£	£	£
1999/2000				
Year ended 30.6.99	48,000	19,200	19,200	9,600
Overlap profits:				
279 days 1.7.98 to 5.4.99				(7,338)
2000/01				
Year ended 30.6.2000	12,000	4,800	4,800	2,400
On Kim — profits to cessation		4,800		
Less overlap relief		(9,748)		
Loss		(4,948)		

	£	£
On Abbie and Julia		
Share to 30.6.2000	4,800	2,400
To cessation (75%:25%)	6,000	2,000
	10,800	4,400
Less overlap relief	(9,748)	(7,338)
	1,052	(2,938)

(Although Kim and Julia have losses available for relief and Abbie has an assessable profit, no further adjustment is needed. This is because the losses are due to overlap relief and *not* because of the allocation of shares of profits.)

Summary of assessments

	Total £	Kim £	Abbie £	Julia £
1994/95	17,968	8,984	8,984	–
1995/96	25,728	12,864	12,864	–
1996/97	18,000	9,000	9,000	–
1997/98	30,000	15,000	15,000	–
1998/99	33,338	13,000	13,000	7,338
1999/2000	48,000	19,200	19,200	9,600
2000/01	(6,834)	(4,948)	1,052	(2,938)
	166,200	73,100	79,100	14,000

It will be noted above that the total profits assessed are £166,200, being the amount of the adjusted profits. In the year 2000/01, Abbie has a profit of £1,052 whereas Kim and Julia both show losses. Kim and Julia are able to claim loss relief in their own names and therefore to make a personal choice as to the way in which that loss is relieved.

Not only does the partnership pay tax on precisely the same figures as it earned, but each individual partner also is assessed on the profits allocated to them in the accounts.

Summary of division of accounting profits

	Total £	Kim £	Abbie £	Julia £
1.8.1994 to 30.6.1995	24,200	12,100	12,100	–
Year ended 30 June 1996	18,000	9,000	9,000	–
Year ended 30 June 1997	30,000	15,000	15,000	–
Year ended 30 June 1998	26,000	13,000	13,000	–
Year ended 30 June 1999	48,000	19,200	19,200	9,600
Year ended 30 June 2000	12,000	4,800	4,800	2,400
1 July 2000 to 31 March 2001	8,000	–	6,000	2,000
	166,200	73,100	79,100	14,000

7.13 However, this does not mean that the tax liability will be the same under a current year basis as under an actual basis. For example, in the above division of accounting profits, all partners make profits in all accounting periods, and yet for taxation purposes there are losses for Kim and Julia in

2000/01. This is because of the duplication of profits in earlier years which are carried forward, in this example, to a period of time in which profits are lower. Because of the need to offset losses fully against other income under *ICTA 1988, s 380,* or fully against profits under *ICTA 1988, s 385,* it may be that the losses will not be effectively relieved, whereas the profits may be chargeable at starting, basic or higher rates.

There is still the effect that tax will be paid in arrears because it is based upon the profits of the accounting period, which may be as much as eleven months 29 days out of step with the financial year. If profits are rising, then the duplication in earlier years is likely to result in a duplication of lower profits and therefore be advantageous from the point of view of cash-flow in all years except the last. In the same way, if profits are falling, to have an accounting date early in the financial year would mean duplication of high profits with no relief until cessation and a consequential cash-flow loss. For most partnerships which are unable to forecast profits accurately for the foreseeable future, the overriding practical need will be to have information available at an early stage. The ability to achieve compliance with tax return time limits is likely to outweigh unknown changes in profits in future years.

A practical solution could be to prepare accounts to 5 April after commencement and also to 30 April after commencement. Before those figures are submitted to the Revenue, a trend of profits for the coming twelve months would be known. If profits are rising, accounts could be submitted to 30 April, whereas if profits are falling, the accounts to 5 April would be used.

Change of partner

7.14 A new partner will apply the rules set out above at 7.6 *et seq*, whereas existing partners will continue to be assessed on a current year basis.

7.15 In the same way, if a partner left a partnership during 1997/98 or 1998/99, that retirement would not trigger a revision of the partnership assessments under the transitional rules. Those rules only apply to sole traders unless, exceptionally, there was at the same time either:

(a)   a cessation of the actual partnership business; or
(b)   a change to the business which is such that the continuing partners cannot be said to be carrying on the same business. [Inland Revenue SAT 1, 6.78].

If either of the above conditions applies, the special rules for cessation set out in Appendix C applied in 1997/98 and 1998/99.

Change between sole tradership and partnership

7.16 Where a sole trader takes a partner, or a partnership is reduced to sole tradership by the retirement of all but one of the partners, then it will be necessary to complete both partnership pages and self-employed pages for that year for the continuing trader.

Notwithstanding the above, there will be no cessation of a trade or commencement of a trade for the individual concerned. Accordingly no entry is made in boxes 3.7 or 3.8 on the self-employment pages.

Insofar as the basis period covers a period during which the individual carried on business exclusively as the sole trader, the self-employment pages are completed including the standard accounting information. Insofar as any period is carried on in partnership, a partnership return (including SAI) and details will be provided by the partnership statement and included in the individual's return on the partnership supplementary sheets.

In the same way as the change is not treated as a commencement or cessation for the sole trader self-employment pages, the same principle applies to the partnership supplementary pages. Accordingly no entry is required in boxes 4.3 or 4.4.

When completing the self-employment pages, do not complete the adjustments section. Instead complete a partnership supplementary page showing the share of partnership profit in box 4.7 and the profit for the period of sole tradership in box 4.8. It may be that, because of a change of accounting date, there will also be additional adjustments included in box 4.8.

If the base period only covers a period of time as a sole trader, then the partnership pages are not required and all entries are included on the self-employment pages.

Conversely, when completing the partnership tax return, the move to or from sole tradership is a cessation or commencement requiring an entry in boxes 3.8 or 3.7 of the partnership tax return.

If a partnership ceased within the fiscal year, and one of its members continued to trade as a sole trader so that accounts were prepared for a period ending after the end of the fiscal year, then partnership trading pages will be required showing standard accounting information. This will be included in the last partnership return even though the accounting date ends after the end of the fiscal year.

Example

Jack and Jill have been in partnership for many years making accounts up to 30 September. On 31 December 2000 Jill retired from the partnership, Jack continued to trade. Accounts are prepared for the year to 30 September 2001.

In preparing the partnership tax return for the year 2000/01 it will be necessary to complete separate sets of trading pages showing:

(a)   SAI details for the year ended 30 September 2000; and
(b)   SAI details for the year ended 30 September 2001.

(This may require the submission of provisional figures corrected when the accounts are available.)

The partnership statement within the return will only include details of the accounts that ended within the fiscal year, i.e. year ended 30 September 2000. A second partnership statement will be required for the accounts for the year ended 30 September 2000.

That partnership statement will divide the profits between Jack and Jill for the period 1 October 2000 to 31 December 2000 and allocate the balance of profits to Jack. Thus the partnership statement includes the profits for the whole of the accounting year, both as a partnership and as a sole trader.

When completing Jill's partnership pages for 2000/01 she will have a base period of 1 October 1999 to 31 December 2000 and will show the sum of her two profit allocations in box 4.7.

When Jack completes his partnership pages for the year 2000/01 it will be for the base period 1 October 2000 to 30 September 2000 showing this base period's profit only at box 4.7.

When Jack prepares his tax return for 2001/02 he has been a partner for part of the basis period (1 October 2000 to 31 December 2000) and a sole trader for part of his basis period (1 January 2001 to 30 September 2001). It would appear that he completes his return as follows:

Self-Employment Pages

Box 3.10	tick
Boxes 3.14 to 3.73	leave blank
Boxes 3.74 and 3.75	basis period is 1 October 2000 to 30 September 2001
Box 3.76	profits for Jack (per partnership statement) for the year ended 30 September 2001
Box 3.77	deduct profits for period as a partner (1 October 2000 to 31 December 2000)
Box 3.83	taxable profits as a sole trader (1 January 2001 to 30 September 2001)

Partnership Pages

Boxes 4.5 and 4.6	basis period is 1 October 2000 to 30 September 2001
Box 4.7	profits for Jack (per partnership statement) for the year ended 30 September 2001
Box 4.8	deduct profits for period as a sole trader (1 January 2001 to 30 September 2001), i.e. the amount shown in 3.83 above
Box 4.13	taxable profits as a partner (1 October 2000 to 31 December 2000)

It would be advisable to indicate in the additional information box 3.116 on the self-employment pages that the accounting detail has been provided on the partnership pages of the previous year giving the reference of that partnership.

Class 4 national insurance should be computed on one sheet only for both of the businesses entering multiple business in the additional information box of both the self-employment and partnership pages.

Successions, mergers and demergers

Complete change of ownership

7.17 Whenever there is a complete change of ownership of a business there will be a deemed cessation followed by a deemed commencement of a new business.

Partial change of ownership

7.18 Wherever there is a partial change of ownership then the existing partnership will be deemed to be a continuing business with the commencement and cessation rules applying to the partners who join or leave providing the original trade continues. [*ICTA 1988, s 113*].

Merger or demerger

7.19 There are a number of different ways in which two businesses can be merged and the tax consequences can be different. The way in which a particular merger or demerger has been carried out is a question of fact.

Example — Continuation of one business following a merger/demerger

ACS and BCS are under different ownership but carry on similar business activities.

ACS could acquire the assets of BCS in which case ACS has continued whereas BCS has ceased and normal cessation rules apply. If some or all of the partners in BCS become partners in ACS cessation and recommencement rules will apply to them only but ACS will be a continuing business. Similar provisions apply on the demerger of a business to form two businesses, if one of the new businesses is the same as the original business then it will be a continuation of the original partnership. Commencement rules will then apply to the second business.

Cessation of both businesses

7.20 It may be that on the merger of ACS and BCS a totally new business carrying on a different trade is created. In such circumstances both businesses will cease at the date of change and an entirely new business will commence.

Continuation of both businesses following a merger

7.21 Where the activities of ACS and BCS are similar then the activities of the merged business, CCS, may be the same as both of the predecessor businesses. Both businesses will be continuing, but unless they have the same accounting dates, the assessable profits of the merged business may initially have to be calculated by reference to separate basis periods. CCS will have a different unique reference number to both ACS and BCS and will require partnership returns from commencement.

Example

ACS and BCS both provide accounting and business services. ACS has two equal partners A Morris and C Jones and makes up accounts to 30 April each year. The partners each have overlap relief of £31,900 brought forward. BCS has three partners, B Watson, C Dainty, S Smith and share profits 40:40:20. They make up accounts to 31 December and have overlap relief brought forward of £8,000, £8,000 and £4,000.

The businesses will merge on 1 January 2001 to form CCS and will make up accounts to 30 April in each year. B Watson will retire on 1 January 2001 and all other partners will then be equal. The adjusted profits after capital allowance have been:

	ACS £	BCS £	CCS £
Year ended 30.4.1999	80,000		
Year ended 31.12.1999		90,000	
Year ended 30.4.2000	84,000		
Year ended 31.12.2000		100,000	
Period ended 31.12.2000	64,000		
1.1.2001 to 30.4.2001			52,000
Year ended 30.4.2002			170,000

The tax return and partnership statement will show:

		1999/2000	
	Total £	A Morris £	C Jones £
ACS			
Year ended 30.4.1999	80,000	40,000	40,000

	Total £	B Watson £	C Dainty £	S Smith £
BCS				
Year ended 31.12.1999	90,000	36,000	36,000	18,000

		2000/01	
	Total £	A Morris £	C Jones £
ACS			
Year ended 30.4.2000	84,000	42,000	42,000

The later accounting date of 31.12.2000 will be a temporary date and will be ignored in computing assessable profits as no notification has been given under *ICTA 1988, s 62a(3)*; however a second set of partnership trading pages and partnership statements will be required for the period 1 May 2000 to 31 December 2000. These profits are taxable 2001/02 but must be included in the final tax return of ACS for 2000/01.

7.21 *Partnerships*

Period

1.5.2000 to 31.12.2000   64,000   32,000   32,000

	2000/01		
	Total £	B Watson £	C Dainty £	S Smith £

BCS				
Year ended 31.12.2000	100,000	40,000	40,000	20,000
Less overlap relief				
Claimed on retirement		8,000		
		32,000		

CCS   *2000/01*

A partnership tax return is required with boxes 3.2, 3.7, 3.97, 3.98 and 3.117 completed together with a tick in box 3.10 and the statement in the additional explanation box that the first accounts end on 30 April 2001. Taxed income for the period 1 January 2001 to 5 April 2001 will be included in boxes 7.7A, 7.8A and 7.9A. The relevant information from those boxes being included in the partnership information for use by the individual partners on their own returns.

C Dainty and S Smith   *2001/02*

Those partners have changed their individual accounting dates from 31 December to 30 April. This will require an adjustment to profits on their individual tax return in box 4.8 on the partnership pages, as follows:

	Total £	C Dainty £	S Smith £
Profits 1.5.2000 to 31.12.2000			
(8/12 of above)	40,000	26,667	13,333

This in turn will give rise to additional overlap profits of the same amount shown in box 4.11 with overlap profit brought forward, as follows:

	C Dainty £	S Smith £
Overlap profits brought forward.	8,000	4,000
Additional — as above	*26,667*	*13,333*
To carry forward (box 4.11)	*34,667*	*17,333*

		2001/02			
	Total £	A Morris £	C Jones £	C Dainty £	S Smith £
CCS					
1.1.2001 to 30.4.2001	52,000	13,000	13,000	13,000	13,000

The above amounts are shown in box 4.7 on the partnership pages of the individual's tax return.

(Note the partnership tax return will also show details of taxed interest at boxes 7.7A, 7.8A and 7.9A, charges in box 3.117, tax deducted from trading income in box 3.98 and sub-contractor tax in box 3.97 for the year ended 5 April 2002).

A summary of taxable amounts is as follows:

	Total £	A Morris £	2001/02 C Jones £	C Dainty £	S Smith £
CCS Year ended 30.4.2001 As ACS					
1.5.2000 to 31.12.2000	64,000	32,000	32,000		
As BCS (8/12 of £60,000 excluding B Watson)	40,000			26,667	13,333
As CCS 1.1.2001 to 30.4.2001	52,000	13,000	13,000	13,000	13,000
		45,000	45,000	39,667	26,333
Overlap relief to carry forward		31,900	31,900	34,667	17,333

	Total £	A Morris £	2002/03 C Jones £	C Dainty £	S Smith £
CCS Year ended 30.4.2002	170,000	42,500	42,500	42,500	42,500

It should be noted that overlap profit belongs to an individual, not the partnership, accordingly the change of profit share (to S Smith) does not affect overlap relief. Each partner will use his own overlap relief should his involvement in the business cease (as B Watson above) or his accounting period alters (as C Dainty and S Smith above).

Corporate partners

7.22 If a partnership has a corporate partner, then two separate computations are required, one for income tax using income tax rules and one for corporation tax. The differences can include a different treatment of interest paid. The amounts in each computation are allocated to the partners both individual and corporate, the amounts from the income tax computation being used by the individual partners and the share from the corporation tax computation (including loan relationship allocations) by the company partners. If the accounting period of the company differs from that of the partnership, the company's share of partnership profits will be apportioned on a time basis to the chargeable accounting periods of the company.

Income other than Schedule D, Case I/II

7.23 All untaxed income of a partnership is to be assessed using the same basis period. Where a partnership has Case I/II income, then the basis period will be that of the trading income. This will apply even where the trading income is a minor part of the partnership business. [Inland Revenue Booklet SAT 1, 5.49–5.51].

Where a partnership commences, or a new partner joins an existing partnership and that partnership has untaxed non-trading income from one or more sources, then all of those sources are aggregated and are deemed to be a second trade or profession. Overlap profits are computed in accordance with the normal rules for trades, and claimed in box 4.66 of the partnership (full) pages of the individual partner.

Where such overlap relief has been computed, it will be relieved on a change of accounting date or on cessation. It should be noted that it is the cessation of being a partner that gives overlap relief, and not the cessation of the source of other income. Accordingly, it is possible that there may be no other income at the time the overlap is available. It is therefore provided that, if the relief exceeds the other income, the excess shall be deducted from the individual's total income for the year of cessation (or change of accounting date). [*ICTA 1988, s 111*]. It is not available to increase a terminal loss claim.

If a partnership does not have any income chargeable under Schedule D, Case I/II, then the computational rules that apply are those for an individual with Schedule D, Case III income (actual fiscal year basis).

7.24   If a partnership has taxed income, e.g. dividends, income from employment, taxed interest, etc., that income is divided between the partners in the profit-sharing ratio of the fiscal year. The attached tax credits, etc. will also be allocated on the same basis, i.e. an actual 6 April to 5 April basis of assessment will apply as for individuals. [Inland Revenue Booklet SAT 1, 5.46 and 5.47].

7.25   If a partnership only has income from a trade or profession plus taxed interest from a bank, building society or other deposit-taker, then the short version of the partnership return may be used by the partnerships and the individual partner. In all other cases the full version of the returns must be used.

Partnership tax return

7.26   The partnership tax return follows the same format as that for individuals described in Chapter 3 above. First, it is necessary to answer the questions as follows:

Question 1 — Did the partnership receive any rent or other income from land and property in the UK?

Question 2 — Did the partnership have any foreign income?

Question 3 — Did your partnership business include a trade or profession at any time between 6 April 2000 and 5 April 2001?

Question 4 — Did the partnership dispose of any chargeable assets?

Question 5 — Did the partnership include
— a company;

— a non-resident;

— a partner in a business controlled and managed abroad?

Question 6 — Are you completing this return on behalf of a European Economic Interest Grouping?

If questions 1, 2 or 4 are answered 'yes', then supplementary pages must be completed as for individuals.

If the partnership carried on a trade or profession, then boxes 3.1 to 3.117 must be completed as appropriate. Separate sheets are required for each trade and each accounting period.

The partnership trading details are very similar to that described for individuals at 3.4 above. If the annual turnover is less than £15,000, accounts may be summarised into three boxes at box 3.24 to box 3.26. In other cases, standard accounting information must be provided at boxes 3.27 to 3.73 and, if a balance sheet is prepared, a summary must be given in boxes 3.99 to 3.115.

A summary of capital allowances is provided in boxes 3.14 to 3.23 with total capital allowances transferred to box 3.70 and balancing charges to box 3.68.

The accounting period is shown in boxes 3.4 and 3.5. Only accounts *ending* in the fiscal year are required to be shown in a partnership tax return. (By contrast an individual return requires completed SAI details on the *earliest* return covered by the accounts of a sole trader, i.e. the commencement date determines the tax return used with box 3.10 (ticked on subsequent returns) — see 3.4 above for further details and an example).

Because only completed accounting periods are included within the return, and no assessment arises on a partnership, no adjustments are needed to the partnership profits or losses, shown at box 3.26 or 3.73. That figure is transferred to box 3.83 (if a profit) and to box 11 of the partnership statement. If the figure is a loss, box 3.84 and box 12 of the partnership statements are used. Box 3.83 then shows '0'.

A separate set of trading pages is required for each accounting period ending within the fiscal year, and for each trade.

If the accounts are provisional then box 3.93 and box 10.1 are ticked, and the reason stated in the additional information box 3.116 on page three. The return should then be amended as soon as the actual information is known.

If no accounts end in the fiscal year box 3.10 is ticked. In the same way, if a sole trader becomes a partnership and the accounts have been included in the tax return of the individual it is not necessary to repeat the details. Instead box 3.10 is ticked and a note made in the additional information box giving the reference of the return in which the accounts are included.

Question 7 of the partnership return asks 'did the partnership receive any other income which has not been included elsewhere on the partnership tax return?'. This will include taxed interest from UK banks or building societies included on a fiscal year basis.

Question 8 requires confirmation of the details shown on the return, Question 9 requires a contact telephone number and Question 10 requires details of any provisional figures used within the return. The return should be signed at the declaration at Question 11.

Partnership statement

7.27   After completing the partnership return, it is necessary to prepare a statement of partnership information. This is a summary of the amounts in the partnership return, divided between the individual partners. A copy of the individual partner's share should be provided to each partner so that they can complete their own personal returns.

If the profits are not shared on a simple percentage basis, then a copy of the division of profits should be submitted to the Revenue, either as a separate summary or by inclusion in the additional information box 3.116 on page three.

Partners' personal expenses and capital allowances

7.28   In certain partnerships, e.g. doctors, dentists etc., it is traditional that partners incur their own expenditure in certain areas. Where such a procedure is adopted, then in order to prepare the partnership return it is necessary to add together the main accounts and the supplementary accounts in providing the standard accounting information in the partnership return. For example, Smith & Jones are doctors. The partnership accounts show employee costs of £21,200. The individual expense claim of Dr Smith shows wife's salary of £3,000. In the similar statement of Dr Jones there is wife's salary of £3,000 and wife's pension of £1,200. The amount to be shown in box 3.51 (employee costs) will be:

	£
Partnership salaries	21,200
Doctor Smith	3,000
Doctor Jones	4,200
	28,400 (entry in box 3.51)

The same will apply to all personal expenses, and also to all disallowable amounts, e.g. private proportions of motor expenses, which should be accumulated and entered in box 3.37. Accordingly, the net business profit for tax purposes calculated in box 3.73 will be that after deducting all allowable individual expenses. The summary of capital allowances will include the allowable capital allowances of the individual partners, and consequentially the net profit for the year at 3.73 will be after all allowable deductions. This is transferred forward into box 3.83 and onto the partnership statement summary at box 11.

In order to divide the profit at box 11, it will normally be necessary to add back the individual expenses and capital allowance claims. The resultant adjusted profit can then be divided in accordance with the partnership profit-sharing ratio. From this can be deducted the individual partners' expense claims and capital allowances to arrive at their appropriate shares at box 11, to be entered in their individual statements.

Chapter 8

Capital Allowances

The changes

8.1   To facilitate the introduction of self-assessment, the principle of having a separate regime for the calculation of depreciation on fixed assets was simplified. Much of the complexity of the previous capital allowances legislation arose from the need to ensure that there was no duplication of additions or disposals of assets, nor gap periods in which such items could fall out of account. With the move to assessments that exactly equal the actual profits earned by the business over the life of the business, the potential for manipulation was reduced and therefore it was possible to introduce a system whereby capital allowances are treated as trading expenses and balancing charges as trading receipts. This was done by rewriting *section 140* of the *Capital Allowances Act 1990* (now *CAA 2001, s 247*). Allowances for individuals and partnerships are therefore given in a broadly similar way to the granting of allowances for corporation tax purposes.

Deduction as a trading expense

8.2   As a result of these changes, capital allowances are no longer dealt with separately but instead are deducted in arriving at the adjusted profits, and the adjusted profits are taken into account for all calculations from the introduction of the new system. [*CAA 2001, s 247*]. The only exception is that transitional overlap relief was calculated on profits before capital allowances. [*FA 1995, s 122(3)*].

Period of account

8.3   The chargeable period for capital allowances is the period for which the accounts are drawn up. [*CAA 2001, s 6*].

Because capital allowances are based upon a period of account, the writing-down allowance will be given by reference to the length of the period of account. [*CAA 2001, s 56(3), s 310(2)*]. Thus, if accounts are made up for a nine-month period, 9/12ths of writing-down allowances will be granted. In the same way, if a period of account is made up for 16 months, allowances will be calculated as 16/12ths of writing-down allowance. To prevent manipulation to achieve higher allowances, it is provided that a period of account for capital allowance purposes cannot exceed 18 months. [*CAA 2001, s 6(6)*]. If the period of account does exceed 18 months, then for the purpose of calculating capital allowances it is divided into periods of twelve months, with the balancing period having restricted writing-down allowances. It would appear that all of the capital allowances so calculated are deducted from the adjusted profits to arrive at the figure to be brought into the assessment computation.

Claims for capital allowances

8.4 Claims for capital allowances are made in the tax return. [*CAA 2001, s 3(2)*]. Under self-assessment, this means that capital allowances claims have to be finalised by twelve months after the normal filing date for the tax return, i.e. twelve months after 31 January following the end of the fiscal year of assessment. Elections for short-life asset treatment, etc. are to be made by the same date. [*CAA 2001, s 85(2)*].

Introduction of the new rules

8.5 The new provisions apply to existing (pre 6.4.94) businesses with effect from the period of account 1997/98. [*FA 1994, s 211(2)*].

For businesses commencing on or after 6 April 1994, the new rules apply from commencement. Capital allowances are calculated based upon the period of account, and the resultant allowances are deducted from the profits or added to the losses for that period.

For examples of periods of account and their relevant writing-down allowances in opening and closing years, see Chapter 6 above. The provisions for the transitional period are set out in Appendix C, and those for a change of accounting date are illustrated in Chapter 10 below.

8.6 To summarise, businesses that commenced before 6 April 1994 will have used the old rules until 1997/98. From the period of account ending in that year onwards, capital allowances and balancing allowances are trading expenses and balancing charges are trading receipts. Before that time, basis periods are calculated and writing-down allowances are only restricted if the assessment is for less than one year. For businesses commencing on or after 6 April 1994, the new rules apply from commencement.

A worked example

8.7 Claire commenced trading on 1 May 1997, making up accounts to 31 December. After three years she changed her accounting date to 31 May. She ceased trading on 31 December 2002.

On commencement she owned a car, valued at £8,000 (with 25% private use). On 30 November 1998 she purchased a computer for £2,000. This machine was part-exchanged on 30 April 1999. The selling price was £500 and the replacement cost price was £4,000. She sold her car on 20 September 2001 for

£2,600, buying a replacement for £16,000. On cessation her car was valued at £11,500 and the computer at £800.

Her adjusted profits before capital allowances were:

	£
1.5.97 to 31.12.97	6,950
Year ended 31.12.98	12,700
1.1.99 to 31.5.2000	23,779
Year ended 31.5.01	14,112
1.6.01 to 31.12.02	11,313

Claire's assessments will be calculated after deducting capital allowances for the accounting period, computed as follows:

	Pool	Car		Capital Allowances
1.5.97 to 31.12.97	£	£		£
Introduced		8,000		
WDA (8/12 × 2000)		1,333 less 25% p/u		**1,000**
		6,667		
Year ended 31.12.98				
Addition	2,000			
FYA—40%/WDA—25%	800	1,667 less 25% p/u = 1,250		**2,050**
	1,200	5,000		
1.1.99 to 31.5.2000				
Less sale	500			
	700			
WDA (17/12)	248	1,771 less 25% p/u = 1,328		1,576
	452			
Addition	4,000			
FYA 40%	1,600 2,400			1,600
	2,852	3,229		**3,176**
Year ended 3.5.01				
WDA	713	807 less 25% p/u = 605		**1,318**
	2,139	2,422		
Year ended 31.5.02				
Sale		2,600		
Balancing charge		178 less 25% p/u = (134)		
Addition		16,000		
WDA	535	3,000 less 25% p/u = 2,250		**2,785**
	1,604	13,000		

	Pool	Car	Capital Allowances
	£	£	£
Forward	1,604	13,000	

1.6.02 to 31.12.02
Taken over at MV   800   11,500
Balancing allowance   804   1,500 less 25% p/u = 1,125   **1,929**

Giving profits after capital allowances of:

1.5.97 to 31.12.97	6,950 − 1,000	=	5,950
Year ended 31.12.98	12,700 − 2,050	=	10,650
1.1.99 to 31.5.2000	23,779 − 3,176	=	20,603
Year ended 31.5.01	14,112 − 1,318	=	12,794
1.6.01 to 31.12.02	11,313 + 134 − (2,785 + 1,929)	=	6,733
			56,730

and assessments of:

	£	£
1997/98		
1.5.97 to 31.12.97	5,950	
1.1.98 to 5.4.98		
95/365 × 10,650	2,772	8,722
1998/99		
Year ended 31.12.98		10,650
(overlap profits £2,772 overlap period 95 days)		
1999/2000		
Year ended 31.5.99		
1.6.98 to 31.12.98		
214/365 × 10,650	6,244	
1.1.99 to 31.5.99		
151/517 × 20,603	6,018	12,262
Additional overlap profits		
214 days 1.6.98 to 31.12.98	6,244	
95 days b/f	2,772	
309	9,016	
2000/01		
Year ended 31.5.2000		
366/517 × 20,603		14,585
2001/02		
Year ended 31.5.01		12,794
2002/03		
1.6.01 to 31.12.02	6,733	
Less overlap profits b/f	9,016	(2,283)
		56,730

(relievable under *ICTA 1988, s 380* against other income in 2002/03 or 2001/02).

8.7   *Capital Allowances*

Notes on Example:

(1)   The basis period for capital allowances will be the same as for the accounts, providing that the length of the period of account does not exceed 18 months. Accordingly, the first capital allowances computation is for the eight months to 31 December 1997, notwithstanding the fact that the assessment for 1997/98 is based upon the period to 5 April 1998.

(2)   It should be noted that the second capital allowance computation is for the year ended 31 December 1998. Accordingly, the addition in November 1998 gives rise to allowances which are taken into account in computing the 1997/98 assessment.

(3)   Because the accounts for the year ended 31 December 1998 are used in aggregate more than once, allowances are given more than once, but with a corresponding reduction in the overlap profits calculated on that period.

(4)   Only one capital allowance computation is required for the period 1 January 1999 to 31 May 2000, as the period is 17 months. Accordingly, the writing-down allowance becomes 17/12ths.

(5)   The final set of accounts can be for more than 18 months (and in this case will be taken wholly into the computation of the 2002/03 assessment). The legislation then provides that, where the accounts are made up for more than 18 months for capital allowances purposes, it must be divided into a period of twelve months with a balancing period. Accordingly, a capital allowances computation will be prepared for the year ended 31 May 2002, followed by a final computation for the period 1 June 2002 to 31 December 2002.

(6)   After computing the capital allowances, they are deducted as trading expenses or, in the case of a balancing charge, treated as a trading receipt to give adjusted profits.

(7)   Assessments and overlap profits are always calculated on the profits after capital allowances (except transitional overlap reliefs, for which see 8.2 above).

(8)   In this example, two overlap profit relief calculations are necessary. The first will be made for the year 1998/99 where the profits for the year ended 31 December 1998 fall into the 1997/98 and 1998/99 computations. Because of the change of accounting date, the assessment for 1999/2000 will be based upon the new year ending in the fiscal year 1999/2000. It is assumed that Claire has given the necessary notice to the Revenue by 31 January 2001. At that stage additional overlap profits are calculated, also based upon the year ended 31 December 1998.

(9)   The overlap profits are deducted in the final year of assessment, 2002/03. Note that this gives rise to a loss, even though the accounts show profits for each and every year. The computations can be proved by taking the total profits less capital allowances and comparing with the actual assessments. In total both amount to £56,730.

(10)   Assuming Claire has no other income, the loss of £2,283 will be relieved against the assessment for 2001/02 by way of an *ICTA 1988, s 380(1)(b)* claim made before 31 January 2005 giving relief for income tax and Class 4 NIC in 2001/02.

Chapter 9

Losses

Loss relief under current year basis

9.1   Under the self-assessment rules, the same principles apply to the calculation of a loss as to the calculation of a trading profit. This means that capital allowances become trading expenses, with balancing charges treated as trading receipts. [*ICTA 1988, s 382(3)*]. Although this simplifies the loss relief claim, it does mean that it is necessary to consider fully the usage of the losses before finalising the claim for capital allowances. It is still possible to disclaim or restrict claims for capital allowances, thus giving an opportunity to minimise the loss of personal reliefs where a loss claim is made.

9.2   Because trading losses are treated in the same way as trading profits, they can be used in the calculation of more than one assessment using the same basis period rules as apply for profits. If an overlap in basis periods occurs, then loss relief is to be given in the earlier of the periods only. [*ICTA 1988, s 382(4)*]. Care must be taken if an accounting date of other than 5 April or 31 March is chosen in such circumstances, as the overlap relief could then be nil, with a very large assessment possible on cessation.

Example

Nigel commences on 6 May 2000 with the following results:

	£
Year ended 5.5.2001	Loss (1,200)
Year ended 5.5.2002	Loss (1,800)
Year ended 5.5.2003	Profit 12,000
Period ending 31.3.2004 (cessation)	Profit 24,500

2000/01
Basis period 6 May 2000 to 5 April 2001.
Assessable   NIL
Loss available
(11/12 × £1,200)   1,100

113

2001/02
Basis period 6 May 2000 to 5 May 2001.

Assessable		NIL
Loss available	1,200	
Less used above in 2000/01	1,100	
	100	
Overlap relief (6.5.2000 to 5.4.01)		NIL

2002/03
Basis period 6 May 2001 to 5 May 2002.

Assessable		NIL
Loss available	1,800	

2003/04
Basis period 6 May 2002 to 31 March 2004.

Assessable		
Year ended 5.5.2003	12,000	
Period ended 31.3.2004	24,500	
	36,500	
Less overlap relief	NIL	36,500

Thus, exactly the correct amount of loss relief is given (£1,100 + £100 + £1,800 = £3,000) and profits assessed (£12,000 + £24,500 = £36,500). However, personal allowances may be lost in earlier years, and higher rate tax may be due in 2003/04.

By comparison, if accounts had been prepared to 5 April with the following results:

	£
Period ended 5.4.2001	Loss (1,100)
Year ended 5.4.2002	Loss (1,750)
Year ended 5.4.2003	Profit 10,850
Period ended 31.3.2004 (cessation)	Profit 25,500

the overall profits are identical but with revised assessments (and loss relief) of:

	£
2000/01 — Allowable loss	(1,100)
2001/02 — Allowable loss	(1,750)
2002/03 — Profits	10,850
2003/04 — Profits	25,500

If loss relief is carried forward it is available earlier (in 2002/03 rather than 2003/04) and the profits do not bunch in the final year, thus reducing the likelihood of a charge to higher rate tax, but possibly increasing the charge to Class 4 NIC.

9.3   Special rules will continue to apply to losses arising during the first four years of assessment. [*ICTA 1988, s 381*]. Any unrelieved losses will be carried forward for relief against future trading profits from the same source. [*ICTA 1988, s 385*]. On cessation it will still be possible to carry losses backwards for three years under terminal loss relief. [*ICTA 1988, s 388*].

As above, the use of a 5 April year-end will ensure maximum use of *section 381* losses.

With a 5 April year-end and a business commencing on 6 May 2000, 47 months could be used in a *section 381* loss claim, i.e.:

2000/01	6.5.2000 to 5.4.01	= 11 months
2001/02	6.4.01 to 5.4.02	= 12 months
2002/03	6.4.02 to 5.4.03	= 12 months
2003/04	6.4.03 to 5.4.04	= 12 months
		47 months

whereas with a 5 May year-end, only 36 months will be available, i.e.:

2000/01	6.5.2000 to 5.4.01	=	11 months
2001/02	6.5.2000 to 5.5.01	= 12	
	Less used above	11	1 month
2002/03	6.5.01 to 5.5.02		12 months
2003/04	6.5.02 to 5.5.03		12 months
			36 months

9.4   From 1996/97 the time limits for loss relief claims were amended, and became one year from the 31 January following the year of assessment for *section 380* and *section 381* claims, and five years from 31 January following the year of assessment for *section 385* and *section 388* claims. [*TMA 1970, s 43*].

Relief for trading losses against other income

9.5   Under the previous legislation, relief for trading losses was given against income from other sources for the year of loss and the year following the year of loss, providing that the trade was carried on in that following year. The relief was given against the full amount of income for the year of claim, restricted only by the availability of loss. Any balance was then available in the other year.

9.6   Under the new legislation, relief for trading losses is given against other income of the year of loss, or against income of the year preceding the year of loss. [*ICTA 1988, s 380(1)(2)*]. As with the previous relief, the claim is not restricted but will be against the full amount of other income, limited only by the availability of loss.

9.7   If the claim is made for a year other than the year of loss then the relief has to be computed in terms of reduction in tax (and Class 4 NIC) liability of the earlier year. The computed relief is then set off in the following order:

(a)   any tax outstanding for an earlier year;

(b)   the final liability for the year of loss, i.e. the amount due on 31 January following the end of the year of loss; or

(c)   any tax due within 35 days following the date of processing of the claim.

If the relief has not been fully utilised above then any further excess will be repaid. No interest will be added to the repayment providing it is used or repaid before 31 January following the end of the year of loss. Any interest payable will be calculated from that date. [*ICTA 1988, s 824(3)*].

9.8   The claim may be made outside the tax return or within the return. [*TMA 1970, 1B Sch, disapplying s 42(2)*]. If the claim is made outside the return then the tax credit should be set off against tax due for earlier years on the date of claim, thus stopping interest accruing on that date.

By comparison if the claim is made within the tax return the relevant date will be the date that the return is entered into the Revenue system. If the return is not likely to be filed for some time due to lack of information, a separate written claim to the Revenue should minimise interest on any outstanding tax.

The claim to carry back to a previous year is shown in the tax return by an entry at box 3.86. If an earlier claim has been submitted then the date of that claim should be given in the additional information box 3.116. In such cases it is also likely that the tax liability for the current year will be lower than the payments on account based upon the liability for the earlier year without deducting the tax credit for the loss brought backwards. A claim to reduce those payments on account can also be made, in practice by submission of form SA303.

If the loss claim is known in sufficient time to incorporate in the tax return of the previous year (e.g. loss in accounts year ended 30.4.01 to be carried back to 2000/01 before submission of that return by 31 January 2002) then the reduction in payment on account can be made within the tax return by ticking box 18.7 and specifying the reason and value of reduction in the additional information box 23.6. If the taxpayer is calculating his own tax, the reduced payment is then entered in box 18.6. The value of a loss claim carried back to the year in question (2000/01 in the above example) should be shown in the additional information box 23.6 and box 18.8 should be ticked if it is to be set against the tax liability of this year. In addition, box 23.4 should be ticked.

9.9   A claim may be made for:

(a)   relief against income of the year of loss;

(b)   relief against income of the preceding year of loss;

(c)   relief against income of the year of loss with the balance carried back against the income of the preceding year; or

(d)   relief against income of the preceding year of loss with the balance carried forward against the income of the year of loss.

Any unrelieved loss will then be carried forward against profits from the same source in future years.

If there are two loss claims available for any given year, then *ICTA 1988, s 380(2)* provides that a loss is set off against general income for the year of loss in priority to a claim brought backward to the year.

As the loss is after the inclusion of capital allowances, there is no longer a need to specifically add capital allowances to the loss claim and therefore *ICTA 1988, s 383* has been repealed. [*FA 1994, s 214(1)(b)*].

The time limit for making a *section 380* loss claim is twelve months after 31 January following the end of the tax year in which the loss was incurred, e.g. relief for 2000/01 must be claimed by 31 January 2003.

9.10 The loss claim is shown on the third page of the self-employment pages (or on the partnership pages). The allowable loss is shown at box 3.84 (4.14) with '0' as the net profit at box 3.83 (4.13). Relief for the loss in the year of loss is made at box 3.85 (4.15) and for the preceding year at box 3.86 (4.16). Any remaining loss is carried forward in box 3.87 (4.17).

Example

9.11 James King (who is single) makes up his accounts to 30 September each year and has the following income:

Schedule D, Case I		*Including capital allowances of*
	£	£
Year ended 30.9.2000 profit	8,000	900
Year ended 30.9.2001 loss	(4,975)	815
Year ended 30.9.2002 profit	4,700	1,300

Other income

		£
2000/01		4,700
2001/02		4,100
2002/03 — Non-dividend	2,600	
Dividend	1,400	4,000

His assessment for 2000/01 would originally be:

	£
Schedule D, Case I	8,000
Other income	4,700
	12,700
Personal allowance	4,385
	8,315

For 2001/02:

Schedule D, Case I	NIL
Other income	4,100
	4,100
Personal allowance	4,535
	NIL

Available for *section 380* loss relief:
Schedule D, Case I (y/e 30.9.2001)   (4,975)

This is available in 2001/02 or 2000/01 and the claim must be made by 31 January 2004.

James claims in 2000/01, giving a revised assessment of:

	£
Schedule D, Case I	8,000
Other income	4,700
	12,700
Less section 380 loss relief	4,975
	7,725
Less personal allowance	4,385
	3,340

James could in theory have claimed relief of £4,100 in 2001/02, carrying the balance of £875 back to 2000/01. As the effect would merely be to increase the unrelieved personal allowances, this would be a pointless claim. In the same way, capital allowances could have been disclaimed but in this example it would not benefit James to do so. Alternatively, James could have carried the loss forward against future profits from the same source under *ICTA 1988, s 385*. This is illustrated at 9.17 below.

Relief for trading losses in opening years

9.12   Special relief for trading losses in the first four tax years of a trade, profession or vocation continues to be available. [*ICTA 1988, s 381*]. The available loss relief is calculated using the same basis period rules as for trading profits. [*section 382(3)*]. If a loss appears in more than one calculation, it is not included in the computation for the second year. [*section 382(4)*]. Therefore the use of an accounting date other than 5 April restricts the period of loss available for claim under this section. This is illustrated at 9.3 above.

In the year of commencement and the three following years of assessment, losses computed can therefore be relieved under *section 380* against other income of the year of loss or of the preceding year; or, under *section 381*, against the total income of the taxpayer of the year three years before the year to which the loss relates. Relief is given to the full extent of total income for that earlier year and is then carried forward against other income of the following years. Relief is given for the earliest year in preference to the later years.

9.13   In order to claim relief under this section, it is necessary to show that the trade was carried on on a commercial basis with a view to profits and that profits can be reasonably expected within a reasonable time thereafter. [*ICTA 1988, s 381(4)*].

The time limit for claim is twelve months after 31 January after the end of the fiscal year to which the loss relates.

The reduction in tax computed for the earlier year is given as tax credit in the year of loss as set out at 9.7 above.

The claim for loss relief under *section 381* will normally be made outside the tax return. If a claim is made within the return, box 3.86 (4.16) should be used with details in the additional information box. The tax credit will then be set off as for a *section 380* claim (see 9.7 above) or repaid. Repayment interest does not arise until 31 January after the tax year of loss, even though the tax relief is computed by reference to the tax paid up to four years earlier.

Example

9.14 Karen Long commenced trading on 1 November 2000, making up her accounts to 30 September in each year. She has other income of £1,000 p.a., was previously employed at £12,000 p.a., and is entitled to a single allowance.

Her accounts show the following (assume no claims for capital allowances):

	£	£
1.11.2000 to 30.9.2001	(33,000)	
Year ended 30.9.2002	2,400	
Year ended 30.9.2003	48,000	

Schedule D, Case I assessments (without loss relief):

2000/01 (1.11.2000 to 5.4.2001)		NIL
Loss available:		
Loss 5/11 × (£33,000)	(15,000)	
2001/02 (1.11.2000 to 31.10.2001)		
Loss 1.11.2000 to 30.9.2001	(33,000)	
Less included in 2001/02	15,000	
	(18,000)	
Profit 1.10.2001 to 31.10.2001		
1/12 × 2,400	200	
Loss available	(17,800)	NIL
2002/03 year ended 30.9.2002		2,400
2003/04 year ended 30.9.2003		48,000

with overlap profits of £200 and an overlap period of 187 days.

Note: The actual overlap periods are 1 November 2000 to 5 April 2001 and 1 October 2001 to 31 October 2001, but where a loss is included in two periods then it is excluded from the second period in computing the overlap profit relief. [*ICTA 1988, s 63A(4)*]. Therefore, the overlap profit will be only for the period 1 October 2001 to 31 October 2001. The overlap period is defined as being, in relation to an overlap profit, the numbers of days in the period in which the overlap profit arose. [*ICTA 1988, s 63A(5)*].

It is therefore considered that, in the above example, the overlap period would be 187 days being both of the periods the first of which has 'Nil' profits and the second a profit of £200. This means that on cessation Karen Long could have profits based, for example, on the year ended 30 September, having only been in self-employment for the period 6 April to 30 September. Normally this will be counteracted by a deduction of overlap profits representing a period of approximately six months. Because of the loss relief claims in opening years, Karen would only have a deduction of £200, which in fact was based on 31 days. This could give unexpected and unpleasant results on cessation.

As an alternative to relief under *section 380*, Karen has the possibility of making a claim under *section 381* against her total income of the three years preceding the year of loss. These claims would be as follows:

	£
Trading loss of 2000/01 available for relief	(15,000)

Available under *ICTA 1988, s 381* in:

(i)   1997/98 (with balance carried forward to)
(ii) 1998/99
(iii) 1999/2000

Giving claims of:

	£	£	£
1997/98 Schedule E	12,000		
Other income	1,000	13,000	
2000/01 *section 381* claim		(13,000)	NIL
Loss available		(15,000)	
Loss used		13,000	
Loss carried forward		(2,000)	
1998/99 Schedule E	12,000		
Other income	1,000	13,000	
Balance of 2000/01 *section 381* claim		(2,000)	11,000

The time limit for claim is 31 January 2003 (being the time limit applicable to 2000/01).

If the above claims were made, personal allowances would be lost in 1997/98. The balance of the loss for 2001/02 could then be relieved under *section 380* as above, or under *section 381*, as follows:

	£
Trading loss of 2001/02 available for relief	(17,800)

Available in:

  (i)   1998/99 (with balance carried forward)
 (ii) 1999/2000
(iii) 2000/01

Giving claims of:

| 1998/99 | total income (net of loss claim) as above | 11,000 | | |
| | *section 381* claim | (11,000) | NIL | |

Loss available for relief	(17,800)		
Claimed 1998/99	11,000		
Loss carried forward to 1999/ 2000	(6,800)		

		£	£	£
1999/ 2000	Schedule E	12,000		
	Other income	1,000		
			13,000	
Balance of 2001/02 *section 381* claim			(6,800)	
				6,200

If the above *section 381* claim was made, personal allowances would be lost in 1998/99.

Relief for national insurance (SSCBA 1992, 2 Sch 3)

9.15 If loss claims are made against income other than trading income, under either *section 380* or *section 381*, then a loss is calculated for Class 4 national insurance purposes, to be carried forward to relieve profits from the trading source. Accordingly, regardless of the claims made above, for Class 4 purposes the unrelieved loss as at 5 April 2002 would be £32,800, being the loss of £33,000 less £200 used in overlap. This would be relieved against the first available profits from the same trade, i.e.:

| 2002/03 | £2,400 |
| 2003/04 | £30,400 |

Therefore the income for Class 4 national insurance purposes in 2003/04 would be:

Schedule D, Case I assessment	£48,000
Class 4 NIC loss	£30,400
Class 4 profits for year	£17,600

Relief is claimed by entering the amount of the claim (£30,400 for 2003/04) in box 3.95 on the tax return for that year. In the case of a partner, the claim is made in box 4.24.

Relief for trading losses carried forward

9.16 Insofar as trading losses are not offset against other income, relief will be available, by claim, against future profits from the same source. [*ICTA 1988, s 385*]. The time limit for the claim is five years after the 31 January following the year of loss. In practice, such loss relief claims are made by way of income tax return entries.

In future years the unrelieved loss brought forward is shown in box 3.88 (on the partnership pages, 4.18) and the amount claimed in the year is shown in box 3.89 (4.19). The claim must be for the full amount brought forward restricted only to the profits for the current year (box 3.83 or 4.13). Although the guidance notes to the tax return do not cover the point, it would appear that any unused losses from earlier years now to be carried forward — i.e. box 3.88 (4.18) less box 3.89 (4.19) — should also be shown in box 3.87 (4.17) as losses not used in any other way.

Example

9.17 James King (who is single) makes up his accounts to 30 September each year and has the following income:

Schedule D, Case I		*Including capital allowances of*
	£	£
Year ended 30.9.99 profit	8,000	900
Year ended 30.9.2000 loss	(4,975)	815
Year ended 30.9.01 profit	4,700	1,300

Other income		
		£
1999/2000		4,700
2000/01		4,100
2001/02 — non-dividend	3,100	
dividend	1,400	4,500

If James King decided not to make a *section 380* claim, but to carry losses forward against future profits from the same source under *section 385,* his assessments would be:

	£	£
1999/2000 Schedule D, Case I		8,000
2000/01 Schedule D, Case I		NIL
2001/02 Schedule D, Case I	4,700	
Less loss b/f	4,975	
Loss c/f	275	
Other income	4,500	
Less personal allowance	4,535	NIL

(with no repayment of tax credits on dividend income).

In practice, the unrelieved personal allowances and dividends carrying a non-repayable tax credit could be retrieved by restricting the capital allowance claims in the year to 30 September 2000. This could be done by amending the tax return for the year to 5 April 2001. The filing date for that tax return would be 31 January 2002, giving a time limit on amending claims for the period of 31 January 2003. If the capital allowances in the year ended 30 September 2000 were restricted to nil, there would be a revised loss claim of £4,160. As this would still leave unrelieved allowances and notional tax credits, it would then be necessary to restrict the capital allowance claim for the year to 30 September 2001 as well to no more than £405, giving a revised assessment of:

	£	£
Profits before capital allowances	6,000	
Less revised capital allowances	405	
Schedule D, Case I profits		5,595
Less loss b/f (y/e 30.9.2000)		4,160
		1,435
Other income — non-dividend		3,100
— dividend		1,400
		5,935
Less personal allowance		4,535
		1,400

The tax chargeable at 10% = 140 being covered by the non-repayable tax credits of £140 giving no liability payable.

Relief for terminal losses

9.18   Where a trading loss is incurred in the last twelve months of the life of a business, then special relief is available. The relief is calculated by taking the loss of the actual period of the final twelve months, augmented by any overlap relief. The available loss is therefore the loss of the fiscal year of cessation (including overlap relief) plus any part of the loss of the final twelve months of trading that falls in the preceding year. A terminal loss cannot be calculated by only identifying the basis period for the trade and taking any computed loss. Once the loss is computed, it is then relieved against trading profits, if any, of the fiscal year of cessation and of the three preceding fiscal years (giving relief against later years in preference to earlier years). [*ICTA 1988, s 388*]. The time limit for claiming terminal loss relief will be five years from 31 January following the fiscal year of cessation. Insofar as the loss relates to the penultimate year, then the time limit will be based upon that earlier year.

The claim is a *TMA 1970, Sch 1B* claim and therefore the value of the claim in tax repayable terms is made for the year of claim (year of cessation, or penultimate year) and no interest is payable on the repayment until 31 January following the end of the year of claim.

The claim will include any corresponding reduction in Class 4 NIC liabilities.

9.19   *Losses*

Example

9.19   Norah Otter ceased trading on 5 April 2002. Her adjusted profits were:

	£
Year ended 5.4.1999	12,000
Year ended 5.4.2000	6,000
Year ended 5.4.2001	2,000
Year ended 5.4.2002 — Loss	(11,000)

She has no other income.

As the fiscal year basis applies there is no overlap profit relief.

Her terminal loss claim will be:

	£	£
2001/02 — Year ended 5.4.2002		(11,000)

Offset against profits of same trade:	
2000/01	2,000
1999/2000	6,000
1998/99 (balance)	3,000
	11,000

Giving a revised 1998/99 assessment of:	
Profit	12,000
Loss relief *section 388*	(3,000)
	9,000

9.20   In computing assessable profits or losses, overlap profit relief is treated as a deduction of the final period.

Example

Oliver Patel ceased trading on 30 June 2002. His adjusted profits (losses) have been:

	£
Year ended 31.12.1999	15,000
Year ended 31.12.2000	12,000
Year ended 31.12.2001	14,000
Period ended 30.6.2002 — Loss	(9,700)

With overlap profits brought forward of £5,800.

He has no other income.

His assessment for 2002/03 would be nil, and he would have a terminal loss claim, computed as follows:

Loss of last twelve months of trading:
Loss of final fiscal year 2002/03
6.4.2002 to 30.6.2002

3/6 × £9,700 loss	4,850	
Overlap relief	5,800	10,650

Loss computation for the
preceding fiscal year 2001/02
1.1.2002 to 5.4.2002

3/6 × £9,700 loss	(4,850)	
1.7.2001 to 31.12.2001		
6/12 × £14,000 profit	7,000	NIL
Terminal loss claim		10,650

(In computing a terminal loss, the two different years of assessment are looked at separately, so that the 'net profit' of £2,150 arising in the part of the terminal loss period falling within 2001/02 does not have to be netted off against the 2002/03 loss and is instead treated as nil.)

The balance of the loss (£4,850) could be used in a *section 380* claim against other income. Oliver does not have any other income in 2002/03 and the terminal loss claim would have reduced the 2001/02 assessment to:

	£
Year ended 31.12.2001	14,000
Less terminal loss	10,650
	3,350
Less section 380 claim (restricted)	3,350

leaving £1,500 unused.

It would appear that the taxpayer could make the claims in the reverse order, giving a *section 380* claim of:

	£
2002/03	
Loss 1.1.2002 to 30.6.2002	9,700
Overlap relief	5,800
	15,500
Claimed in preceding year (*section 380(1)(b)*)	14,000
Unrelieved	1,500

followed by a *section 388* terminal loss claim:

	£	£
Loss of last twelve months of trading:		
Loss of final fiscal year 2002/03		
6.4.2002 to 30.6.2002		
(restricted by *section 380* claim)	NIL	
Overlap relief (balance)	1,500	1,500

Loss computation for preceding
  fiscal year (2001/02)

1.1.2002 to 5.4.2002	NIL	
1.7.2001 to 31.12.2001	NIL	NIL
Terminal loss claim		1,500

Giving assessments of:

2002/03	NIL
2001/02 (£14,000 — *section 380* £14,000)	NIL
2000/01 (£12,000 — *section 388* £1,500)	10,500
1999/2000	15,000

The Revenue Inspector's Manual confirms that, providing that the taxpayer makes his *section 380* claim first and allows it to become final before making a *section 388* claim, the Revenue will not insist on the terminal loss claim being made first.

9.21   Where a loss is incurred in the penultimate period then it may well only partially fall into a terminal loss claim. This again will give the taxpayer a choice of ways in which loss relief claims can be made. In computing profits for Class 4 national insurance, it must be remembered that any loss claim against non-trading income will form a separate loss relief to carry forward for Class 4 purposes only. This can mean that the use of a loss in a *section 380* claim against non-trading income will result in unrelieved losses for Class 4. In that circumstance it is not possible to make a terminal loss claim for Class 4 'losses' only. The Class 4 loss can only be carried forward. [*SSCBA 1992, Sch 2.3(4)*]. However it would appear that the cessation of a trade does not prevent the carry forward of the Class 4 loss for use against profits of subsequent trades in later years.

If the adjusted results of Oliver had been:

	£
Year ended 31.12.1999	15,000
Year ended 31.12.2000	12,000
Year ended 31.12.2001	(9,700)
Period ended 30.6.2002	14,000

With overlap profits brought forward of £5,800 and no other income, his assessments would then be:

	£	£
1999/2000 (year ended 31.12.1999)		15,000
2000/01 (year ended 31.12.2000)	12,000	
Less section 380 loss relief	9,700	2,300

	£	£
2001/02 (year ended 31.12.2001)		NIL
2002/03 — 6 months to 30.6.2002	14,000	
Less overlap profits	5,800	8,200

If it was decided not to make a claim under *section 380* to carry the relief back for the year ended 31 December 2001 to the year 2000/01, then the relief would normally be carried forward under *section 385*. Insofar as relief was not available under *section 385*, then a terminal loss relief claim would be possible. Continuing the above example with *section 385* relief and then *section 388* relief the assessments would be:

	£	£
1999/2000 (year ended 31.12.1999)		15,000
2000/01 (year ended 31.12.2000)	12,000	
Less terminal loss relief (*section 388*)	1,500	10,500
2001/02 (year ended 31.12.2001)		NIL
2002/03 6 months to 30.6.2002	14,000	
Less unused losses b/f (*section 385*)	(9,700)	
	4,300	
Less overlap relief	(5,800)	NIL
Unrelieved losses	(1,500)	

Terminal loss claim:

Loss of final fiscal year:

	£	£
6.4.2002 to 30.6.2002 — Profit	4,300	
Overlap relief	(5,800)	1,500
Loss of preceding fiscal year restricted to unused loss (*section 388* loss fully used in 2002/03 above)		NIL
		1,500

Available in:

	£
2002/03	NIL
2001/02	NIL
2000/01	1,500

Restriction of relief in respect of farming and market gardening

9.22 The additional restrictions in *ICTA 1988, s 397* continue to apply to ensure that loss relief will only be granted to farmers and market gardeners where the business has made a profit in at least one of the preceding five years (unless a competent farmer or market gardener could not have expected a profit).

This restriction applied where there was not an adjusted profit before capital allowances. With the introduction of the treatment of capital allowances as a trading expense, this would have altered the test under *section 397*. It is therefore provided that in carrying out the test under *section 397* the profit shall be computed without regard to capital allowances, thus keeping the previous test intact.

See Chapter 11 at 11.9 for notes on farmers' averaging.

Relief for losses on unquoted shares

9.23 When an individual had subscribed for shares in a qualifying trading company and those shares have resulted in an allowable loss for capital gains tax purposes, then it is possible for him to elect to treat the loss as being an income tax loss. [*ICTA 1988, s 574*].

Relief under this section is given against other income for the year of loss; alternatively, the taxpayer may elect for relief against other income for the year preceding the year of loss.

Where a claim is made for relief in the current year, a further claim can be made for any balance of the loss to be given against general income of the preceding year. [*ICTA 1988, s 574(1)(2)*].

The time limit for claiming relief under *section 574* is twelve months from 31 January following the year of loss. [*ICTA 1988, s 574(1)*].

For shares issued on or after 6 April 1998, the trade carried on by the qualifying company must be such as to justify the test under Enterprise Investment Scheme (EIS) relief for qualifying companies. [*ICTA 1988, s 576(4)*].

Change of accounting date

9.24 When an accounting date is changed so that the new date is earlier in the fiscal year then additional overlap relief is computed. If the relevant period is a loss then the additional relief will be nil. (See Chapter 10 for computational details.)

Where an accounting date is changed to bring it nearer to 5 April, then overlap profits will be apportioned to the period and the amount will be deducted from the assessable profits or added to an allowable loss. This can have the effect of enhancing a loss.

Example

Joshua Knight (who is single) has the following trading results:

Schedule D, Case I (no capital allowances)

		£
Year ended 30.4.2000	Profit	71,000
Year ended 30.4.01	Loss	(12,000)
Period ended 31.12.01	Profit	4,000
Year ended 31.12.02	Profit	30,000

Joshua has overlap relief brought forward of £51,000 for 340 days.

He has other income of £4,600 per year.

Assuming loss relief is claimed in 2000/01 under *section 380*, his assessable income for the years 2000/01 to 2002/03 will be as follows:

Computation of *section 380* loss claim — 2001/02

Loss year ended 30.4.01	(12,000)	
Profit period ended 31.12.01	4,000	
Overlap profits $\frac{245}{340} \times 51,000$	(36,750)	
Claimed in 2000/01	(44,750)	

2000/01		
Schedule D, Case I	71,000	
Less section 380 loss claim	44,750	26,250
Other income		4,600
		30,850
Less personal allowance		4,385
		26,465

2001/02		
Schedule D, Case I		NIL
Other income		4,600
		4,600
Less personal allowance		4,535
		65

2002/03		
Schedule D, Case I		30,000
Other income		4,600
		34,600
Less personal allowance (say)		4,600
		30,000

Thus by changing the accounting date from April to December, during which period a profit of £4,000 was earned, overlap relief of £36,750 has been brought into the computation, and relieved at higher rates in 2000/01.

Chapter 10

Change of Accounting Date

The objectives of the legislation

10.1 One of the prime objectives of the new legislation is to give complete freedom as to choice of accounting date, both on commencement and during the life of the business. At the same time, the Revenue are concerned to ensure that there could be no tax advantage obtained by changing an accounting date. Although the rules introduced are almost neutral, the Revenue have still included anti-avoidance legislation where rapid changes take place (i.e. two changes within five years), unless the later change is made for a bona fide commercial reason.

A period of account of less than twelve months ending in the next fiscal year

10.2 When an accounting date is for a period that is less than twelve months ending in the next fiscal year, then the assessment will be based upon the twelve months ending with the new accounting date. [*ICTA 1988, s 62(2)(a)*]. This gives further overlap profits that can be calculated and carried forward for overlap relief. [*ICTA 1988, s 63A*]. See the example at 10.8 below.

A period of account of less than twelve months ending in the same fiscal year

10.3 If the accounts are made up to a new accounting date for a period of less than twelve months, and that period falls within the same fiscal year as the previous accounting date, then the old date is ignored and profits are calculated for the longer period of account, i.e. over twelve months to the new accounting date. [*ICTA 1988, s 60(5)*]. See the example at 10.9 below.

Overlap relief will be allowed where two periods of account end in the same fiscal year and they are aggregated to form the assessment. See 10.4 below.

A period of account of more than twelve months ending in the next fiscal year

10.4 If the new accounting date is based upon a period of account of more than twelve months, but not more than 18 months, then the whole of the profit of that accounting period will form the basis of assessment of the fiscal year in which the accounts end. [*ICTA 1988, s 62(2)(b)*]. Because the period of account is more than twelve months, writing-down allowances will be expanded pro-rata. Overlap relief will then apply. [*ICTA 1988, s 63A*]. This is calculated by taking the number of days in the period of account less the number of days in the year of assessment. That proportion of the overlap period relief already available will then be deducted from the profits, or added to the losses, of the long period of account. See the example at 10.10 below. For periods of account exceeding 18 months, see 10.12 below. For enhancement of a loss claim see 9.24 above.

A period of account of more than twelve months such that there is a fiscal year without accounts

10.5 Where a change of accounting date results in a fiscal year without accounts ending in that year, then the legislation deems a period of accounts to have ended on the new accounting date in that year and the assessment will be based upon the period of twelve months ending with that date. [*ICTA 1988, s 62(2)(a)(5)*]. The assessment for the next year will be based upon the period of twelve months ending with the new accounting date in that year. The overlap profits will be calculated and will be available to carry forward. See the example at 10.11 below.

Conditions for change of accounting date

10.6 Except in the first three years of trading (see 10.15 below), it will be necessary to satisfy certain conditions for a change of accounting date to apply. These conditions are set out in *ICTA 1988, s 62A*.

In order to be a valid change:

(a)   the accounting period must not be for a period exceeding 18 months; and
(b)   notice must be given to the Revenue by 31 January following the end of the year of assessment in which the new accounting date first falls, and either:
    (i)   no change of accounting date has taken place in the five years of assessment preceding the year of change; or
    (ii)   the notice of change of date given to the Revenue contains the reason for change and an officer of the Board is satisfied that the changes are made for a bona fide commercial reason. The Revenue have 60 days in which to respond to the notice or else its right of challenge is removed. There is a right of appeal against a refusal by the Revenue to allow the change.

Notification can be given within the tax return by a tick in box 3.12, or if this is a second change by a tick in box 3.13 with the reason for change set out in the additional information box 3.116.

10.7 If the above conditions are not satisfied, then the assessment will be based upon the profits to the old accounting date. Providing the conditions are satisfied in the following fiscal year, the change will be deemed to have taken place in the second year to which the new accounting date has been used. The effect of these provisions will be that the overlap relief will be calculated upon the profits of the second (i.e. twelve-month) period rather than the first (long or short) period using the new accounting date.

Because of the existence of the change of accounting date rules, a taxpayer will be able to claim credit for overlap profits at any time during the life of the business. This is achieved by extending the accounting period to cover a period of not more than 18 months, or by shortening the period to end in the same fiscal year as the last year end (providing that such a change has not taken place in the five previous years and the relevant notice is given).

Examples of change of accounting date

A period of account of less than twelve months ending in the next fiscal year

10.8 Colin Davies, who commenced trading on 1 June 1994 and who makes up his accounts to 31 December in each year, decides to change his accounting date to 30 June with effect from 2000.

His adjusted profits after capital allowances are:

	£
Year ended 31.12.99	42,000
6 months to 30.6.2000	24,000
Year ended 30.6.01	54,000

His overlap profits brought forward are £9,500 with an overlap period of 95 days.

The first year with the new accounting date will be the fiscal year 2000/01. Accordingly, his assessments will be:

	£	£
1999/2000 (old date)		
Year ended 31.12.99		42,000
2000/01 (new accounting date)		
12 months ended 30.6.2000		
6/12 of 42,000	21,000	
Period to 30.6.2000	24,000	45,000
2001/02 (new date)		
Year ended 30.6.01		54,000

As the period from 1 July 1999 to 31 December 1999 (184 days) has been assessed twice, that amount will be added to the overlap profits brought forward as follows:

	Overlap profits £	Overlap period
Brought forward	9,500	95 days
2000/01	21,000	184 days
Carried forward	30,500	279 days

In computing the capital allowances for the period to 30 June 2000, only 6/12ths writing-down allowance will be available.

A period of account of less than twelve months ending in the same fiscal year

10.9   Doreen Ely, who makes up her accounts to 31 May, decides to change her accounting date to 31 December with effect from 2000.

Her adjusted profits are:

	£
Year ended 31.5.99	30,000
Year ended 31.5.2000	35,000
7 months to 31.12.2000	7,000
Year ended 31.12.2001	48,000

Her overlap profits brought forward are £30,900 with an overlap period of 309 days.

Her assessable profits are:

	£	£	£
1999/2000 year ended 31.5.99			30,000
2000/01 1.6.99 to 31.12.2000			
Year ended 31.5.2000	35,000		
7 months to 31.12.2000	7,000	42,000	
Less overlap profits released		21,400	20,600
2001/02 year ended 31.12.2001			48,000

As the assessment for 2000/01 is based upon more than twelve months, part of the overlap profits will now be released. This is calculated in the following way:

Number of days in period of account	580
Number of days in year of assessment	366
Number of days released	214

Overlap profits released 214/309 × £30,900 = £21,400.

	Overlap profits £	*Overlap period*
Brought forward	30,900	309 days
Released	21,400	214 days
Carried forward	9,500	95 days

Capital allowances will be calculated separately for each period of account, with 7/12ths writing-down allowances given in the period to 31 December 2000.

133

A period of account of more than twelve months ending in the next fiscal year

10.10   Where accounts are prepared for more than twelve months and a period of account ends in each fiscal year, the basis period is then the period of account. As that period is for more than twelve months, overlap relief will be given based upon the number of days in the extended period less the number of days in the year of assessment.

Freda Gray, who has made up her accounts to 30 September for many years, decides to change her accounting date to 31 January.

Her adjusted profits are:

Year ended 30.9.99	£14,000
16 months to 31.1.2001	£24,400

Her overlap profits brought forward are £9,350 with an overlap period of 187 days.

Her assessments will be:

	£	£
1999/2000 year ended 30.9.99		14,000
2000/01 16 months to 31.1.01	24,400	
Less overlap relief	6,150	18,250

As the 2000/01 assessment is based on more than twelve months, part of the overlap profits brought forward are released.

Number of days in the period of account	489
Number of days in the year of assessment	366
Number of days released	123

	Overlap profits	*Overlap period*
	£	
Brought forward	9,350	187
Days released		
123/187 × 9,350	6,150	123
Carried forward	3,200	64

Capital allowances will be based upon the period of account, giving writing-down allowances for the 16 months to 31 January 2001 of 16/12ths.

A period of account of more than twelve months such that there is a fiscal year without accounts

10.11   To consider the assessments if the change is for a period of more than twelve months, a further example is required. If the periods of account are prepared such that there is one fiscal year without any accounts ending in that year then:

(a)   the basis period for the fiscal year without an accounting period ending within the fiscal year is the twelve-month period based on the new accounting date ending in that year; and

(b) the basis period for the following tax year is the period of twelve months ending on the new accounting date.

This creates additional overlap profits. Continuing the above example of Doreen Ely:

She subsequently discovers that her new accountancy date is unsatisfactory, as staff are unwilling to undertake stocktaking at the New Year and, because of the seasonable nature of her business (sale of Easter eggs), she is holding very high stocks. She gives notice of the proposed change to the Revenue on 30 August 2003, setting out the reason for change and receives clearance for the change.

Her adjusted profits are:

	£
Year ended 31.12.01	48,000
17 months to 31.5.03	103,200

Her overlap profits brought forward are £9,500 with an overlap period of 95 days.

Her assessable profits are:

		£	£
2001/02	Year ended 31.12.2000		48,000
2002/03	Year ended 31.5.2001		
1.6.01 to 31.12.01	214/366 × 48,000	28,065	
1.1.02 to 31.5.02	151/516 × 103,200	30,200	58,265
2002/03	Year ended 31.5.2003		
	365/516 × 103,200		73,000

	Overlap profits £	*Overlap period*
Brought forward	9,500	95 days
Overlap		
1.6.2000 to 31.12.01	28,065	214 days
Carried forward	37,565	309 days

Capital allowances will be based upon the period of account 1 January 2002 to 31 May 2003, giving 17/12ths writing-down allowances.

If the Revenue does not give clearance, the assessment for 2002/03 will be based upon the profits of the year ended 31 December 2002. Doreen Ely can apply again for clearance in 2003/04. If there are five clear years between changes, i.e. first change in 2000/01, next change in 2006/07 or later, then the Revenue's clearance is not required.

Accounts for more than 18 months

10.12   It would appear that making up accounts for a period in excess of 18 months will not be encouraged by the Revenue. In those circumstances, accounts should be prepared for two periods.

In practice, if accounts are prepared for a period of more than 18 months, then in the fiscal year in which the change takes place the conditions in *ICTA 1988, s 62A* will not be met and the assessment will be based upon the profits of the twelve months ending on the 'old' accounting date. However, if accounts continue to be made up to the 'new' accounting date, the conditions may well be satisfied in the next fiscal year, or the fiscal year after that.

Example

10.13   Cynthia makes up her accounts to 30 June in each year. She changes her accounting date to 31 March by making up accounts for 21 months to 31 March 2003.

Her basis periods will be:

2001/02   Year ended 30.6.2001
2002/03   Year ended 30.6.2002   (being 12/21 of accounts to 31.3.2003)
2003/04   1.7.2002 to 31.3.2004   (being 9/21 of accounts to 31.3.2003
plus accounts to 31.3.2004)

Overlap relief will be given on 274 days of overlap profits.

Note: Capital allowances will be computed for the periods of the year ended 30 June 2002, and 1 July 2002 to 31 March 2003 (9/12 WDA) with both amounts being deducted from the profits of the 21 months to 31 March 2003 before apportionment.

By comparison, Charles makes up his accounts to 31 December and then changes his accounting date to 30 September by making up accounts for the 21 months to 30 September 2002.

His basis periods will be:

2000/01   Year ended 31.12.2000

2001/02   Year ended 31.12.2001 (being 12/21 of accounts to 30.9.2002)

(*Note*: The assessment would be based upon the new accounting date (*section 62(5)*) if the accounting period had not exceeded 18 months. However, this provision (the first condition in *section 62A*) is not satisfied, and therefore the old date applies.)

2002/03   Year ended 31.12.2002 (9/21 of accounts to 30.9.2002 plus 3/12
of accounts to 30.9.2003)

(*Note*: The accounts ending in the fiscal year are for a period of more than 18 months, so that the first condition in *section 62A* is not satisfied and therefore the old date applies.)

2003/04   Year ended 30.9.2003

(*Note*: Overlap profits computed for the period 1 October 2002 to 31 December 2003 to carry forward.)

Failure to give notice

10.14 If notice is not given to the Board by the relevant date, the adjusted profits after capital allowances for the accounting periods must be apportioned to provide assessments based upon profits to the old accounting date. [*ICTA 1988, s 62A(3)*]. Such apportionment will continue until the taxpayer has given notice to the Revenue of the change within the time limit. This will normally mean that for the following fiscal year of assessment the new accounting date will apply.

Changes in first three years of trading

10.15 The qualifying conditions for change of accounting date do not apply to changes in the two years following the year of commencement. Instead, the normal opening year rules apply as set out in Chapter 6. However, where the new date chosen in the second year falls more than twelve months after commencement, then the basis period is the year ending with the new date. [*ICTA 1988, s 62(2)(a)*].

Example

Simon commenced business on 1 July 2000 and makes up his accounts as follows:

6 months to 31 December 2000
9 months to 30 September 2001
12 months to 30 September 2002.

This basis period will be:

2000/01	1/7/2000 to 5/4/01	(*section 61(1)*)
2001/02	1/10/2000 to 30/9/01	(*section 62(2)(a)*)
2002/03	1/10/01 to 30/9/02	(*section 60(3)(b)*)

(*Note*: Although the period of account ending in 2001/02 is far less than twelve months, the normal rule of taking the first twelve months of trading in *section 61(2)(a)* is overriden, because the period from commencement of trading to the end of that accounting period is more than twelve months and there has been a change of accounting date. [*section 61(2)(b)*].)

10.16   Where the change occurs in the third year and the period of account is for more than twelve months, then the assessment will be based on that long period of account minus overlap relief, i.e. normal change of accounting date rules apply

10.17   If the business ceases within the first two years then actual fiscal year basis of assessment applies throughout. [*ICTA 1988, s 63*].

Chapter 11

Other Sources of Income and Capital Gains

Principles of self-assessment

11.1 The introduction of self-assessment and the current year basis has had a far-reaching effect on the way all taxes are assessed and collected.

The basic principle of calculating the liability to tax by reference to the rules of a schedule continues to apply. Having arrived at the quantum of the assessable income, then those amounts are aggregated to form one self-assessment.

Because the taxpayer is making one self-assessment, he will only deal with one tax office and he will only have one tax reference. That tax office and reference may be different to any partnership or employer's tax office or reference.

11.2 In the case of partnerships, the partnership return and statement will be forwarded to the partnership tax district. The resultant division of income from all untaxed sources will be on the basis of the profit-sharing ratio of the period of account.

Accordingly, having arrived at the income chargeable under Schedule D, Case III, etc. for the period of account, this is divided between the partners in the profit-sharing ratio for the accounting period. Effectively, therefore, a different basis arises when Schedule D, Case III income is received by a partnership compared with the receipt of the same income by an individual.

The same applies to all untaxed income received by the partnership, e.g. Schedule D, Case I or II, Schedule A lettings, Schedule D, Cases IV and V overseas income. The division of income from taxed sources will be based upon the profit-sharing ratio of the fiscal year. The amounts to be divided will be the amounts received and the related tax (or tax credits) for the fiscal year.

Schedule D, Case III

11.3 The basis of assessment under Schedule D, Case III has changed from the preceding year basis (in most instances) to an actual basis on all occasions. [*ICTA 1988, s 64*]. As with trading income, the provisions apply to new sources from 6 April 1994. In the case of existing sources, the old rules apply if the source ceased before 6 April 1998. [*FA 1994, 20 Sch 5*].

Example of a new source

11.4   Ingrid James opened a National Savings investment account in June 1998.

Her income from that account was:

		£
Year ended	5 April 1999	1,800
	5 April 2000	1,750
	5 April 2001	1,650
	5 April 2002	1,500

Her Schedule D, Case III assessments are all on an actual basis:

	£
1998/99	1,800
1999/00	1,750
2000/01	1,650
2001/02	1,500

Schedule D, Cases IV and V

11.5   Similar rules apply to overseas income as to UK income. If the source is a foreign trade, profession or vocation chargeable to tax under Schedule D, Case IV or Case V, it is to be assessed as though it were a Schedule D, Case I source. That is, the current year basis of assessment applies, with overlap relief as for Schedule D, Cases I and II. [*ICTA 1988, s 65(3)*].

Other sources of Schedule D, Case IV and Case V income are to be treated as for Schedule D, Case III above, i.e. on an actual basis. [*section 65(1)*].

Schedule D, Case VI

11.6   Income tax under Schedule D, Case VI is computed on the full amount of profits or gains arising in the year of assessment. [*ICTA 1988, s 69*]. This applies to sources of Schedule D, Case VI income arising on or after 6 April 1994, and to existing sources with effect from 1996/97.

If, exceptionally, a partnership receives Schedule D, Case VI income, a current year basis of assessment will apply, together with overlap relief, as a second deemed trade. See 7.24 above.

Lloyd's underwriters

11.7   The profits of a Lloyd's underwriter are assessed on a special basis known as the 'distribution' basis.

The profits of a calendar year are assessed for the year of assessment corresponding to the underwriting year in which the profits are declared.

This means that the profits for the calendar year 1996 will be closed by Lloyd's on 31 December 1999, and its profits declared in June 2000 and will be assessed to tax in 2000/01. For self-assessment the filing and paying dates will apply to that year in the normal way.

Double taxation relief in respect of overlap profits

11.8   Where profits are assessed twice in opening years, the excess profits charged to tax are known as overlap profits and are available for deduction as overlap relief in the year of cessation etc.

If the profits that are charged twice and included in overlap profits have suffered foreign tax then the foreign tax will be available for credit relief twice. [*ICTA 1988, s 804*]. The amount so claimed will be carried forward and will be clawed back in the year in which overlap relief is claimed. If excess credit has been given the excess is recovered by way of an amount chargeable in the fiscal year in which overlap relief is claimed. This is shown on the tax return at box 18.4 (for further details see help sheet IR260 — overlap).

Example

J Mann commenced in business on 1 October 1998 making accounts up to 30 September 1999. Included in his profits for that year of £30,000 are foreign profits of £4,000 on which foreign tax of £1,500 has been paid. These assessments are (using months):

1998/1999	1.10.98 to 5.4.99 (6/12 × 30,000)	15,000
1999/2000	1.10.98 to 30.9.99	30,000

with overlap profits of £15,000.

For double tax relief he will be assessed on (included above):

1998/1999	6/12 × £4,000	£2,000
with foreign tax credit of £750		
1999/2000		£4,000
with foreign tax credit of £1,500		

(*Note*: The Revenue help sheet suggests that the total foreign tax credit of £1,500 + £750 = £2,250 could be claimed over the two years in different proportions for each year, i.e. up to £1,500 in 1998/99 and the balance in 1999/2000.)

Assuming that J Mann is liable at 23% in 1998/99 and 40% in 1999/2000, the actual foreign tax credit claimed will be:

1998/99	£2,000 @ 23%	460
1999/2000	£4,000 @ 40%	1,600
		2,060
Foreign tax borne		1,500
Foreign tax allowed twice on overlap profits		560

J Mann will carry forward overlap profits of £15,000 on which additional tax credit has been allowed of £560.

If J Mann ceased on 31 December 2002 with profits for the 15 months to that date of £45,000 (including foreign income of £5,000 on which £1,250 foreign tax paid), his assessment and tax credit would be:

(Assume basic rate for 2002/03 is 22%)

2002/03 (1.10.01 to 31.12.02)		Profits	45,000
Less overlap relief			15,000
			30,000

Foreign tax credit £1,250 on income of £5,000. If tax rate is 22%. UK tax on same income is £1,100.

Relief available in 2002/03 for foreign tax is:

Tax credit relief (before overlap relief)	1,100
Less additional tax credit allowed	560
Allowable tax credit relief — 2002/03	540

If the foreign income in the final period had been £1,000 with foreign tax paid of £200, the calculation would be:

UK tax on foreign income	
£1,000 at 22%	220
Restricted to foreign tax paid	200
Less additional tax credit allowed	560
Tax credit relief recovered — 2002/03	(360)

Similar rules apply on a change of accounting date, i.e. additional overlap relief may be created or withdrawn, giving rise to double relief or withdrawal as in opening and closing years.

Farmers' averaging provisions

11.9   Farmers' profit averaging provisions, under *ICTA 1988, s 96*, continue to apply under self-assessment. However, previously the provisions applied to the profits before capital allowances. From 1997/98, capital allowances become a deduction as a trading expense and, accordingly, the averaging now applies to profits after capital allowances.

11.10   Where a claim is made for farmers' averaging to apply, the time limit for claims is twelve months following 31 January after the second year of the period. Any claim of the first year that consequently requires amendment, but would otherwise be out of time, is deemed to become a claim of the second year, and therefore to be in time.

The effect of the claims on the tax chargeable for the first year is computed. That amount is then added to or deducted from the amount payable for the second year. Thus any additional liability does not attract an interest charge, provided that it is paid by 31 January following the end of the second year. Any amount repayable can be deducted from the payments on account or balancing payment of the second year, and any excess is repayable, but interest is not added until after 31 January following the second year. [*TMA 1970, 1B Sch*].

Example

Joe Grundy, a farmer, has the following trading profits after capital allowances:

Year ended 30 April 1998	32,200
Year ended 30 April 1999	2,000
Year ended 30 April 2000	22,000

Joe made payments on account for 1998/99 of £3,600 per instalment.

Set out his tax liabilities and payment dates on the assumption that he has no other income and is single. Joe makes all possible averaging claims as early as possible. He always files his tax return in August.

	Profits before averaging	*Profits after averaging*	
1998/99 (70% = £22,540)	32,200	32,200	17,100
1999/2000	2,000	2,000	17,100
		34,200	
1999/2000	17,100		
2000/01 (75% = £16,500)	22,000		

1998/99

Schedule D, Case I before averaging	32,200	
PA	4,195	
	28,005	
27,100 at 20/23%	6,104	
905 at 40%	362	
Class 4 NIC (25,220 − 7,310) at 6%	1,075	7,541
Less payments on account		7,200
Due 31.01.2000 balancing payment 1998/99		341
payments on account 1999/2000		3,770
		4,111
Due 31.07.2000 payment on account 1999/2000		3,771

1999/2000

Schedule D, Case I after averaging with 1998/99	17,100	
PA	4,335	
	12,765	
Tax 1,500 at 10%	150	
11,265 at 23%	2,591	
Class 4 NIC (17,100 − 7,530) @ 6%	574	3,315

Paid on account for 1999/2000		7,541
Repayable		(4,226)

Repayable re 1998/99

Schedule D, Case I after averaging	17,100	
PA	4,195	
	12,905	
4,300 at 20%	860	
8,605 at 23%	1,979	
Class 4 NIC (17,100 − 7,310) @ 6%	587	3,426
Original liability—1998/99		7,541
Repayable by Revenue		(4,115)

Due 31.1.2001 payment on account 2000/01		1,657
Due 31.7.2001 payment on account 2000/01		1,658

2000/01

Schedule D, Case I (no averaging available)	22,000	
PA	4,385	
	17,615	
1,520 at 10%	152	
16,095 at 22%	3,541	
Class 4 NIC (22,000 − 4,385) @ 7%	1,233	4,926
Less payments on account		3,315
Due 31.01.2002 balancing payment 2000/01		1,611
payment on account 2001/02		2,463
		4,074
Due 31.07.2002 payment on account 2001/02		2,463

The original payments on account for 1999/2000 are based upon the liability shown in the 1998/99 tax return (£7,541) that is before averaging. It is possible to make a claim to reduce those payments on account based upon the eventual liability of 1999/2000 (£3,315) but not taking into account the expected repayment for 1998/99 of £4,115.

If the payments are reduced below £1,657 each, then interest will be charged on the shortfall.

The Revenue will repay the excess tax for 1999/2000 after processing the return, however a claim to reduce the payments on account could be made as soon as a reasonable estimate of the liability was available, and the repayment (or reduction of the amount due 31 July 2000) obtained at an earlier date.

By comparison the tax repayment based on 1998/99 of £4,115, arising because of the averaging claim, will be made in the tax return. That amount is shown on the 1999/2000 return by ticking box 18.5 and showing the claim in the additional information box. As it is a claim of 1999/2000 no interest arises on the claim provided repayment is made by 31 January 2001.

The averaging claim carried back does not affect the calculation of the payment of account of the earlier year but does affect the payment for the year following the second year because that is based on the profits as assessed in the second year. This applies equally to an averaging claim that gives rise to an increased liability for the earlier year. That extra amount is entered in box 18.4 on the second year return. The liability for the second year is then reduced because of the average with the consequential reduction of the payments on account for the following year.

The adjustment is shown in box 3.81 on the self-employment pages of an individual or box 4.12 for a partner.

The profits taken into an averaging claim is after reduction by any claim for overlap relief.

Capital gains

11.11 The taxpayer must include computations of capital gains and capital losses within the tax return. Any capital gains tax payable will be due on 31 January following the end of the year of assessment. Under self-assessment the taxpayer must make a claim for capital losses within the tax return. If a claim is not made then loss relief will not be granted. [*TCGA 1992, s 16; TMA 1970, s 42*]. *FA 1995, s 113* provides that losses of 1996/97 and subsequent years are to be deductible from capital gains in preference to capital losses of earlier years brought forward.

In computing a capital gain or capital loss it is necessary in many instances to use a valuation. This should be indicated by a tick in column B and also in the first 'yes' box on page CG8. Valuations necessarily require the exercise of judgement, and more than one figure may equally be sustainable. The basis of valuation should be shown in the further information section of the capital gains pages (pages CG4, 5 or 6). A copy of any valuation obtained should be attached and the reason for the valuation stated. If the taxpayer believes that the valuation is a considered figure, then it should be regarded as the final figure subject to the Revenue's right to enquire into the tax return. If the Revenue do not enquire into a valuation figure within the normal enquiry period, i.e. twelve months from 31 January following the end of the year of assessment (or later if the return is filed later), then it cannot challenge that valuation at a later date unless it is 'unreasonable'.

If the taxpayer believes that the figure is provisional then it should be shown as such in the further information section with a tick in box 23.3 and full details of when the correct information is likely to be available shown in the additional information box 23.6. The provisional figure should be corrected as soon as the missing information is available.

11.12 Details of any reliefs claimed are shown in column G with a tick in the second 'yes' box on page CG8. When a claim is to be made for rollover relief under *TCGA 1992, s 152* or relief for compulsory acquisition of land under *TCGA 1992, s 247*, then it will be possible to make a provisional claim if the re-investment into relevant assets has not taken place by the time that the return is filed. The taxpayer will make a declaration that he intends to make a qualifying acquisition within the relevant time period (three years from the date of disposal). The capital gains liability is then computed on the assumption that a valid claim has been made. If the taxpayer subsequently purchases a qualifying asset, no adjustment is necessary. If the taxpayer fails to satisfy the conditions of the provisional claim, the capital gains tax is recomputed and becomes payable, together with interest, from 31 January following the end of the year of disposal. [*TCGA 1992, ss 152, 153A, 247A*].

Where a claim involves EIS deferment relief the claim must not be made until the taxpayer has received form EIS3 from the company into whom the investment has been made. The claim form E1S3 (1998) must accompany the tax return or claim. The claim is made by writing 'EIS deferral relief' in column G on page CG2 next to the relevant disposal and entering the amount claimed. If the form is not issued until after the tax return has been filed then a stand alone claim must be made. This can be made up to five years after 31 January following the tax year in which the EIS shares are issued. [*TCGA 1992, 5B Sch 6; ICTA 1988, s 306(1)*]. The EIS3 will not be issued until at least four months after the company commences trade, and commencement of trade can be up to two years after the date of investment, which in turn can be up to three years after the date of disposal giving rise to the gain being deferred. CGT must be paid and then reclaimed when a valid claim can be made.

11.13   Where an individual who has been a UK resident for at least four of the last seven years temporarily leaves the UK, then capital gains arising after the date of departure but within the fiscal year of departure are chargeable in the year of departure. Capital gains of subsequent years are chargeable in the year of return. A temporary absence is a period of less than five complete fiscal years. [*TCGA 1992, s 10A*].

As a taxpayer will not be certain as to his period of absence when completing his self-assessment return for year of departure, he may exclude gains made after departure. If he returns within five years then capital gains tax will be payable. Interest will run from the 31 January following the end of the relevant fiscal year, but the latest date for assessing such gains is extended until two years after 31 January following the fiscal year of return. [*TCGA 1992, s 10A(7)*].

Pension contributions

11.14   A taxpayer may pay personal pension premiums in 2000/01 and elect to carry those contributions back to the preceding year (or the year before that year if there are no net relevant earnings in the preceding year). [*ICTA 1988, ss 619, 641*]. Similar rules apply to RAP's (but not personal pensions or stakeholder pensions) for 2001/02 and subsequent years. [*ICTA 1988, s 619*].

From 6 April 2001, the personal pension legislation includes stakeholder pension premiums. From that date all such premiums paid by an individual (employed or self-employed) are net of basic rate tax. If a carry-back claim is required then it must be made before the premium is paid. It is expected that the claim form will be included in the application form provided by the pension provider (i.e. the claim is effectively made to the insurance company). The claim and premium must be made before 31 January following the year to which the carry-back claim is made. [*ICTA 1988, s 641A introduced by FA 2000*]. It will be too late to make a carry-back claim when the tax return is completed if the premium has already been paid.

The relief claimable by a carry-back claim is calculated by reference to the tax chargeable for the earlier year, but relief is given by way of repayment, set-off, treatment as a payment on account or otherwise in the actual year of payment. [*TMA 1970, Sch 1B*].

In the case of a retirement annuity, a claim for 2000/01 may be made in writing outside the tax return at any time, providing that the pension premium has been paid before the submission of the claim. Alternatively, a claim may be made within the tax return. The resultant relief is then treated as a tax credit for the actual year of payment and will be relieved as set out in 3.15 above.

11.15 A claim cannot be quantified before the tax due for the earlier year has been calculated. The tax return for the earlier year must therefore have been completed and returned first.

No repayment of tax will be made where tax is outstanding for any earlier year. Relief will then be given by set-off.

If a claim is not set off as above, but is processed within 35 days of a payment being due (i.e. between 27 June and 31 July or 28 December and 31 January), then relief will be given against the tax due payable at the end of that period.

If no set-off is available under the above provisions, then a repayment will be made.

Interest is, however, only due from 31 January following the end of the fiscal year in which the pension premium is actually paid. [*ICTA 1988, s 824(30)*].

Example

11.16 John pays a retirement annuity contribution of £10,000 on 30 December 2000 but elects for the payment to be deemed paid in 1999/2000. John will receive relief in 1999/2000 at 40%, i.e. £4,000.

John is due to make a payment on account of £6,000 on 31 January and on 31 July 2001 based upon his 1999/2000 liability, together with a balancing payment for 1999/2000 of £4,200 due on 31 January 2001.

John's final tax liability for 2000/01 (before pension payments) is £10,400 and relief for the personal pension payment in that year would be £3,600 if the amount was not the subject of a carry-back claim.

Payments due:

	£	£
31 January 2001		
Balance of 1999/2000	4,200	
Less relief for personal pension	4,000	
	200	
Payment on account 2000/01	6,000	6,200

	£	£
31 July 2001		
Payment on account 2000/01		6,000

	£	£
31 January 2002		
Payable for 2000/01	10,400	
Payments on account	12,000	
	(1,600)	
Payment on account 2001/02	5,200	3,600

	£
31 July 2002	
Payment on account 2001/02	5,200

(*Note*: If the 2000/01 liability is known at an early stage, a claim under *TMA 1970, s 59A* (see 4.4 above) could have been made to reduce the payments on account, giving a repayment of £1,600, and altering the amount due on 31 January 2002 to £5,200. Alternatively the Revenue will credit interest on £800 from the date of payment of the first instalment, and on £800 from the date of payment of second instalment, to 31 January 2002.)

This should be compared with the tax payments due if a carry-back claim was not made:

	£	£
31 January 2001		
Balance of 1999/2000	4,200	
Payment on account 2000/01	6,000	10,200

	£	£
31 July 2001		
Payment on account 2000/01		6,000

	£
31 January 2002	
Liability (before pension payment)	10,400
Less relief for personal pension	3,600
	6,800
Payments on account	12,000
	(5,200)
Payment on account 2001/02	3,400
Repayable	(1,800)

31 July 2002
Payment on account 2001/02   3,400

Notes:
(1)   The result of making a carry-back claim is that the payable amount at 31 January 2002 will only be reduced by £6,800, not by £10,400 as above.
(2)   When the 2000/01 liability is known, a claim under *TMA 1970, s 59A* claim (see 4.4 above) could be made to reduce the payments on account, giving a repayment   of   £5,200   and   altering   the   amount   due   on 31 January 2002 to £3,400 payable. Alternatively, repayment supplement would be paid on £5,200 when the Revenue make the repayment of £1,800.

Thus, if a retirement annuity premium is paid, the taxpayer should first consider which tax year will give the greater relief. John (above) received £4,000 relief by claiming relief in 1999/2000 compared with £3,600 in the year 2000/01. Secondly, the cash-flow implications should be considered. In the above example, the 31 January 2001 payment is reduced by carry-back, whereas without carry-back the reduction takes effect on 31 January 2002. However, the 2001/02 payments on account are not reduced when a carry-back claim is made. Where carry-back is not claimed, a corresponding adjustment is due on 31 January 2003, i.e. the amount is increased by the relief which had effectively been granted a second time when relief was claimed in the year of payment.

11.17   Similar considerations apply where personal pension or stakeholder pension contributions are made. However, as the claim must be made at or before the premium is paid, the decision must be made well before the completion of the application form. This may well be before the tax adviser has been consulted. Furthermore the premium must be paid by 31 January following the relevant year (ten weeks earlier than for RAPs) and the claim made at the time of payment (between one year and 21 months earlier than for RAPs). Maximum flexibility will be retained where the taxpayer has an existing RAP policy.

Chapter 12

The Penalty Regime

Penalties

12.1 In order to control and police a self-assessment system, it is necessary to have a comprehensive armoury of penalties available to the Revenue authority. The UK system of self-assessment is no exception. The Revenue will automatically charge interest from the due date of payment. To compensate, repayment interest will, in most instances, be paid on overpaid tax from payment date (see Chapter 4 above).

In addition to interest for late payment, there is a surcharge of 5% if tax is not paid by 28 days from the final due date. This surcharge will be increased by a further surcharge of 5% of the tax unpaid six months after the normal due date (see 12.2 below). Such a surcharge is treated as though it is income tax for the purpose of charging interest. However, a surcharge is not taken in addition to a further tax-geared penalty. Surcharges do not apply to companies.

An automatic penalty applies for failure to file an income tax return by the due date. If a return is not filed by 31 January following the end of the fiscal year, or three months after the date of issue if that is later (providing that full notification of liability has been made), then there is a penalty of £100 (restricted to the tax liability shown in the return). If the return has not been filed by six months after the filing date, a further penalty of £100 is imposed. The Commissioners can set aside the flat-rate penalty if there is a reasonable excuse for failure.

If the failure continues after a year, a penalty can be imposed of an amount up to the tax liability that would have been shown in the return. On application by the Revenue to the Commissioners, a daily penalty can be imposed.

Similar penalties apply to each partner for failure to file a partnership return, but without restriction as to tax due.

The new regime makes it essential that accounts and tax returns are filed by the due date, and that tax is paid by the due date. The penalties for failure to meet such deadlines can be high.

Surcharges

12.2 To prevent the taxpayer using the Inland Revenue as a cheap form of loan finance, *TMA 1970, s 59C* provides for a surcharge where tax is not paid on time.

That section provides that where tax remains unpaid 28 days from the due date, it will be increased by a surcharge of 5%. Furthermore, when any tax remains unpaid on the day following the expiry of six months from the due date, the surcharge on the tax then outstanding is a further 5%. The surcharge will not be charged in addition to a tax-geared penalty.

12.3 The surcharge will be charged by way of notice served by the Revenue on the taxpayer. The taxpayer may appeal against that notice within 30 days. [*section 59C(5)(7)*]. The Commissioners may set aside the surcharge if it appears to them that the taxpayer had a reasonable excuse throughout the period of default for not paying the tax. The inability to pay the tax is not in itself a reasonable excuse. Alternatively, the Board of the Inland Revenue may mitigate or remit the surcharge at their discretion. [*section 59C(9)–(11)*].

Interest will be charged on any surcharge not paid within 30 days of the date that the *notice* is issued. [*section 59C(6)*]. A surcharge is not charged on late-paid payments on account.

In the same way, if a tax return is corrected by the Revenue or amended by the taxpayer, then the due date for payment becomes 30 days after the notice of amendment. [*TMA 1970, 3ZA Sch*].

12.4 Similar rules apply where a self-assessment is amended following enquiries by the Revenue. Such enquiries will result in a closure notice informing the taxpayer that the enquires are complete and giving the Revenue's conclusions. If the enquiry officer considers that an amendment of the taxpayer's return is necessary, the closure notice will make the necessary amendments.

Any extra tax which becomes due as a result of the amendment must be paid on or before the day following the end of the period of 30 days beginning with the day on which the closure notice was given. [*TMA 1970, Sch 3ZA para 5(2)*]. If the tax remains unpaid 28 days following the end of that period, then a surcharge will be applied. [*section 59C*].

The taxpayer may appeal against any amendment made by the closure notice but this does not automatically lead to the postponement of the extra tax. In a case like this, *TMA 1970, s 55(2)* provides that the extra tax should normally be paid as if no appeal had been made. However, the taxpayer may appeal to the Commissioners under *section 55(3)* for postponement of some or all of the extra tax payable.

A worked example of interest and surcharge

12.5 Susan has a final liability for 2000/01, due on 31 January 2002, of £2,100. She pays £1,000 on 28 February 2002. On 31 March 2002 the Revenue issues a notice of surcharge. She pays a further £600 on 31 May 2002. On 2 August 2002 the Revenue issues a further surcharge notice. Susan pays the balance of her liability and surcharges on 31 August 2002.

Her interest and surcharge payable will be (assuming 10% p.a. interest):

Surcharge

	£	£
On tax outstanding at 28 February 2002		
5% × £1,100	55	
On tax outstanding at 31 July 2002		
5% × £500	25	80

Interest	£	£
1 February to 28 February		
10% 28/365 × £2,100	16	
1 March to 30 April		
10% × 61/365 × £1,100	18	
1 May to 31 May		
10% × 31/365 × £1,155	10	
(including surcharge unpaid after 30 days)		
1 June to 31 August		
10% × 92/365 × £555	14	58
		138

(Note that the second surcharge is paid within 30 days of the notice and therefore does not attract interest.)

Assessments and determinations

Determination of tax where no return delivered

12.6 Under self-assessment, the Revenue will not normally issue an assessment to the taxpayer. However, if a taxpayer does not file a tax return, the Revenue will be able to raise a determination on him under *TMA 1970, s 28C*. Such a determination will be treated as if it were a self-assessment. The Revenue will make the determination to the best of its information and belief and it may include income tax and capital gains tax for the year of assessment. The determination may include both the amount chargeable and the amount payable, i.e. the amount due after deducting income tax deducted at source and tax credits.

Any tax payable under the determination is deemed to be due on the same day as the normal tax which would have been due had the taxpayer self-assessed. This tax is collectible and cannot be postponed. A self-assessment filed within twelve months of the date of determination will supersede the determination.

The Revenue cannot issue a determination more than five years after the 31 January following the year of assessment.

12.7 The above provisions deal with the situation where the taxpayer has not filed a tax return. It should be remembered that the onus is on the taxpayer to report sources of income within six months from the end of the fiscal year in which those sources arise. Failure to do so will give rise to the penalties set out in *TMA 1970, s 7*, i.e. an amount not exceeding the amount assessable for the year and which is not paid by the due date (see also 12.12 below).

Assessment where a loss of tax is discovered

12.8 A less common situation may well be where the taxpayer has not notified the Revenue of a source of income and therefore a tax return has not been submitted. This situation is dealt with by *TMA 1970, s 29*, which provides that the Revenue may raise an assessment where they discover a loss of tax.

As the enquiry system does not of itself give rise to penalties, it must be expected that the Revenue will be looking to make 'discoveries' during the course of an enquiry, thus enabling them to issue assessments and charge penalties.

An assessment may be raised if an officer discovers:

(a) that any profits which ought to have been assessed to tax have not been assessed;

(b) that an assessment to tax is or has become insufficient; or

(c) that any relief which has been given is or has become excessive. [*section 29(1)*].

It is not a discovery if the taxpayer has delivered a return which was made in accordance with the normally accepted accounting practice prevailing at the time when the return was made.

12.9 Furthermore, if a taxpayer has made a tax return, then unless there has been fraudulent or negligent conduct, either by him or by somebody acting on his behalf, the Revenue are precluded from re-opening an enquiry after they have informed the taxpayer that they have completed their enquiries into his return. In the same way, if the period in which the Revenue could commence enquiries has expired, the Revenue cannot open an enquiry into the return unless they can show fraud or negligence. If an enquiry has been conducted into a taxpayer's return and the Revenue have issued notice that they have completed their enquiries, then the Revenue again are precluded from making a discovery (except for fraud or negligence), unless the discovery could not have been reasonably expected to have been made on the basis of the information available to the Revenue during the course of the enquiry.

For the purpose of the phrase 'information available to the officer', the Revenue are deemed to have such information available to them if:

(a) it is contained in a person's tax return in respect of the relevant tax year or either of the two previous tax years, or in any accounts, statement or documents accompanying the return;

(b) it is contained in any claim made by the taxpayer;

(c) it is contained in any document, account or particulars which are produced to the Revenue for the purpose of the enquiry; or

(d) it is information which could reassurably be expected to be inferred by the Revenue from the information falling within (a), (b) or (c) above or which has been notified in writing by the taxpayer to the Revenue. [*section 29(6)(7)*].

If the Revenue makes a discovery, then penalties will arise under the existing legislation.

Penalty for late filing of tax return

12.10   It must be remembered that the tax return must be filed by 31 January, or three months after the date of issue. This is an absolute time limit and will result in a flat-rate penalty of £100 if the filing date is missed. If the failure continues for a further six months, the penalty will be increased by a further £100. The fixed penalties cannot exceed the liability to tax shown in the return for the year. If the tax return has not been filed one year after the filing date, then the penalty is increased to the tax liability shown by the return. An appeal against such a penalty may be made to the Commissioners. [*TMA 1970, s 93*].

The Revenue will accept a return received on 1 February without imposing a penalty provided it was placed in the tax office letter box before commencement of work. If that day is not a working day, then the return should not receive a penalty provided it is in the tax office before it opens on the next working day. This is based upon the case of *Steeden v Carver* [1999] STC 283.

12.11   In addition, the Revenue can apply to the Commissioners for a penalty of up to £60 per day for continued failure to file a tax return. However, if this application is made before the second £100 penalty then that second penalty will not be applied.

The Commissioners can, on appeal, set aside the flat-rate penalty if it appears to them that there is a reasonable excuse for the failure to file a tax return during the period of default. Similar penalties also apply to partnership returns. [*TMA 1970, s 93A*].

Notification of chargeability

12.12   The penalty for failure to notify chargeability by 6 October following the end of the fiscal year in which the income arises is a penalty of an amount up to the tax which remains unpaid as at 31 January following the year of assessment. [*TMA 1970, s 7(8)*]. This rule was introduced from 1995/96. It should be noted that, in the case of a new business, notification will be required before the end of the first trading period in many instances.

Example

12.13   Jenny commenced trading on 1 November 2000. She makes her accounts up to 31 October 2001. The income first arose in the fiscal year 2000/01 and therefore the latest date for notification is 5 October 2001.

The Schedule D tax liability, based upon the period 1 November 2000 to 5 April 2001, will be due on 31 January 2002, a mere three months after the end of the first period of account. It will be seen that, if the first trading period had been the year ended 28 February 2002, payment would actually be due on 31 January 2002, before the end of the first accounting period. Obviously the taxpayer would have to use a best estimate and correct that estimate after the end of the period, with a charge to interest on any underpayment.

Keeping of records

12.14 To complement this brief review of penalties, it should be noted that records must be maintained for one year from the 31 January following the fiscal year of assessment, increased if the return is filed late to the anniversary of the quarter date of filing, or in the case of a trade, profession, vocation or letting for five years from 31 January following the year of assessment. The penalty for failure to retain records is an amount of up to £3,000. [*TMA 1970, s 12B(5)*].

Usually, the taxpayer is not required to keep the original documents, merely to preserve the information contained in them. [*TMA 1970, s 12B(4)*]. In some cases, however, the original documents must be kept, i.e. when they relate to:

(a) dividend vouchers;
(b) certificates of tax deduction;
(c) C1525 (tax deducted from subcontractors in the construction industry); and
(d) foreign tax credits. [*TMA 1970, s 12B(4A)*].

However, a certificate of dividends and tax credits issued in respect of a nominee holding may be substituted for the actual vouchers.

If dividend vouchers are not retained, then third party evidence of the amount of dividend income may be accepted by the Revenue. [*TMA 1970, s 12B(5B)*].

Subcontractors vouchers are normally filed with the tax return. However it is good practice to keep a photocopy of the vouchers in case of loss in the post (or by the Revenue).

Production of documents

12.15 If a taxpayer is under enquiry, then the Revenue may issue a notice requiring the production of documents that are in the taxpayer's power or possession. If the taxpayer fails to produce documents as required by a notice under *TMA 1970, s 19A*, then a penalty will be imposed under *TMA 1970, s 97AA*. This will be a penalty of £50, together with a daily penalty for continued failure of an amount not exceeding £30 per day for each day the failure continues after the date on which the penalty of £50 is imposed. If the penalty is imposed by the Commissioners, the maximum amount is £150 per day.

Interest on penalties

12.16 *TMA 1970, s 103A* imposes interest upon late payment of penalties. It is charged from the date on which the penalty becomes due and payable until payment.

Claims

12.17   Many time limits were altered by the introduction of self-assessment. The general rule becomes that a claim must be made by five years from the 31 January following the end of the year of assessment. [*TMA 1970, s 43(1)*]. This is approximately nine weeks shorter than the previous time limit of six years. This new general rule was introduced for 1996/97, except for existing partnerships, when it applied from 1997/98.

The treatment of such claims is dealt with in *TMA 1970, Sch 1A*. This gives the Revenue the power to determine the form in which claims are made and allows for amendment or alterations to such claims.

However, many claims are to be made in the tax return. [*TMA 1970, s 42*]. As that return must be complete and final by twelve months after the 31 January following the end of the year of assessment, the normal time limit becomes one year and ten months after the end of the fiscal year for claims such as these.

Certain elections can be made outside the tax return. For example, elections to carry back a personal pension contribution to the previous year must be made by 31 January in the year of payment from 2001/02. Notification of a change of accounting date must also be made by 31 January following the fiscal year of change.

Other time limits have been brought into line with claims made in the return and become one year after 31 January following the end of the fiscal year. [*FA 1996, s 135, 21 Sch*].

Error or mistake claims

12.18   In the past many claims could have been made under the provisions for an error or mistake claim. [*TMA 1970, s 33*].

Nowadays, error or mistake claims will not be allowed where a tax return has been completed on the basis of the practice generally prevailing at the time that the tax return was made, nor where the error or mistake is in a claim included in the return. [*TMA 1970, s 33(2A)*]. Where a claim is allowed, notice must be given no later than five years from the 31 January following the end of the year of assessment. [*section 33(1)*].

12.19   Similar rules apply for partnership statements as well as partnership returns, allowing for errors or mistakes to be corrected within five years of the filing date. The claim is made by the representative partner and, if the partnership statement is amended, the amendment is binding on all partners and the Revenue will give each partner a notice of the amendment and also amend each individual partner's personal return. [*TMA 1970, s 28B(4)*].

Assessments for 1995/96 and earlier years

12.20   If an assessment to income tax or capital gains tax for 1995/96 or any earlier year is issued after 6 April 1998, then the self-assessment interest and surcharge provisions will apply. [*TMA 1970, s 59C, s 86*]. This means that if an old-style tax return was issued and completed for that earlier year by 31 October following the year of assessment (and therefore *TMA 1970, s 88* cannot apply), interest will run under *TMA 1970, s 86* from 31 January following the end of the year of assessment.

The Revenue have announced that interest will not be charged on Schedule D, Case I assessments for 1995/96 or 1996/97 that are increased because of the cessation of the business and the exercise by the Revenue of their transitional powers under *FA 1994, 20 Sch 3*. Interest will, of course, run on the original assessment from the normal date. Interest will also run on the uplift from 30 days after the date of issue. The announcement does not cover interest on revised Schedule D, Case III etc. assessments (see 6.53 above).

Example

12.21 In 1994 Nigel sold farmland which was to be used for housing development, giving rise to a capital gain of £500,000. This was clearly shown upon the tax return to 5 April 1995 but the Inland Revenue did not assess it.

In December 2000 the Revenue become aware that an assessment for 1994/95 capital gain has not been issued. On 3 January 2001 they issue an assessment charging tax of £197,680.

Because the assessment is for the year 1995/96 or earlier and was issued after 6 April 1998, the rules of self-assessment apply. Interest therefore runs from 31 January following the end of the fiscal year, i.e. from 31 January 1996 to 3 January 2001. Furthermore, if the tax remains unpaid 28 days after the normal due date, then a surcharge will become due. The normal due date is 30 days after the issue of the notice of assessment, i.e. 2 February 2001, and the 5% surcharge would apply if the tax was unpaid by 2 March 2001. The surcharge would increase to 10% six months from the due date, i.e. on 2 August 2001.

Penalties on employers

Forms P14 and P35

12.22 Automatic penalties are payable by employers who do not send in year-end forms P14 and P35 by 19 May, or who send in incorrect returns. The penalty for failure to file by 19 May is £100 for every 50 employees (or part of 50) for each month, or part of a month, that the return is late. [*TMA 1970, s 98A*]. In addition, interest is charged if PAYE and national insurance contributions for any year ending 5 April are paid later than 19 April. [*Income Tax (Employment) Regulations 1993, reg 51*].

Form P60

12.23 The form P60 is normally part of the P14 pack or its computer equivalent. Employers are required to give forms P60 to employees who worked for them at 5 April not later than 31 May, e.g. for an employee on 5 April 2002 the form P60 must be given to that employee by 31 May 2002.

If an employer fails to provide the information to the employee by the deadline and the Inland Revenue become aware of that failure, then they will remind the employer of his obligation and encourage compliance. The purpose of the new obligation is to enable employees to be able to complete their tax returns accurately and in good time. Providing the employer provides the information in such time that the employee can comply with his obligations to the Revenue, then generally no penalty will be imposed by the Inland Revenue on the employer. However, if the employer persists in failing to comply, or the amount of tax involved is significant, then the Inland Revenue will consider taking penalty proceedings. A penalty of up to £300 per form may be imposed by the General or Special Commissioners. The Commissioners can order a further penalty of up to £60 per form for each day that the failure continues.

The Revenue will not generally consider taking any action to recover penalties unless an employee tells them of an employer's failure.

Forms P11D and P9D

12.24   An employer is obliged to file a form P11D or form P9D, for each employee for whom benefits have been provided or expense payments made, by 6 July. In addition the employer will be required to give the employee a copy of the relevant form P11D or P9D.

Failure to file by the due date can give rise to an initial penalty of up to £300 per form being imposed by the General or Special Commissioners, together with a further penalty of up to £60 per form for each day that the failure continues. These are the maximum penalties available, covering a wide range of circumstances, and the Revenue do not normally ask the Commissioners to impose the maximum penalty. However, if a form is not filed by the due date and the case is listed for hearing before the Commissioners, then even if the breach has been remedied before the hearing, i.e. the relevant forms filed, it is still possible for the Revenue to continue with the hearing and to ask for a penalty to be imposed for late filing.

Where the Inland Revenue discover that an employer has provided incomplete information or that forms P11D or P9D contain errors, they will normally ask the employer to provide an explanation of the error before penalty action is considered. If the employer can show that the error or omission is entirely innocent, no penalty will arise. Therefore a genuine mistake made in good faith, e.g. in the calculation of a figure shown on the form, will not give rise to a penalty.

In practice the Inland Revenue pursue very few P11D/P9D penalties to the Commissioners, instead preferring to arrange voluntary settlements with the employer to collect any tax and national insurance due. Where a form P11D or P9D is incorrect or incomplete, there is a maximum penalty of £3,000 per form.

In addition to completing the form P11D or P9D and forwarding it to the Revenue by 6 July, the employer will also have to provide a copy of the form P11D to his employees. He will be obliged to provide a form to all employees in service on 5 April. In the case of employees who have left since that date the form may be sent to the last known address. If the employer fails to provide a copy of the form P11D or P9D to the employee, then the Revenue can ask the Commissioners to impose the same penalty on the employer as for failure to file the form with the Revenue, i.e. up to £300 per form plus a further penalty of up to £60 per day. However, it will be the policy of the Inland Revenue not to ask for penalties initially, but to remind the employer of his obligations and to encourage compliance. Penalties will only be imposed where the failure persists or the amount of tax involved is significant.

An employer does not automatically have to give a copy of form P11D or P9D to employees who left during the tax year. However, if such an employee requires a copy of the form, then the employer must provide the information within 30 days of the written request, or by 6 July following the end of the relevant tax year if later. The employee is only allowed to make one written request. [*Income Tax (Employment) Regulations 1993, reg 46AA*]. Again, failure to comply can result in the General or Special Commissioners imposing a penalty of up to £300 per form together with a daily penalty of up to £60 per form. In practice the Revenue will encourage compliance rather than automatically apply for a penalty.

Third parties

12.25 A third party providing a benefit to an employee is required to provide written details of that benefit, including its cash equivalent value, to the employee by 6 July following the end of the tax year.

This requirement does not normally involve the Inland Revenue. If an employee does not receive such notification, and informs the Inland Revenue of the failure, then the Revenue will contact the third party to persuade it to comply with its obligation. Only in the last resort will the Inland Revenue consider taking the matter to the General or Special Commissioners for a penalty of up to £300 per form together with up to £60 per day for continued failure.

Although the Inland Revenue can also require the third party to make returns of such benefits directly to them, this will not be done automatically. If the third party fails to comply with the notice, the Revenue can apply to the Commissioners for the usual penalty of up to £300 per form and a continuing penalty of up to £60 per day. For an incorrect or fraudulent return the penalty is up to £3,000 per return.

Chapter 13

Enquiries

13.1 The Board of Inland Revenue is charged with the care and management of inland revenue. In the words of its Code of Practice, the Board wants us all 'to pay the right amount of tax: no more, no less' and will do everything it reasonably can to help make sure this happens.

These words were carefully chosen but they do not come from any of the Inland Revenue's publications specifically concerned with tax investigations. They are to be found in Code of Practice 11, which deals with enquiries into self-assessment returns. [Appendix A]. They cover not only those people intent on evasion but also those who pay too little (or too much) tax through neglect or ignorance.

Indeed, the Inland Revenue's definition of 'investigations' for the benefit of its own inspectors does not mention the word 'evasion' at all.

13.2 The Revenue's Investigation Handbook defines investigations into the financial affairs of businesses and business owners as follows:

> *'An accounts investigation consists of a fundamental review of the accuracy and completeness of the records underlying the accounts and/or a review of the private financial affairs of the directors (or of the taxpayer in the case of unincorporated businesses) to establish whether business profits have been understated.' (IH 1000)*

This definition underlines the ethos inherent in the self-assessment return in that there is, at least in theory, no in-built assumption that the return is incorrect at the start of an enquiry whereas in earlier times an investigation was not started unless the inspector had reason to believe that a tax return was incorrect.

The definition was not designed to encompass investigations concerning the operation of the PAYE Regulations or the Construction Industry Tax scheme though it could be adapted without strain.

13.3 Apart from certain powers vested in the General and Special Commissioners of Tax, all statute law concerned with the process of investigation is contained in the *Taxes Management Act 1970* at least in relation to individuals, partners and trustees. The company rules are now found in *FA 1998, Sch 18*. These provisions are based on the following tenets:

160

(1) The definition of:

(a)   a series of responsibilities to be met by those chargeable to tax;
(b)   a series of responsibilities to be met by those delivered of a return;
(c)   time limits within which those responsibilities must be discharged;
(d)   parameters as to how those responsibilities are to be discharged.

(2) The conferment of power on tax inspectors to check that responsibilities have been discharged in the required manner by equipping them with:

(a)   tools to gather information from the taxpayer and third parties about the taxpayer's financial affairs either directly or through the General and Special Commissioners;
(b)   the right to enquire into any self-assessment return without reason;
(c)   the right to amend self-assessment returns and to raise discovery assessments;
(d)   the right to determine interest and penalties on those persons found to have failed to meet their responsibilities.

The *Taxes Management Act* also provides, in most cases, that wherever the inspector has a right to act, then the taxpayer has a right of appeal against that act whether to the General or Special Commissioners of Tax.

The taxpayer's responsibilities

Notification of liability — TMA 1970, ss 7 and FA 1998, 18 Sch 2

13.4   The onus of responsibility to 'join the club' is put squarely on to the taxpayer's shoulders by *TMA 1970, s 7* and *FA 1998, 18 Sch 2* in that every person who is chargeable to tax (individual, company, trust or other body) must notify chargeability within six months of the end of the year of assessment (twelve months from the end of the accounting period for a company).

Under *section 7(3)* and *7(7)* a person is relieved from notifying chargeability if, had he completed a self-assessment return for that year, he would not be taxable on any source of income by virtue of that income being covered by reliefs and/or allowances.

Section 7 also provides for a penalty for failure to notify chargeability. [*s 7(8)*]. This is unusual in that most penalty sections are contained in *TMA 1970, ss 93* to *99A*. The main penalty provisions are considered in Chapter 12.

Making a return — TMA 1970, ss 8, 8A, 9, 12AA and FA 1998, 18 Sch 3

13.5   Any person who is sent a return by an officer of the Board of Inland Revenue of income, capital gains or profits chargeable to corporation tax must make or deliver that return and supply any information in support of it as may be reasonably required within the time specified.

13.6 *Enquiries*

It is of interest to contrast the wording in the 'modern' *s 8* and *FA 1988, 18 Sch 3* with the wording prior to the run up to self-assessment.

In the days prior to *Finance Act 1989*, the return of income or profits had to be 'computed in accordance with the taxes acts' and had to 'specify each separate source of income and the amount from each source'. The onus was clearly on the taxpayer's shoulders to ensure that the tax return was correct whether or not he knew the law.

13.6 Now, in the case of an individual, for example, under *TMA 1970, s 9* every return is to include a self-assessment, i.e. 'an assessment of the amounts in which, on the basis of the information contained in the return and taking into account any relief or allowance ..., the person making the return is chargeable to income tax and capital gains tax for the year of assessment'.

Since it is the Inland Revenue's responsibility to specify the form of the self-assessment return then the onus of responsibility has shifted onto the Inland Revenue to ask the right questions within the return so as to ensure that an honest answer will produce the correct tax bill. This is why the Revenue has to supply a comprehensive (though some would say incomprehensible) tax calculation guide with the self-assessment return that must cover every combination of circumstances known to the tax system.

Be that as it may, if we revert to the definition of an investigation (see 13.2 above) it will be seen that testing the information underlying the figures in the tax return is as fundamental a part of the process as it ever was.

Records to be kept for the purposes of returns — TMA 1970, s 12B

13.7 *Section 12B* is designed to ensure that the information is available for the production of figures for inclusion in the self-assessment boxes and for testing through the investigative process. Prior to the advent of self-assessment there was no statutory responsibility to keep such records for the purposes of income tax although the PAYE Regulations have always provided such a responsibility in so far as business records impinge on wages.

Sub-section (1) requires the person who may be required to make a return to keep 'all records as may be requisite for the purpose of enabling him to make and deliver a correct and complete return for the year or period'.

Where the taxpayer is carrying on a trade, profession or other business, alone or in partnership, these records must be kept for a period approaching six years being the period from the fifth anniversary of the 31 January next following the year of assessment or period.

Sub-section (3) defines the records that should be kept by a taxpayer in business as including:

(a)   those showing all amounts received and expended 'and the matters in respect of which the receipts and expenditures take place'; and

(b)   in the case of a trade involving the dealing in goods, records of all sales and purchases of goods made in the course of that trade; and

(c)   all supporting documents relating to the items mentioned above.

The impact of the Finance Act 2001 on enquiries

13.8   The *FA 2001, Sch 29* includes various amendments to the 'machinery of assessment'. The vast majority relate to enquiries. Why have there been so many changes in this area? Part of the answer lies in a collaborative research study carried out by the Chartered Institute of Taxation and the Revenue, and published in October 2000 under the title 'Income Tax Self-Assessment Enquiries'.

The collaborative research study

13.9   The study was launched in December 1999 in order to:

(a)   carry out a review of all the process and procedures involved in an Income Tax Self-Assessment Enquiry that have an impact on the taxpayer or agents, consulting with interested parties both from within and outside the Revenue;

(b)   highlight those areas which were working well and those where improvements were required; and

(c)   make recommendations on improvements which could be put in place.

The study involved the extraction of a wide range of views on enquiries from a selection of Revenue officers, members of the Chartered Institute of Taxation and the Association of Taxation Technicians, and other agents. These views were canvassed through a preliminary study, then by a carefully structured questionnaire with a final follow-up stage to review the issues raised.

The study covered a range of issues. In some cases, no definite proposals were forthcoming. In others, the consultees were broadly in favour of legislative change. These areas included proposals:

(a)   that the Revenue be able to resolve minor queries without the need to open a formal *s 9A* enquiry, perhaps by means of a written request for information (most consultees considered that there was a 'strait-jacket' approach to many enquiries);

(b)   to replace all references to 'the giving of notice' in the legislation with 'the date of issue' to avoid some of the problems encountered particularly in relation to the date of opening a *s 9A* enquiry (although there might be some need to extend the existing time limits to take account of postal delays);

(c)   that there should be a separate capital gains enquiry power, totally distinct from any power to enquire into the income tax sections of the return (although it was accepted that careful thought would be needed before any legislative changes could be implemented as this would have wide ranging effects on the way self-assessment operates);

(d)   that, in larger cases and those involving corporation tax self-assessment, the Revenue and the taxpayer should be able to agree to litigate a point whilst the enquiry was still going on (although concern was expressed that changes would add an additional layer of complexity to the system, perhaps resulting in delays and errors);

(e) that the existing 'cumbersome' completion procedure (with its successive 30-day periods to allow the taxpayer to amend his return and the Revenue to make a counter-amendment) should be streamlined to provide for the enquiry inspector to make any necessary amendments to the return in his closure notice (counter-balanced by the taxpayer having a right to amend his tax return whilst the enquiry is carrying on).

Amendments made by the Finance Act 2001

13.10 Many of the above suggestions have found their way into the *Finance Act 2001* (usually with effect from 11 May 2000), e.g.,

(a) a taxpayer may now amend his own return even though an enquiry has commenced, although the amendment will not take effect until the enquiry is completed and may be superseded by the inspector's closure notice (*TMA 1970, new s 9B*);

(b) the legislation makes provisionn for the joint referral of questions arising during an enquiry to the Special Commissioners (however, the implementation of these rights requires the passing of regulations by the Lord Chancellor and at the time of writing these had not been published) (*new ss 28ZA to 28ZE*);

(c) the completion procedure has been streamlined along the lines proposed in the study, with the enquiry inspector amending the taxpayer's return in his closure notice where appropriate and the taxpayer having the right to appeal against the amendments (*new s 28A*).

The *Finance Act* also tidies up some other areas which had attracted criticism, e.g.:

(a) the 'window' for opening an enquiry has been brought into line with other time limits under the self-assessment regime, i.e. for a return delivered on time, the enquiry must be commenced on or before the 31 January in the year after the normal filing date (the previous wording meant that the deadline ran out on 30 January in that year) (*new s 9A(2)*);

(b) where an enquiry is opened into an amendment made by the taxpayer to his return, and the 'window' for enquiring into the return as a whole has closed or the return has already been the subject of a completed enquiry, the scope of the new enquiry is limited to matters to which the amendment relates or which are affected by it (*new s 9A(5)*) – this was always the Revenue's practice but now it is backed up by statute;

(c) where the Revenue makes a so-called 'repair' amendment to the taxpayer's return under the *new s 9ZB*, the taxpayer has the legal right to reject the amendment (*s 9ZB(4) and (5)*).

At the time of writing, the Revenue has not produced the updated version of its Enquiry Handbook so it is still unclear how far these changes will affect its existing practices on enquiries. It may be that they will have little substantial effect on the way enquiries are handled.

The Inspector's powers to mount enquiries into self-assessment returns

The right to enquire and make 'discovery' assessments — TMA 1970, ss 9A and 29, FA 1998, 18 Sch 24

13.11 Tax inspectors did not possess a general right to enquire into a person's financial history or tax returns until the introduction of self-assessment. Prior to this event, the inspector could not take up a tax return for investigation without any reason nor could he select an individual or company for enquiry or investigation at random. The information gathering powers conferred on inspectors by *s 20* run counter to this comment up to a point for reasons that will be discussed later on.

TMA 1970, s 9A

13.12 *Section 9A* is fundamental both to the self-assessment system and the process of tax investigation.

If a person (individual, trust or company) has made a self-assessment return then an 'officer of the Board' may make enquiries. The section does not stipulate what form those enquiries may take nor does it provide that the Inland Revenue should give any reasons for enquiries being made. The section stipulates that the Revenue must give a notice that a return is under enquiry. The standard form of notice is as follows:

> 'Thank you for your tax return for the year ending 5 April [   ]. I am writing to tell you that I intend to make some enquiries into this return. I have written to your tax adviser [name] to ask for the information I need.
>
> I enclose a copy of our Code of Practice. It explains how we make enquiries and how we keep our promise of fair treatment under the Revenue's Service Commitment to you.
>
> When you have read the booklet [leaflet in aspect cases], please contact me if you require further information.'

Section 9A enables the Inland Revenue to have virtually a free hand in organising the function of an investigation as it so wishes. In practice this means that if an enquiry is to be made into a self-assessment return then that enquiry can range from a simple question about the basis behind one aspect of the return to a full enquiry in which every part of the return may be given close examination without any need for the inspector to justify his actions.

There are two restrictions on the process of enquiries made under *s 9A*:

(a)   the enquiry has to be started within a period of time known as 'the enquiry window'. Once that window has been closed then *s 9A* is irrelevant (and so are the information gathering powers conferred by *TMA 1970, s 19A* — see 13.48). The Inspector can only open up an expired self-assessment return by making a discovery and an estimated assessment under *TMA 1970, s 29* (see 13.19); and

(b) there can only be one enquiry under *s 9A* into a self-assessment return, therefore the Revenue must ensure that this opportunity is not thrown away on an unimportant matter within the enquiry window.

13.13 The enquiry window is defined under *TMA 1970, s 9A(2)* as:

(a) in the case of a return delivered or amendment made on or before the filing date, the period of twelve months after the filing date (as from 11 May 2001 — see 13.10). The Revenue has accepted that the *s 9A* notice must actually be delivered no later than the last day of the specified period (see Inland Revenue Tax Bulletin Special Edition April 2000) so for a 2000/01 return filed on time, the notice must be delivered no later than 31 January 2003 (twelve months after the filing date of 31 January 2002);

(b) in the case of a return delivered or amendment made after that date, the period ending with the quarter day next following the first anniversary of the day on which the return or amendment was delivered or made.

The quarter days are defined as 31 January, 30 April, 31 July and 31 October.

Aspect enquiries

13.14 The Enquiry Handbook (EH160) lists the following examples of an aspect enquiry:

(a) a query about the amount of personal pension relief claimed;

(b) a check of the admissibility of an employee's claim for a deduction for travel expenses;

(c) a query about the valuation of a property on which a capital gain has been made;

(d) an examination of the individual items making up a debit for motor expenses in the standard accounts information (SAI).

The instruction goes on to state that these are mere examples and that any box on the self-assessment return or any entry in the 'free format' spaces could be the subject of an aspect enquiry. Enquiries which are directed at several aspects of the return will still be aspect enquiries wherever the scope of the enquiry falls short of a full examination of the return.

Full enquiries

13.15 A full enquiry is one that seeks to test the veracity of the return as a whole. This does not mean that every last aspect of the return must be examined in full detail but the inspector selects aspects of the return for a full review as benchmarks enabling him to become satisfied as to the veracity of the whole return. Clearly, therefore, the standard accounts information supplied in a business return is likely to be given the deepest possible review in the first instance and if this process leads to the discovery of fraud or neglect then the whole of the return for that year, and earlier years under certain conditions, will be reviewed in depth.

If the self-assessment return under full enquiry is that belonging to a company director then his company accounts will come under scrutiny should matters be discovered leading the inspector to believe that the director has received some form of benefit, asset or money derived from the company which has not been taxed via the company's returns.

The relationship between aspect and full enquiries

13.16 The fact that a return has been selected for an aspect enquiry, as opposed to a full enquiry, does not mean that any amendment to the self-assessment is immune from the imposition of a financial penalty on the grounds of neglect, nor does it mean that the case will escape a full enquiry although once an aspect enquiry is completed by the issue of a notice of completion (see 13.73) and the enquiry window has passed the only way that either the tax return as a whole or the aspect covered in the enquiry can be re-opened is via a discovery (see 13.19).

The Inspector may discover some matter whilst making an aspect enquiry that questions the reliability of the return as a whole. This may cause the Inspector to switch the process of enquiry on to full enquiry lines.

13.17 Aspect enquiries can develop into full enquiries but there can be no reverse process. Once a case has been designated as a full enquiry then the Inspector is instructed to work the case through to its conclusion on full enquiry lines.

If an aspect enquiry case is reclassified as a full enquiry then the inspector must make his decision quite plain to the agent and taxpayer. There is no set procedure for the changeover, but once this has happened, and the matter has been made plain, then the Inspector will have to visit new areas of the tax return and re-visit others in depth in order to comply with full enquiry procedures therefore the switch over may be quite seismic.

13.18 The taxpayer has a right at this time (as at any time during a *TMA 1970, s 9A* enquiry — see 13.69) to ask the Commissioners for an order compelling the Inspector to issue a closure notice [*s 28A(4)*] and may well be tempted to do so if it is felt that the Inspector is upping the ante on the grounds that he has been unsuccessful in getting a satisfactory result from the aspect enquiry.

Indeed, pre-emptive action may be the best way forward in cases where it is felt that the Inspector is about to switch over to a full enquiry because once he has switched over he is unable to switch back again.

The Inspector must satisfy the Commissioners that he has reasonable grounds for not giving a notice of completion. [*s 28A(6)*]. The threat of such an application may dissuade the inspector from further enquiry or force his hand open so that matters may still be addressed on aspect enquiry lines.

The circumstances that trigger a switch over to a full enquiry may be obvious on occasions but if they are not obvious then the switch will come as a complete surprise to the agent and taxpayer, therefore aspect enquiries and their ramifications should not be underestimated.

Discovery and TMA 1970, s 29

13.19 Under *s 29*, prior to the introduction of self-assessment, the Inspector had to be satisfied that a tax return afforded correct and complete information concerning profits and chargeable gains so he had an implied right to enquire into aspects of the return but he could not mount an investigation unless:

(a)   he had discovered that profits had gone unassessed because he had come across information which gave him reason to believe either that a tax return was incorrect or that a person was chargeable to tax but had failed to notify chargeability; or

(b)   he had inspected a tax return and was dissatisfied with the contents.

Once either of these events had occurred then *s 29* (pre self-assessment) gave him the right to raise an assessment to tax to the best of his judgement or in an amount that in his opinion ought to be charged.

A person receiving such an assessment then had a right of appeal against it. The onus was then on that person to show that the assessment was incorrect. This gave the Inspector the opportunity to investigate that person's financial affairs.

Such an assessment could be raised even if there was a pre-existing assessment covering the same period that was already under appeal. The same event, facts or reasoning could be used also to raise assessments under an alternative statute, such as capital gains tax and Case 1 Schedule D (say on suspected profits from the purchase and resale of a property on the grounds that it was an 'adventure in the nature of trade').

Moreover, for 1983–84 and later years *TMA 1970, s 36(1)* provides the authority for making assessments outside the normal time limit where there has been a loss of tax attributable to the fraudulent or negligent conduct of the taxpayer or of a person acting on his behalf. The assessment can be made up to 20 years after 31 January next following the relevant year of assessment.

13.20 *TMA 1970, s 29* remains in force in a modified form but the advent of self-assessment has reduced its rôle as a tool of investigation in the vast majority of cases where there is a pre-existing self-assessment return.

If a self-assessment return is already in existence for a given year of assessment but the enquiry window has expired or an enquiry has commenced and been completed by the issue of a notice under *TMA 1970, s 28A* (see 13.73) then an 'officer of the Board' can raise an assessment under *TMA 1970, s 29* but only under certain conditions. An assessment can be raised if either:

(a)   he has discovered information leading him to believe that the taxpayer, or a person acting on his behalf, has been fraudulent or negligent in respect of that year of assessment [*sub-section (4)*]; or,

(b)   following the expiry date for making an enquiry into that return under the self-assessment rules [*s 9A*], or the date when the taxpayer had been informed that his enquiries were complete [*TMA 1970, s 28A(1)*], the officer discovers that profits have gone unassessed even though fraud or neglect may not have occurred and at the time when the final date for a *s 9A* enquiry has passed, the Inspector could not reasonably have been expected to be aware of the situation giving rise to the discovery, given the information made available to him at the time. [*sub-section (5)*].

13.21 However, if no self-assessment return exists for a given year of assessment because the taxpayer has not made one (either because he has failed to notify chargeability or the return is late) then the officer of the Board may raise an assessment under *TMA 1970, s 29* as before, so long as a discovery has been made. If a return has been issued to a taxpayer but he has failed to make the return then it is more likely that the Inspector will take steps to require the submission of the return and then proceed to carry out a full enquiry under normal self-assessment rules rather than raise a discovery assessment.

13.22 *Section 29* relies wholly on a 'discovery' having been made by the Inspector.

Cases such as *R v Kensington Commissioners ex p Aramayo* 6 TC 279 and *R v St Giles and St George Commissioners ex p Hooper* 7 TC 59 support the idea that the concept of 'discovery' is broadly based. It does not mean merely the discovery of a fact that would have triggered an investigation had it been known at the time that the self-assessment return was still current for an enquiry. The dicta in these cases shows that an inspector can make a discovery at any time if he honestly comes to the conclusion from information available to him that tax has gone unassessed.

13.23 However, self-assessment has brought with it one important curb on the inspector's very wide remit to make a 'discovery'.

Part of the ethos of self-assessment is that taxpayers should have certainty that their tax affairs are not going to be turned over willy-nilly after the window for enquiries has been closed. Consequently, the principles already established by *Cenlon Finance Co Ltd v Ellwood* 40 TC 176 and *Olin Energy Systems Ltd v Scorer* 50 TC 592 have been incorporated in the current *s 29*.

In the *Cenlon* case, the Inspector determined an appeal against an estimated assessment in certain agreed figures under *TMA 1970, s 54*. In considering the appeal the Inspector had dealt with a specific matter and accepted that it was not taxable. A subsequent Inspector disagreed and raised an assessment under the 'old' *s 29*. It was accepted that a discovery had been made but because all relevant information was before the first inspector the terms of *s 54* barred the Revenue from making an assessment on the grounds that the determination had rendered the first assessment as determined final and conclusive.

In the *Olin* case an Inspector had agreed certain computations that had been based on the erroneous belief that the losses from one trade could be set against the profits of another trade carried on by the same company. A subsequent Inspector issued a further assessment based on his discovery that the computation was incorrect. It was held that the second Inspector was precluded from making an assessment on the grounds that since the allowability or otherwise of losses was fundamental to any tax computation in which they were claimed, the first Inspector must be assumed to have covered the point in issuing a determination under *s 54*. Therefore the first assessment was final and conclusive.

13.24 In essence the new rules provide that information that is already in the hands of the Inland Revenue *within the enquiry period* cannot be used to justify a discovery assessment once the self-assessment has become final unless either:

(a)   the self-assessment is incorrect due to fraudulent or negligent conduct; or

(b)   the Inspector, at the time when the final date for a *TMA 1970, s 9A* enquiry has passed, 'could not have been reasonably expected, on the basis of the information made available to him before that time, to be aware of the situation' giving rise to a discovery.

Apart from the common sense embodied in this proviso, legislators may well have had dicta in the case of *Nicholson v Morris* 51 TC 95 in mind. Taxpayers sometimes excuse their own failures by trying to cast the blame on the Inland Revenue by pointing out that the Inspector should have been aware of information that might have been found in another file or at another tax office. As Walton J said at page 110, in the case of *Nicholson v Morris*:

> '... it is idle for any taxpayer to say to the Revenue, "Hidden in your vaults are the right answers: go thou and dig them out of the vaults." That is not a duty on the Revenue.'

In summary it is quite clear that established tax case dicta on discovery makes it likely that inspectors will only be inhibited from taking up a small minority of cases after the self-assessment enquiry window has been shut for that particular year, so long as the fundamental parameters of a discovery can be demonstrated.

Self-assessment and the onus of proof

13.25 The advent of self-assessment has given tax advisers welcome respite from one of the most familiar problems they had under the old regime — namely having to explain to clients why they are essentially guilty as regards allegations of tax fraud and neglect until they have proved their own innocence.

Appellants against assessments under *TMA 1970, s 29* will, of course, still have the problem. The inspector must make an assessment in an amount or further amount that in his opinion ought to be charged to make good the loss of tax to the Crown [*s 29(1)*] so the taxpayer still has to dislodge an assessment.

13.26 However, it may not be so apparent that the problem still persists even under self-assessment and will arise if the taxpayer refuses to come to an agreement with the inspector and as a result the inspector issues a closure notice amending the taxpayer's return under the new *s 28A(2)*. The taxpayer will presumably lodge an appeal to the Commissioners under *TMA 1970, s 31(1)*, probably on the grounds that the amendment is excessive and not in accordance with the facts. The taxpayer will still have to disprove the inspector's amendment, rather than the other way around.

In tax investigation cases the taxpayer's predicament is not quite so clear-cut. If the appeal is against an assessment made under *s 29* then the onus first rests on the Inspector to show the Commissioners that the assessment has been raised to make good a loss of tax attributable to fraudulent or negligent conduct [*TMA 1970, s 29(4)*] or to a situation of which he could not reasonably be expected to have been aware at the relevant time. [*s 29(5)*]. Once this onus is discharged, then the taxpayer must start his uphill struggle to dislodge the assessment. Where no return has been filed, the Inspector is not under any duty to show fraud or negligence so the burden of proof will be on the taxpayer from the start.

The classification and selection of aspect and full enquiry cases

13.27 Practitioners were well aware of the fundamental process of accounts classification in the Revenue in the days prior to self-assessment in that all accounts were classified either 'A' — Accept, 'R' — Review or 'E' — Examine, but that knowledge did not really help in assessing whether any particular set of accounts was going to be taken up for investigation.

If a set of accounts and tax computations was classified 'A' then it went through on the nod with no further checks. An 'R' case was one in which the reviewing Inspector felt that aspects of the return deserved a fairly thorough review but that did not mean necessarily that any questions would be asked of the taxpayer. The classification of cases into the 'aspect' group is very similar to the process of classifying a case as an 'R' case.

An 'E' case was one which the reviewing Inspector believed was a potential investigation case possibly because there was already information on file which clearly indicated that the return or accounts were incorrect (such as a return of interest paid) or there were good reasons for the Inspector to believe that some probing of the accounts would lead directly to the case being taken up for a full investigation.

However, this did not mean that the case would be investigated automatically. For example, the Inspector deputed to examine the accounts and tax computations had to become convinced that there was sufficient reason to mount an investigation, i.e. he had to have reason to believe that the return was incorrect on the basis that he could not mount such an investigation unless he could justify the raising of a 'discovery' assessment under *TMA 1970, s 29* (see 13.19 above).

13.28 The classification procedure under self-assessment has enabled the inspector to shed this thought process and it has brought with it two extreme situations that increase certainty that a case will be given a review (but not necessarily a full review) on the one hand, but introduces a 'wild card' element on the other.

First, if a self-assessment return exhibits certain characteristics (see 13.32), or the circumstances connected with the non-submission of a return exhibit certain characteristics, then there is certainty that the case will be subject to review. A case may be processed without further query following the review but often the review will lead to an enquiry.

The enquiry may start out as an aspect enquiry, but with the possibility of conversion to a full enquiry, or it may commence as a full enquiry.

Secondly, because *TMA 1970, s 9A* bestows on the Inspector the right to make enquiries without reason (see 13.12), the Inspector can pick a case at random and subject it to a full review. This is the wild card element. It is calculated to instil respect in the system to the extent that people will be dissuaded from submitting incorrect returns knowingly.

Section 9A has also enabled the Inland Revenue to be far more structured and directional in its approach to full enquiry work. Given that the Inspector now has the right to subject a self-assessment return to a full enquiry it follows that he also has the power to target certain classes of taxpayer for full enquiry with no inhibition. For example, a local district may decide to target 5% of all the self-employed taxi drivers in its catchment area or all the owners of Chinese restaurants in a particular town.

13.29 The very structure of a self-assessment return, particularly in respect of returns made by the self-employed, partnerships and companies, also lends itself to better targeting and a more coherent structure to investigations policy nationally. This is because the standard accounts information boxes in the SA return demand that information has to be entered on the return in a standard format.

Notwithstanding the problems that might arise because people are unsure which box applies to a particular expenditure, all businesses with a given trade classification will have presented their 'accounts' in the same way, therefore any anomalies, such as an unusually low gross profit rate or a high stock turnaround compared with the rest of similar businesses in the country as a whole (or just in a given geographical area), may easily be thrown up for a full enquiry during the process of computerising the results. This is referred to in the Revenue's manuals as 'automated risk assessment'. This approach is likely to lead to more accurate selection of cases each year as more and more data is collected via the standard accounts information in the SA return.

13.30 Once a self-assessment return has been submitted it will be classified either for an aspect or full review or it will be processed without further ceremony. However, a return that has been processed without immediate review cannot be said to have been accepted by the Revenue until the enquiry window has closed since it can be taken up either for an aspect or full review during that period.

13.31 The process by which a case is taken up for review is a mixture of automatic selection, selection based on certain statistical criteria and selection based on the inspector's view that the return is inaccurate for one reason or another.

The degree of risk inherent in the self-assessment return is fundamental to the selection process. Procedures have been introduced to ensure that various defined segments of the taxpaying population undergo some percentage of review, albeit that the percentage coverage reflects the perceived degree of risk in that segment. This strategy is based on the view that whilst the Revenue must put great effort into tackling major cases of abuse, nevertheless much tax may be lost over thousands of small cases involving small amounts of tax individually but amounting to a large loss in the aggregate. Segmentation is discussed in 13.34 *et seq.*

Mandatory review

13.32 Certain cases must undergo a so-called 'mandatory review' because they exhibit a higher degree of risk that the return will be incorrect, or they cannot be passed through on the nod because of some technical aspect such as a change of accounting date. They will contain one or more of the following attributes:

(a)   there was a failure to notify chargeability;
(b)   there was a late filing of a return;
(c)   the case has been nominated as a potential enquiry case;
(d)   capital gains have been returned;
(e)   there has been a change of accounting date;
(f)   the return contains provisional or estimated figures;
(g)   a post-transaction ruling has been given so a check is required that the circumstances are as previously described;
(h)   the case is one that is inherently more complicated or high profile than a normal case because of some aspect such that it requires permanent review.

A mandatory review does not necessarily lead either to an aspect or a full enquiry but in the larger cases it is likely that virtually all aspects of the return will be reviewed over time possibly under a deliberate rolling programme of review. Rolling programmes of review giving rise to aspect enquiries into pre-defined areas of such firms' accounts have been initiated for the very large companies in preference to subjecting them to random or full enquiries (see 13.15 and 13.33).

Random enquiries

13.33 Whilst mandatory review cases do not necessarily lead to an aspect or full review those cases selected under the random enquiry procedure almost always will be taken up for full enquiry. There are a number of reasons why cases are selected in this way.

The fact that any case is capable of being selected for full enquiry by this procedure renders all self-assessment returns capable of investigation, therefore no taxpayer can discount the possibility of a full review entirely.

One can do no better than quote the text of paragraph EH173 of the Revenue's Enquiry Handbook in describing the rationale for random enquiries:

'There are two main reasons for taking up random enquiries.

1.   Deferrence – by creating a presence in all parts of the population (not just those we perceive as "higher risk") all taxpayers should be aware that there is a chance of their returns being subject to enquiry.

2.   To obtain a better understanding of the nature and extent of detectable non-compliance within different segments of the taxpaying population. This will also help us to refine our strategy and methods of selecting individual cases for enquiry.

To achieve these ends:

(a)   the random sample of cases for enquiry will be structured to ensure that different groups within the population, and different geographical areas, are properly represented;

(b)   it is essential that these cases are worked to the same standards as cases selected on the basis of risk; and

(c)   the nature of any non-compliance must be accurately recorded so that we can learn as much as possible about the reasons for it.

The Revenue has published figures suggesting that there will be 7,500 to 10,000 cases randomly taken up for full review each year. Clearly data will be generated over time that will test this rationale but even if the results from randomly based full enquiries are lower than for cases selected on stronger criteria the chances are high that random cases will be a permanent part of the Revenue's weaponry simply because of the deterrent effect, even though this effect may not be capable of accurate quantification.

Segmentation and the selection process

13.34 The Revenue has defined six main segments of the taxpaying population as:

(a)   small business taxpayers (turnover less than £15,000);

(b)   medium business taxpayers (turnover £15,001 to £250,000);

(c)   large business taxpayers (turnover greater than £250,000);

(d)   very large business taxpayers;

(e)   non-business taxpayer with complex affairs;

(f)   non-business taxpayer with non-complex affairs.

Each segment has been assigned a level of risk in terms of tax compliance, which presumably will be reassessed at intervals based on the results of full and aspect enquiries into that segment through time. The level of risk then determines the percentage of cases in each segment that will be targeted for full and aspect enquiries annually. [EH 180–186].

13.35 The levels of risk in each segment are based on a series of 'risk rules' that have been programmed in to the Revenue's computer system. There are a series of 'core risk rules' used to assess all self-assessment returns and then a secondary series differing in various respects depending on the segment that covers a particular return. This enables a tuned approach, which should raise the success rate in each segment by reducing the number of 'duds'.

For example, applying the risk rules for large business taxpayers to a business with a turnover of less than £15,000 would be valueless since there are likely to be few occasions when the smaller business return will require an aspect enquiry. For this reason aspect enquiries on small businesses under self-assessment are statistically far less likely than before but any enquiries that are undertaken will be far more likely to be full enquiries than before.

The same principle prevails in the medium and large business segments. Statistically full enquiries are likely to be a higher proportion of all enquiries in the medium business segment but not so high as in the small business segment. Equally, aspect enquiries will predominate in the very large business segment.

The segment covering non-business taxpayers with complex affairs is likely to yield some good results for the segmentation approach since it embodies all company directors and all individuals with income exceeding £100,000 annually as well as taxpayers such as Lloyd's underwriters.

It is something of a misnomer to treat directors as 'non-business taxpayers' since by far the largest proportion of this class of taxpayer does not consider that they and their companies are mutually exclusive, notwithstanding the finer points of company and commercial law, nor is it the Revenue's experience that directors' tax compliance problems are unconnected with tax compliance issues affecting their companies.

For example, the benefits legislation (and lack of compliance thereto) links the two classes of taxpayer if nothing else. Consequently the opportunity to take up a director's personal self-assessment return on full and aspect enquiry lines through the segmented risk process gives a second bite at the company 'cherry'.

The Inspector's choice

13.36 Consideration of the previous comments concerning the process of selection of a case for full or aspect enquiry will show that there is now far greater opportunity for the automation of selection. Even the risk factors used to pick cases from each segment of taxpayers could be totally automated by defining certain anomalous business relationships within the trading and profit and loss accounts or balance sheets as the trigger points for an enquiry.

Total automation of the selection process does not exist because the Revenue still chooses to rely on the streetwise intelligence and experience of its Inspectors to pick a high proportion of cases.

Sometimes the choice may simply rely on the Inspector's gut feeling but on many occasions there is prima facie evidence on the file that may tip a case from aspect to full enquiry or may spark off a full enquiry even though, viewed separately, each individual factor in the selection matrix may not be sufficient to trigger an enquiry.

The integration of objective and subjective criteria in the selection process is achieved:

(a)   by deciding what proportion of a particular taxpaying segment is to be subjected to full review; then

(b)   deducting those cases that are to be reviewed randomly or under mandatory selection; so

(c)   leaving a percentage in each category to be taken up using traditional selection techniques based on past experience.

If the quota for that particular segment is not filled by this point, the Inspector still has the right to fill in by selecting cases on whatever criteria he chooses. This may involve, for example, targeting certain business sectors for review simply because they belong to that class and for no other reason.

The commencement of an enquiry

13.37 Under *TMA 1970, s 9A(1)*, the Inspector must give notice of enquiry that he intends to enquire into a return. This is achieved through a letter which should contain either of the two following statements:

If the taxpayer is represented then the letter will say:

'Thank you for your tax return for the year ending 5 April [   ]. I am writing to tell you that I intend to make some enquiries into this return. I have written to your tax adviser [name] to ask for the information I need.

I enclose a copy of our Code of Practice. It explains how we make enquiries and how we keep our promise of fair treatment under the Revenue's Service Commitment to you.

When you have read the booklet [leaflet in aspect cases], please contact me if you require further information.'

At the same time a letter is sent to the agent as follows:

'I have today issued to your client (name) a notice under *s 9A Taxes Management Act* of my intention to enquire into his/her [200.. /00..] return. A copy of the notice is attached.'

The letter to the agent should then go on to request the information regarded as necessary for checking the return.

If the taxpayer is unrepresented then the notice must say:

'Thank you for your tax return for the year ending 5 April [ ]. I am writing to tell you that I intend to make some enquiries into this return.

I enclose a copy of our Code of Practice. It explains how we make enquiries and how we keep our promise of fair treatment under the Revenue's Service Commitment to you.

When you have read the booklet [leaflet in aspect cases], please contact me if you require further information.'

The letter should then go on to request the relevant information.

The Inspector is instructed in the strongest possible terms not to give a reason or reasons for the enquiry.

13.38 EH302 states:

'Neither the section 9A notice nor any covering letter to an agent should state that the return is under enquiry because you are not satisfied that it is correct. Nor should you give reasons for thinking that the return may be incorrect, in order to justify your enquiry.'

The logic for this instruction is quite clear. The fact that it is obvious that a full review is under way does not necessarily mean that the Inspector suspects fraud or neglect.

13.39 As stated previously (see 13.15 above), first, the fundamental object of a full review is to test the veracity of the return as a whole and so the inspector may find no compliance failure yet will have carried out his job correctly and completely (all other things being equal). Secondly, the case may have been picked out through the random selection procedure therefore it may well not exhibit any characteristics that would render it suitable for selection under any other criterion yet still be capable of a full enquiry. Indeed all randomly selected cases have to be worked on full enquiry lines.

The nature and tenor of the Inspector's questions may well give some indication that fraud or neglect is suspected but the agent should be none the less wary even if the letter gives no such indication.

13.40 There are some variations on the standard opening letter. These may arise because:

(a)   either the return was not intended for enquiry but a taxpayer amendment has been received within the period when a full or aspect enquiry can take place; or

(b)   because the case was starred for an aspect or full enquiry within the enquiry window but had not been taken up before the amendment was received.

In either case the letter will make it plain that the enquiry relates to the return 'as amended'.

On the other hand, if a taxpayer amendment is received after the enquiry window has closed, then, whilst this enables the Inspector to enquire into the nature of the amendment, the Inspector is instructed not to use this as an excuse to mount an enquiry into the wider aspects of the return.

The instructions state (EH337) that 'It would be unfair if, having missed or rejected the opportunity to enquire into the original return, we were to direct an enquiry at the return simply because the taxpayer, by making an amendment to it, had opened another window'. Consequently the letter that opens the enquiry makes it plain that it will be confined to the amendment.

This approach has now been enshrined in statute with effect from 11 May 2001. [*TMA 1970, s 9A(5)*].

13.41 Should the taxpayer's amendment made outside the enquiry window give rise to the view that the case should be subjected to a full enquiry then the Inspector can either raise a discovery assessment (or indicate his intention to raise such an assessment if needs be) or note the case as a potential enquiry case for next year, in which case it must be given a mandatory review (see 13.32).

13.42 Whichever circumstance triggers the *TMA 1970, s 9A* enquiry the opening letter will be accompanied by some or all of the following material:

(a) a short Code of Practice where it is felt that the enquiry will be straight-forward and will not yield information suggesting that penalties may apply. There may be occasions when the initial enquiry yields information leading the Inspector to believe that more extensive enquiries are necessary in which case a full code will be issued at that point;

(b) a full Code of Practice (CoP 11 or, in the case of a company CoP 14) when the enquiries are more extensive at the outset and may result in the discovery of a culpable position. A CoP 11 must be issued in all cases of random selection, therefore it may give comfort to the agent and client that the case is a random selection in those cases where it is quite clear that the taxpayer's affairs are so straightforward that they would not normally warrant a full enquiry;

(c) leaflet IR162 may be issued. This explains the 'faster working' approach to self-assessment enquiries (see 13.44). An invitation to a 'faster working' approach is unlikely to be issued in cases where the inspector has strong suspicions that serious neglect or fraud may have occurred.

An overview of the full enquiry process

13.43 Most full enquiries fit into a general pattern first because the legislation defines the structure guiding the process at a fundamental level and secondly because the Inspector has a particular methodology laid down for him by his training and manual of instructions. That pattern is of course capable of modification and disruption (not necessarily in a destructive way) the more that human aspects are brought into the equation and the more that the taxpayer/agent gets involved in influencing the course of the enquiry.

13.44 In 1997 the Inland Revenue issued a supplement to Special Edition 2 of the Tax Bulletin entitled 'A Better Approach to Enquiry Work under Self-Assessment (Faster Working)'. This was a significant document not because it introduced the idea of a contract between the Inspector and the taxpayer/agent aimed at speeding up the process of enquiry work but because it laid down the view both of the Inland Revenue and practitioners' bodies as to what constituted the most efficient way of carrying out a full enquiry quickly *without compromising thoroughness and quality.*

Consequently the methodology contained in this document must be regarded as the 'industry standard' for most types of full enquiry at local district level notwithstanding that the timetable imposed on the methodology is predictably far too tight in many cases.

The methodology, without the timetable and procedures tied specifically to the timetable, is reproduced below as the clearest statement possible of what one may call the 'surgical' approach to a full enquiry.

The faster working enquiry model

1. Fact-finding phase

13.45 Opening: s 9A notice to taxpayer, opening letter to agent

- Request for factual information and informal request for business records.
- Records requested to include link papers where relevant.
- Private records to be requested where direct bearing on return.
- Agent to obtain records from taxpayer and review them.
- Opportunity for disclosure right from the start.

Initial discussion between Revenue and agent

- Nature of records, extent of private side review.
- Arrangements for making records available.
- Responses to factual questions.
- Accountancy points not dependent on records examination.

Examination of records and private side

- Records to be examined on site, at agent's premises or in Revenue office according to convenience of all parties.
- If at Revenue office, records to be sent back to agent/taxpayer at end of examination unless otherwise agreed.
- If on-site or at agent's premises, agent to be available for all or part of time to answer queries on how figures fit together.
- Revenue staff to bear in mind that on-site record examination not an opportunity to search premises.
- Private side review to be carried out where appropriate.
- Revenue to make clear what private records are required.
- Agent to have chance to review private bank statements etc. before examination by Revenue within agreed time scale.

2. Investigative phase

Discussion of findings with agent

- Revenue to outline areas of concern, including third party information where appropriate.
- Payment on account to be sought if appropriate.
- Possibility of closing down case at this point if all concerns met.

Discussion of findings between agent and taxpayer

- Agent and taxpayer to be given opportunity to answer Revenue's concerns.
- Possibility of closing down case at this point if all concerns met.

Interview with taxpayer

- Interview where areas of concern remain.
- Broad areas for discussion agreed in advance (i.e. an agenda, but not a questionnaire).
- Flexibility for 'supplementary' questions, but recognition that questions outside agreed agenda may need further research.

Proposals for settlement

- Revenue to set out terms for settlement.
- Where possible settlement proposals to be arrived at through negotiation, and not presented on a 'take it or leave it' basis.

Thinking time

- Opportunity for agent to discuss settlement terms with taxpayer.
- Further negotiation where appropriate.

Settlement

- Contract settlement with associated paperwork (including where appropriate Certificate of Disclosure and Statement of Assets).
- If no agreement, formal channels.

The fact that few full enquiries or investigations follow such a pattern so clinically in practice does not detract from its value as a statement of best working practice. However, it should not be regarded as the only way of working in the full enquiry environment.

Fundamentally this model relies on the Inspector managing the enquiry and calling the shots. This may not be the best way forward in some circumstances. For example, the Inspector may well have to ask a whole series of what are superfluous questions in reality and may require third party information (including access to much from the agent's working papers) which proves to be of little use.

Interestingly, in the collaborative research study discussed in 13.9, 705 of the Revenue staff consulted thought that faster working had proved ineffective.

An alternative enquiry model

13.46 Another technique, equally valid as a best practice technique, is for the taxpayer and his agent to take the initiative away from the Inspector with the Inspector's consent.

In normal circumstances (and with the full appreciation of tax law that the agent should be providing), the taxpayer is faced with the following possibilities:

(a)   there is nothing to disclose or nothing to disclose apart from some minor matters that are virtually immaterial;

(b)   either through ignorance, failure to keep adequate records or other forms of relatively benign neglect, the true position is unknowable but the Inspector has the power to impose a solution if a position acceptable to both sides cannot be negotiated;

(c)   there is probably deliberate and material tax compliance failure either with or without the characteristics noted in (b) which may or may not amount to fraud.

In any of these cases, once the inspector has set out on a course of full enquiry, the agent and taxpayer have the option to ask the Inspector to back off for a reasonable length of time whilst a thorough review of the taxpayer's compliance history for that year is carried out with a view to providing the Inspector with all relevant information for negotiations (where necessary) to take place.

Not only is it the taxpayer's prerogative to make a full disclosure of the position in order to mitigate penalties where these may become appropriate but the Revenue recognises this technique as a valid way forward for normal tax investigation work and indeed it is the only way forward in cases where the Revenue feels the wish to reserve the right to consider mounting a prosecution for tax evasion (as embodied in standard Special Compliance Office procedures).

If this approach is suggested to the Inspector he will often become party to an agreed programme of work which should be the minimum amount required to meet the Inspector's need to test the accuracy of the return as a whole.

The agent then has the opportunity to influence the scope and depth of the work to be done and to carry it out at a pace and in an order that is best suited to his operational parameters.

In either of the three circumstances outlined above, the information produced by this method of working should be designed to meet the Inspector's need to become satisfied that he has enough to reach a satisfactory conclusion to his enquiries.

Further aspects of the full enquiry process under self-assessment

13.47 The following parameters of enquiry work have been discussed so far:

(a)   There is no in-built assumption that the return is incorrect at the start of a full enquiry whereas in earlier times an investigation was not started unless the Inspector had reason to believe that a tax return was incorrect.

(b)   *Section 12B* is designed to ensure that information is available for the production of figures for inclusion in the self-assessment boxes and for testing through the enquiry process.

(c)   The Inland Revenue will not give any reasons for enquiries being made but the Inspector must give a notice that a return is under enquiry.

(d)   Every part of the return may be given close examination without any need for the Inspector to justify his actions.

(e)   The only restriction on the process of enquiry is that it has to be started within a period of time known as the 'enquiry window'. Once this has been closed the Inspector can only open up an expired self-assessment return by making a discovery capable of an assessment under *TMA 1970, s 29*.

(f)   Because *TMA 1970, s 9A* bestows on the Inspector the right to make enquiries without reason, the Inspector can pick a case at random and subject it to a full review.

(g)   The process by which a case is taken up for review can now be a mixture of automatic selection, selection based on certain statistical criteria as well as selection based on the Inspector's view that the return is inaccurate for one reason or another.

It should be noted that the purpose of this chapter is not to set out all the processes and procedures that might apply if a client is guilty of tax evasion but to set out the enquiry process in the self-assessment context.

These are all operational procedures leading up to the full enquiry itself but there are also a number of significant processes and procedures that apply during the self-assessment enquiry process that are specific to it rather than general to the process of tax investigation as such.

These are connected with information gathering, the management of the enquiry by both the inspector and the agent, and the completion of the case given that there must be a formal conclusion to the enquiry if it is not concluded by the informal process of a settlement offer and acceptance.

Statutory notices for information

TMA 1970, s 19A

13.48 *Section 19A* was introduced to support the general enquiry powers contained in *TMA 1970, s 9A*. It is a powerful tool for securing information from the taxpayer. It is to be distinguished from the pre-self-assessment arrangement whereby inspectors had to refer to the General Commissioners under *TMA 1970, s 51* for a notice to be sent to the taxpayer requiring information to be sent to them. Inspectors usually used this avenue as a last resort.

Under *s 19A* an officer of the Board can issue a notice to the taxpayer (but to no-one else) at the outset of an investigation or subsequently requiring 'such documents as are in the taxpayer's possession or power' and 'such accounts or particulars' as he may reasonably require. A time limit for the production of this information (of not less than 30 days) can be imposed and failure to comply will lead to a penalty of £50, followed by daily penalties which can be determined by the inspector without reference to the General Commissioners. [*TMA 1970, s 97AA(1)* and *(2)*, see 13.50].

Given the strength of this power the Inspector is instructed to issue an informal notice for the production of information and to state the deadline for its production. This notice is usually incorporated in the formal letter that has to be issued for the Revenue to comply with *TMA 1970, s 9A*.

It will encompass all the information that the Inspector might reasonably be expected to require at the commencement of the enquiry but it should not request information that could not be requested under a formal *TMA 1970, s 19A* notice.

13.49 The types of information covered by a *s 19A* notice are as follows:

(a)   documents such as bank statements and other business books and records 'in the person's possession or power'; and

(b)   the accounts of the business if they are in existence; and

(c)   any 'particulars' that the inspector may reasonably require such as explanations of how figures in the accounts have been arrived at (which may be incorporated in the agent's 'link papers') or the source or destination of bank credits and debits. The term 'particulars' also encompasses the creation of accounts if these do not exist and the production of capital statements since this type of information does not have to be in existence at the outset to be required under the heading of 'particulars'.

This section does not entitle the inspector to require that a taxpayer attends a meeting nor does it confer rights of access to business premises. It does not cover documents that have been brought into existence for the purposes of an appeal nor documents that relate to an earlier year for which the enquiry window has closed.

The restrictions on *s 19A* do nothing to curb the inspector's remit with respect to his ability to test the veracity of entries in the tax return. This section is as powerful in its own way as a notice under *TMA 1970, s 20(3)* when issued to third parties for information in connection with the taxpayers return.

13.50 Failure to comply fully with a *TMA 1970, s 19A* notice will invite the imposition of a penalty under *TMA 1970, s 97AA*. The inspector can impose an initial penalty of £50 plus up to £30 per day for every day that the requisite information is not forthcoming though he will give 14 days' notice of this intention. The matter can be referred to the General Commissioners for the imposition of penalties up to £150 per day.

13.51 Practitioners and taxpayers are often dismayed by the request for access to private bank accounts and other private information under *TMA 1970, s 19A* when a business is under full enquiry.

Even the Revenue appears apologetic about the request for such information. EH398 states: 'We take the view that a *TMA 1970, s 19A* notice *can* in principle be issued for the production of information or copies of information contained in "non business" records' and instructs its officers only to ask for such information where they believe that they can show that it is reasonable to ask for such information in the circumstances.

Practitioners point out that a request for access to an interest bearing account to check the accuracy of the interest included in the tax return is not a reasonable request since this check can be achieved simply by supplying a statement from the bank.

The justification for access to non-interest bearing private bank accounts would appear even less reasonable unless the inspector has already established that the business information in the tax return is fundamentally flawed, yet *TMA 1970, s 19A* does not restrict access strictly to business orientated books and records in a business case.

The collaborative research study discussed in 13.9 revealed a polarisation of views on this point. As might be expected, the vast majority of tax advisers (around 85%) considered that enquiry inspectors should not request private bank account details as a matter of course. On the other hand, a minority of Revenue staff (31%) supported this view (see section 5.3 of the study). The study also makes the point that the Enquiry Handbook guidance (which states that private bank accounts should only be requested once a link has been established) is not followed on a consistent basis in practice.

13.52 There is a right of appeal against a *TMA 1970, s 19A* notice. Practitioners may feel justified in taking an appeal when private financial information is requested, certainly when it is requested at the outset of a full enquiry. Appeals connected with the process of full review are dealt with at 13.60 to 13.70 below.

Inspectors necessarily have to assume that a document is in existence when the wish list for the *s 19A* notice is compiled but documents may not exist for many reasons. The client may have failed to keep such documents or may have lost them or may not have considered such information worthy of documentation in the first place. Consequently it may be impossible fully to satisfy the notice.

However, practitioners and taxpayers should be aware that the request for 'particulars' can cover the generation of information that exists in a form other than a pre-existing document and that failure to keep documents defined by *TMA 1970, s 12B* (see 13.7) may invite a penalty of up to £3,000. [*s 12B(5)*].

TMA 1970, s 19A can only cover information necessary to enable the inspector to carry out a review of a self-assessment return within the enquiry window. It cannot be used to require the production of information pertinent to an earlier year nor can it be sent to a third party for information relevant to the taxpayer's self-assessment return. These areas are the province of *TMA 1970, s 20*.

TMA 1970, s 20

13.53 *Section 20* is to be contrasted with and distinguished from *s 19A* in a number of important ways.

Fundamentally the inspector can use the powers vested in *s 20* as an alternative to *s 19A* when a self-assessment return is open and at any other time whereas *s 19A* is restricted to an open self-assessment return. A *s 20* notice can cover the production of information directly from the taxpayer and from third parties but *s 19A* is more likely to be used for the production of information from the taxpayer *per se* when the enquiry window is open.

Moreover, it enables the Inland Revenue to carry out an investigation without a pre-existing *s 29* discovery assessment or self-assessment return at all.

The structure of each sub-section of *s 20* is similar to that applying to *s 19A*. *Section 20(1)* requires the taxpayer under investigation to deliver 'such documents' as are in the person's possession or power and which, in the inspector's 'reasonable opinion' contain or may contain information relevant to that person's tax liability and 'such particulars' as the inspector may reasonably require as being relevant to that liability.

Section 20(2) echoes *s 20(1)* in terms of the scope of information that can be required but there is a major difference in that permission for the issue of a notice for information issued under *s 20(1)* must first be given by a General or Special Commissioner [*s 20(7)*], whereas the Board of Inland Revenue can authorise a notice for information under *s 20(2)* if the Board has reasonable grounds for believing that the taxpayer has failed, or may fail to comply with his responsibilities under tax law, and that this failure is likely to lead to serious prejudice to the proper assessment or collection of tax. [*s 20(7A)*].

The most important part of *s 20* for the purposes of enquiries under self-assessment is *s 20(3)* because this covers access to third party information that is not covered by *s 19A*.

13.54 A notice issued under *s 20(3)* requires virtually any third party within UK jurisdiction to supply access to such documents as are in that person's possession or power which in the inspector's reasonable opinion contain or may contain information relevant to any tax liability to which a taxpayer is or may become liable. Documents which came into existence wholly more than six years before the date of the notice are exempt from it. [*s 20B(5)*].

Section 20(3) even covers much of what most practitioners regard as their working papers but only in respect of a named taxpayer and mainly in respect of those papers that contain 'workings or other analytical information showing how an entry in the accounts, returns or other information submitted to the Inland Revenue was arrived at'. [Statement of Practice 5/90].

Notices under *s 20(1)* and *s 20(3)* cannot be issued by an inspector of taxes unless express permission has been given by a General or Special Commissioner. In fact, the taxpayer and the third party, in the case of a notice under *s 20(3)*, must be given the opportunity to supply the requisite information voluntarily before the inspector seeks such permission. [*s 20B(1)*]. A time limit of 30 days is usually attached to the request.

Proceedings before a Commissioner for formal permission enabling the inspector to issue a notice are *ex parte*. However, the Commissioner must not give permission unless he is satisfied in all the circumstances that the inspector is justified in proceeding under *s 20* and the taxpayer in most cases has a right to receive a written summary of the reasons why the inspector applied for consent in the first place. [*s 20(8E)*].

Amendments and the enquiry process — TMA 1970, ss 9ZA, 9ZB and 28A

13.55 Either the taxpayer or the Revenue may amend a self-assessment within certain time limits and under certain conditions.

There are a number of occasions when either party might wish to amend the self-assessment as follows:

(a)   the taxpayer may discover an innocent error in the return after it has been made; or

(b)   the taxpayer may have deliberately submitted an incorrect or incomplete self-assessment which he wishes to put right.

Before 11 May 2001, there was a third situation where the taxpayer might wish to amend his tax return and that was on completion of an enquiry by an inspector. The *Finance Act* (as discussed in 13.11) now provides that the inspector's closure notice will make any amendments to the return which he considers necessary, thereby dispensing with the need for the taxpayer to do so (in fact, very few taxpayers used to make the amendments in practice).

The inspector may wish to amend the self-assessment for the following reasons:

(c)   the inspector may discover what is probably an innocent error; or

(d)   the inspector wishes to make a 'jeopardy' amendment during the course of an enquiry in order to protect the Revenue's interests and to force the making of a payment on account pending completion of the enquiry; or

(e)   the inspector may amend the return by means of the closure notice with which he indicates completion of his enquiry.

Amendments by the taxpayer — TMA 1970, ss 9ZA and 9B

13.56 The taxpayer may make an amendment to a self-assessment at any time up to twelve months following the filing date. Before 11 May 2001, a taxpayer could not amend his self-assessment once an enquiry had commenced. [*TMA 1970, old s 9(5)*]. With effect from that date, a taxpayer is not prevented from amending his return whilst an enquiry is in progress but the amendment does not take effect until the enquiry is completed. In the meantime, the amendment does not restrict the scope of the enquiry but the inspector may take it into account (together with any matters arising) in the enquiry. [*s 9B(2)*]. If the inspector in his closure notice states that the taxpayer's amendment has been taken into account in formulating his own amendments to the return, the taxpayer's amendment will not take effect. The same result occurs where the inspector states in the closure notice that he has concluded that the amendment is incorrect. [*s 9B(3)*].

If a taxpayer's amendment is received *before* the enquiry window has closed this may precipitate an enquiry by the inspector. He may have had no intention of taking up a case for enquiry during the period afforded by the enquiry window but a taxpayer amendment is an occasion when the inspector must decide whether to carry out an enquiry. Because the enquiry window has not closed the inspector then has the right to enquire either into the amendment *per se* or into the return generally under the aspect or full enquiry procedure.

Inspectors are instructed normally to take up the whole return for enquiry rather than restrict the enquiry to the subject of the amendment (see 13.57 *et seq.*).

Bearing in mind that the period of the enquiry window is determined by the date when the return is received, or twelve months from the filing date at the latest, whereas the deadline for an amendment is twelve months from the filing date, a taxpayer amendment might be made after the closure of the enquiry window. In these circumstances, the inspector must limit his enquiry to matters to which the amendment relates or which are affected by the amendment (*s 9A(5)* introduced by the *Finance Act 2001* with effect from 11 May 2001 – see 13.40).

If, however, enquiries concerning the taxpayer amendment made at this time throw doubt on the return as a whole, then the inspector is instructed to proceed on discovery lines (see 13.19–13.24).

An amendment may not be made by the taxpayer following the expiration of the twelve month period. Although the taxpayer may not be able to amend a self-assessment after the twelve month period he may apply to have the self-assessment opened under the error or mistake provisions (see 13.79).

There is no prescribed format for a taxpayer amendment but the inspector is advised that the following features must be present for a taxpayer amendment to be valid. It should:

(a)   be in writing; and
(b)   be signed by the taxpayer or by someone who could validly have signed the return, or someone who would, at the time the amendment was made, have had power to sign the return had it been made then. For example, someone holding a power of attorney granted in the interim; and
(c)   give a clear indication of the terms in which the self assessment is to stand amended.

If the inspector is in any doubt about whether any of these features are present he is instructed to make a Revenue amendment within the appropriate time limit and advise the taxpayer and his or her agent of his reasons for doing so.

Amendments by the Inspector — TMA 1970, ss 9ZB, 9C and 28A(2)

13.57 The Inland Revenue may make an amendment to a self-assessment:

(a) at any time during the nine months beginning with the day on which the return was delivered (this is normally known as a 'repair'); or

(b) during an enquiry; or

(c) on completion of an enquiry when the inspector issues the closure notice (see 13.73 below).

Amendments made during the nine months beginning with the day when the return was delivered usually take the form of a 'repair' to the self-assessment, i.e. the correction of a mathematical error or an error in principle following the discovery of an obvious mistake of some kind. [*s 9ZB*].

The correction is of no effect if the taxpayer gives notice rejecting it before the end of the period of 30 days beginning with the date of issue of the notice of correction (*s 9ZB(4)* and *(5)* introduced by the *Finance Act 2001* with effect from 11 May 2001).

Should the inspector discover matters leading him to believe that a self-assessment is incorrect which would have been taken up as an enquiry had the enquiry window still been open he cannot make an amendment but must proceed by way of a discovery (see 13.19).

Amendments made during the course of an enquiry are termed 'jeopardy amendments'. These may be made at any time during the course of an enquiry and may be made on several occasions as further facts unfold. They are designed to bring tax into charge as a holding operation pending completion of the enquiry. [*s 9C*].

They may be put in place because the taxpayer has refused to make a general payment on account of tax that is not in dispute, or of tax that has arisen due to some form of discovery during the enquiry, or for the following reasons:

(a) the taxpayer intends to dispose of assets; or

(b) the taxpayer intends to become non-resident; or

(c) the taxpayer intends to apply for bankruptcy; or

(d) the taxpayer may be about to go to prison.

13.58 The jeopardy amendment has the effect of replacing the original self-assessment so tax is collectible as if it were the taxpayer's self-assessment subject to the taxpayer's right to make a postponement application and the inspector's right to oppose the application before the Commissioners.

The inspector must be of the opinion that there would be 'a loss of tax' to the Crown if a jeopardy amendment were not put in place but the Revenue's opinion as to the meaning of the phrase 'a loss of tax' is that it can include delay in paying tax for an unreasonable time owing to the default of the taxpayer.

Inspectors are asked to consider making such an amendment when the taxpayer refuses to cooperate but only after a strong *prima facie* or actual deficiency in the return has been established.

Further jeopardy amendments can be made as new information emerges during the enquiry process suggesting that the current amendment is inadequate. Alternatively the inspector can apply to the Commissioners to have further tax under the original amendment put into charge.

Whilst the taxpayer can appeal against the jeopardy amendment at the time it is made there is no right to have the appeal heard until such time as the inspector has issued a closure notice signifying completion of the enquiry ([*TMA 1970, s 31(2)*] and see 13.73). He will do this unless the taxpayer is invited to make a voluntary offer in restitution for admitted tax compliance infringements.

13.59 Amendments made by the inspector's closure notice are dealt with at 13.73 to 13.79.

The use of the Tax Tribunal procedure in enquiry work

13.60 Self-assessment has virtually eliminated the Revenue's need to raise estimated assessments. This has removed the threat of a listing of the appeal for hearing by the General Commissioners as one of the main pressure points in enquiry and investigation work. Inspectors can no longer threaten to 'list the appeal' in order to force practitioners and their clients into providing answers to the questions arising from the inspector's investigation of a tax return.

13.61 It should be noted, however, that if a *TMA 1970, s 29* assessment is raised on discovery lines then the old system of appeal and listing still prevails. Inspectors cannot use *s 19A* to get access to information but they still have recourse to the Commissioners. They still have recourse to the General Commissioners under *reg 10 of SI 1994 1812* and, on occasions, to the Special Commissioners under *reg 10 of SI 1994 1811*.

These regulations enable the Commissioners to require taxpayers to produce information in the same way as inspectors can do under *TMA 1970, s 19A*. However, *TMA 1970, s 20(1)* and *(2)* may also be used by inspectors for the purposes of getting information from taxpayers in connection with the issue of discovery assessments.

The advent of fixed penalties and surcharges to underpin the submission of self-assessment returns has created a new class of appeals to be heard by the Commissioners. For example, an appeal can be brought under *TMA 1970, s 100B(1)* against a fixed penalty for the late filing of a tax return on the grounds of reasonable excuse but the Commissioners must be convinced that the excuse subsisted for the whole of the default period. [*s 93(8)*].

Other classes of appeal also continue to exist notwithstanding the introduction of self-assessment. For example the process of negotiating tax-geared penalties by reference to the mitigation factors concerning cooperation, quality of disclosure and size and gravity arising from the discovery of additional tax due to neglect and fraud still exist. The potential for an appeal against a penalty imposed by the inspector has not changed.

However, whilst such matters can feature in enquiry work they are not a feature that needs to be considered in depth here since nothing new has emerged from the introduction of self-assessment.

13.62 The main positions to be covered in this section are as follows:

(a)   an appeal against a request for documents and particulars under *TMA 1970, s 19A* and a subsequent failure to comply with a notice [*s 19A(6)* to *(11)*];
(b)   an appeal against a Revenue amendment [*s 31(1)(a)* and *(5)*]; and
(c)   an application for a direction that the enquiry is complete [*s 28A(4)* to *(6)*].

An appeal against the request for information under TMA 1970, s 19A

13.63 As noted in previous paragraphs the information powers under *s 19A* are powerful and therefore they are capable of being onerous.

Inspectors have got a job to do but they often have little idea of the problems that can be caused both to practitioners and their clients by the request for information to the nth degree of detail within short time limits in cases that do not warrant such an approach.

Equally practitioners have a responsibility to their clients to educate them in proper business and private financial housekeeping, bookkeeping and document retention in order to meet the basic standards implicit in self-assessment as a whole and *TMA 1970, s 12B* in particular.

13.64 The rationale for *s 19A* is based on the assumption that the inspector will only request information that he 'may reasonably require for the purpose of determining whether, and if so the extent to which (i) the return is incorrect or incomplete or (ii) in the case of an enquiry which is limited under *section 9A(5)* ... of this Act, the amendment to which the enquiry relates is incorrect'. The statute gives pointers to the way in which such a notice could be challenged.

Fundamental to this process is that information is in existence as a matter of fact in document form or is capable of being brought into existence in the case of any 'particulars' that might be requested.

13.65 Consequently in an appeal against a *s 19A* notice under *s 19A(6)*, possible lines of opposition to the production of such information might include the fact that it does not exist in document form as a matter of fact nor can it be produced in the form of a 'particular' or that it is unreasonable of the inspector to request the information either on the grounds of cost or that it is irrelevant to the year in question or otherwise.

A defence against a *s 19A* notice on the basis of the costs that would be involved in supplying information might receive some support from decided cases. In considering an appeal against matters connected with a notice under *s 20* in the case of *Kempton v Special Commissioners and CIR* [1992] STC 823 Mummery J said:

'. . . In some cases, having regard to all the circumstances, including the amounts involved and the likely cost of compliance, it may not be reasonable for an inspector to require at one sweep extensive particulars going back over a number of years . . .'

It is unlikely that Commissioners would throw out a *s 19A* notice solely on the grounds of cost but this factor coupled with other reasonable points of defence might sway them.

13.66 The Commissioners are able to take the following courses of action when determining an appeal against a *s 19A* notice:

(a) confirm the notice; or
(b) confirm that part of the notice which they consider reasonable in the circumstances; or
(c) set the notice aside on the grounds that the request is unreasonable.

The Commissioners' decision is final. There is no appeal to a higher court against their decision under *s 19A*. [*s 19A(11)*].

One of the grounds for an appeal may be that the inspector has not allowed sufficient time for the production of information. Commissioners do not have a remit to vary the time allowed but most inspectors would probably accept a variation rather than compromise the whole notice or might suggest that the Commissioners grant an adjournment of the hearing to a later date to give more time for the taxpayer to comply if he felt that the Commissioners were unsympathetic.

13.67 What constitutes an 'unreasonable' request must be decided in the context of the case and the nature of the information being requested.

A trader may not have kept daily cash sales records as a matter of fact therefore such a daily record could not be produced. However, an idea of annual sales might be gleaned from the production of particulars, such as the analysis of his business and private bank accounts, his estimate of business and private cash expenditure and a capital statement as at the commencement and cessation of the year in question.

The initial request for the daily sales record might have been reasonable since the inspector is entitled to assume that the trader has complied with *s 12B* and that any trader in that trade would normally keep a daily record of cash sales. If he persisted in that request after being told that no such document exists then that would be an unreasonable request but he could reasonably request some form of construction of cash sales generally by other means. The trader might complain that the cost of such an exercise would warrant the request as unreasonable. The Commissioners might consider the inspector's request for particulars in these circumstances as wholly reasonable but ask the inspector to temper the depth of information required without setting the notice aside. The inspector may give concessions in order to dissuade the Commissioners from eroding the notice.

The case of *Scott (trading as Farthings Steak House) v McDonald* [1996] STC (SCD) 381 provides the parameters for the outer limits of the term 'unreasonable' in the tax context. This case should be reviewed if a practitioner believes that an inspector has gone far beyond his remit.

13.68 The Special Commissioners' judgment in the case of *Mother v Inspector of Taxes* (SpC 211) covered most of the areas of argument about information requested in a *s 19A* notice.

In this case the inspector issued a *s 9A* notice of intention to enquire into the taxpayer's self-assessment but did not specify a time limit for the production of the information requested with the notice.

Information was not forthcoming so the original request was repeated in the form of a *s 19A* notice asking for:

(a)   all books and records, including bank statements, paying-in books and cheque book stubs for the taxpayer's property management business for the year ended 31 March 1997; and

(b)   dividend counterfoils for the year ended 5 April 1997.

The taxpayer appealed on the following grounds:

(a)   that it was unreasonable for the inspector to have omitted a time limit from the *TMA 1970, s 9A* notice; and

(b)   that it was unreasonable to expect her to produce the documents relating to the property management business as she operated as a managing agent for other companies whose affairs would necessarily be disclosed to the Revenue if she complied strictly with the terms of the notice; and

(c)   that there was no statutory authority for the inspector to require production of paying-in books and cheque book stubs; and

(d)   that not all of the counterfoils were available for production.

The Commissioner did not accept that there was no statutory authority enabling an inspector to request bank paying-in books and cheque book stubs but accepted that if there were never any cheque book stubs within the possession or power of the taxpayer, then the inspector could not demand documents that never existed.

He also accepted that the limits of the *TMA 1970, s 19A* notice extended only to the minimum amount of information concerning other taxpayers as possible and compatible with aiding the inspector in dealing with the appellant's tax affairs.

With regard to the missing dividend counterfoils, the taxpayer had to attempt to obtain replacement copies from the companies concerned at her own expense. If the companies concerned could not comply, and she could show evidence of that to the inspector, no further action on her part would be required as the missing documents would no longer be in her possession or power.

An appeal against a Revenue amendment — TMA 1970, ss 9C(2) and (3), 28A(2) and 31(1)(a) and (b)

13.69 The circumstances in which a Revenue amendment (a 'jeopardy amendment') may be made during the course of an enquiry were considered at 13.57 and 13.58. Such an amendment may well imply that the inspector has established, at least in his own mind, that additional tax is payable over and above the tax arising from the original self-assessment notwithstanding that enquiries are not yet complete.

At the end of an enquiry the inspector must issue a closure notice under *s 28A(2)*. This must inform the taxpayer that the enquiry is at an end and state the inspector's conclusions as to the amount of tax that should be contained in the taxpayer's self-assessment and as to any claims or elections into which he has enquired. Where appropriate, the closure notice will also make amendments to the taxpayer's return to give effect to the inspector's conclusions. The taxpayer then has 30 days to appeal against the amendment (*TMA 1970, new sections 31* and *31A* introduced by the *Finance Act 2001* with effect from 11 May 2001).

This contrasts with the position before 11 May 2001 where the inspector had to request the taxpayer to make his own amendment within 30 days. If the taxpayer did not comply with this request (and most did not), the inspector then had 30 days to make his own amendment. The taxpayer then had a further 30 days to appeal.

If a jeopardy amendment was issued during the course of the enquiry and was appealed at the time it was issued then both appeals stand even though the later amendment creates the new self-assessment. Consequently both appeals have to be considered by the Commissioners if the case reaches the stage that they are asked to make a determination.

The fact that the inspector has issued a closure notice making an amendment, which is then appealed against, does not signify that the next move is automatically to refer the matter to the Commissioners for a contentious hearing. The circumstances surrounding final resolution of an enquiry case are considered in 13.73 to 13.78.

An application for a direction that the enquiry is complete — TMA 1970, ss 28A(4) to (6)

13.70 One of the most important innovations brought in with self-assessment is the process whereby the taxpayer and his agent can apply to the Commissioners to order the inspector to issue a closure notice. Arguably this is merely equivalent to the process whereby the taxpayer could list his appeal for hearing by the General Commissioners in pre-self-assessment days but this is not really the case.

Under the old system the taxpayer had to prove his 'innocence' in order to have the appeal determined in the figures he considered correct. If the original estimated assessment was in much higher figures than those acceptable to the taxpayer then he had to be able to show good cause why the figures to be determined should be lower. There were few occasions under the old rules when the taxpayer initiated the process of listing the appeal.

13.71 Under the new system the inspector must be able to justify why he should be allowed to continue with the enquiry. In those cases where there is genuine cause for questioning the inspector's insistence that the enquiry must continue the matter will be obvious to the Commissioners. At the very least the inspector may be forced to slim down the depth and breadth of his enquiry and may even be forced into revealing his hand if there is some form of hidden agenda at work.

There are cases when inspectors ask far too many questions, or request far too much information, or make big issues out of minor points of adjustment, or who exhibit a failure to understand commercial accounting points and the like. They may be inhibited in their approach if they are under threat of a listing by the taxpayer. However, the taxpayer may well render himself exposed if the inspector is taking a responsible position and the listing is merely an attempt to prevent the inspector from doing a proper job. Experienced practitioners will be able to spot the right cases for this approach.

13.72 The points made in relation to information gathering, the amendment of the self-assessment and the role of the Tax Tribunal in enquiry work may be summarised as follows:

(a)   Under *s 19A* an officer of the Board can issue a notice to the taxpayer (but to no-one else) at the outset of an investigation or subsequently, requiring 'such documents as are in the taxpayer's possession or power' and 'such accounts or particulars' as he may reasonably require.

(b)   *Section 19A* can only cover information necessary to enable the inspector to carry out a review of a self-assessment return within the enquiry window. It cannot be used to require the production of information pertinent to an earlier year nor can it be sent to a third party.

(c)   Fundamentally the inspector can use the powers vested in *s 20* as an alternative to *s 19A* whether a self-assessment return is open or not whereas *s 19A* is restricted to an open self-assessment return. A *s 20* notice can cover the production of information directly from the taxpayer and from third parties relevant to the taxpayer's financial affairs but *s 19A* is more likely to be used for the production of information from the taxpayer *per se* when the enquiry window is open.

(d)   Either the taxpayer or the Revenue may amend a self-assessment within certain time limits and under certain conditions.

(e)   The taxpayer may make an amendment to a self-assessment at any time up to twelve months following the filing date but, if the enquiry has commenced, the amendment will not take effect until the closure notice has been issued and not even then if the inspector states that he has taken the amendment into account in his own conclusions or that the amendment is incorrect.

(f)　The inspector may make a jeopardy amendment to the self-assessment at any time during the course of an enquiry. This is an amendment designed to bring tax into charge as a holding operation pending completion of the enquiry.

(g)　Whilst the taxpayer can appeal against the jeopardy amendment at the time it is made, there is no right to have the appeal heard until such time as the inspector has issued a notice of completion of the enquiry.

(h)　It should be noted, however, that if a *s 29* assessment is raised on discovery lines then the old system of appeal and listing still prevails.

(i)　The rationale for *s 19A* is based on the assumption that the inspector will only request information that he 'may reasonably require for the purpose of determining whether, and if so the extent to which the return is incorrect or incomplete or in the case of an enquiry which is limited under *section 9A(5)* ... of this Act, the amendment to which the enquiry relates is incorrect.' The statute gives pointers to the way in which such a notice could be challenged.

(j)　An appeal may be brought to the Commissioners on the grounds that it is unreasonable for the inspector to request the information (or part of it) contained in the *s 19A* notice.

(k)　At the end of an enquiry the inspector must issue a closure notice under *s 28A(2)*. This must inform the taxpayer that the enquiry is at an end and state the inspector's conclusions as to the amount of tax that should be contained in the taxpayer's self-assessment and as to any claims or elections into which he has enquired. Where appropriate, the closure notice will also make amendments to the taxpayer's return to give effect to the inspector's conclusions.

(l)　The taxpayer then has 30 days to appeal against the amendment.

(m)　One of the most important innovations brought in with self-assessment is the process whereby the taxpayer and his agent can apply to the Commissioners to order the inspector to issue a closure notice in respect of the enquiry. [*TMA 1970, s 28A(4) to (6)*].

Completion of the enquiry — TMA 1970, s 28A(1)

13.73 Under *TMA 1970, s 28A(1)* all enquiries under self-assessment must be completed by the formal issue of a closure notice informing the taxpayer that he has completed his enquiries. However, not all enquiries will end this way. In some cases, the enquiry will come to an end as the result of a contract settlement.

A contract settlement will arise if:

(a)　there has been a failure to notify chargeability such that a financial penalty arises under *TMA 1970, s 7(8)*; or

(b)　the self-assessment return has been delivered late such that there is a financial penalty under *TMA 1970, s 93*; or

(c)　during the course of his enquiry, the inspector discovers matters leading to an additional tax liability that suggest that the taxpayer has been neglectful or fraudulent, and he has invited an offer from the taxpayer in consideration of no proceedings being taken against him.

In any of these cases if an offer has been made by the taxpayer (usually to include a financial penalty in recognition of wrongdoing) and accepted by the Inland Revenue then it is known as a 'contract settlement'.

13.74 A closure notice is issued in all other circumstances and whether or not additional tax has arisen from the inspector's enquiries. If additional tax does arise then the inspector must set out the reasons why, in his opinion, more tax is payable.

As mentioned above, the system before 11 May 2001 involved the inspector setting out his conclusions and inviting the taxpayer to make his own amendments to the return. The form of notice of completion in these cases was as follows:

> **'Notice of completion under Section 28A(5) Taxes Management Act 1970**
>
> I wrote to you on [date] to tell you that I would be making enquiries into [your tax return for the year ended 5 April [year] [the amendment to your tax return for the year ended 5 April [year] made on [date of amendment]. I have now completed those enquiries.
>
> In my opinion your self-assessment for this year should be [£000000.00]. I enclose an explanation of how I have arrived at my figure.
>
> The law allows you to amend your self-assessment within 30 days from the date you receive this notice. [Before you take any action, I suggest you discuss this notice with your adviser who has been sent a copy.]
>
> You may amend your self-assessment to the above figure or any other amount which you consider is correct. An amendment form (SA533) is enclosed for you to use.
>
> If I do not receive your amendment within the 30 day time limit, or I do not agree with your amended figure, I will amend your self-assessment to the figure I have suggested.
>
> You have the right to appeal against any amendment that I make.'

At the time of writing, the Revenue has not published the new version of this notice. Presumably, the first two paragraphs will remain the same but the rest of the notice will set out any amendments to the return made by the inspector, explain the right of appeal and inform the taxpayer (if relevant) that his tax adviser has been sent a copy of the notice.

13.75 The taxpayer or his agent, even under a contract settlement, may request a closure notice. There is nothing to be gained by such a move since the terms of any successfully concluded contract settlement will include formal acceptance by both sides that all relevant matters have been dealt with so that the enquiry is now complete. Indeed, as the Revenue states in its leaflet IR160 (enquiries under self-assessment – how settlements are negotiated):

> 'We will not seek to take advantage of the fact that no formal closure notice has been issued. If any additional liabilities, relating to the years

covered by the enquiry, come to light at any time after all the payments required under the contract have been made, we will not under any circumstances seek to amend your self-assessment. We will instead cover any such liabilities by means of a Revenue assessment, against which you would have a right of appeal [presumably under *TMA 1970, s 29*].'

On the other hand something may be lost by insisting on the issue of a closure notice since the inspector must then follow the strict procedure laid down for this purpose. This may mean that tax is put in charge earlier than would be the case if the taxpayer was waiting for the Revenue to accept the contract offer because the issue of such a notice starts time limits running so precipitating action for recovery of tax.

13.76 Where there is no contract settlement, the enquiry must be completed by the issue of a closure notice. The notice should include a statement by the inspector reflecting all the matters that have been the subject of enquiry, therefore it must include coverage of matters that have not yielded additional tax as well as matters that have.

It is in the taxpayer's interest to ensure that all matters have been noted since this may ensure that grey area situations are not re-visited at a later date if the taxpayer's returns are reviewed again.

It is equally in the inspector's interests to ensure that he has covered all relevant matters before the notice is issued since he has no opportunity to do so afterwards, except in those cases where information comes to light leading to a discovery assessment such that the matter is then dealt with on conventional investigation lines.

Moreover, he has no further opportunity to alter the figures once the notice has been issued therefore he must pitch his figures such that they are the highest that can be justified in the circumstances but are not too high as to render them undefendable should the case end up as a contentious hearing before the Commissioners.

The issue of the closure notice is therefore a crucial stage in the enquiry process.

13.77 By this time all negotiation should have been completed and the taxpayer and his agent should be fully aware of the additional tax that will be stated in the notice. Unless the case is one which has produced a position of impasse so that the matter has to be heard at a contentious hearing before the Commissioners, the inspector and the taxpayer's agent (or the taxpayer) should have agreed the final outcome as to additional tax.

If matters are proceeding amicably the agent will be mindful of the inspector's problem that he has to pitch figures in the closure notice at a given level as noted above (see 13.76). Equally, the inspector should have agreed with the agent what figure would be acceptable to him to avoid the danger of the taxpayer appealing against the amendment contained in the closure notice. Neither the taxpayer nor the Revenue is likely to relish the idea of contentious proceedings before the Commissioners, so there will be a strong incentive to find a figure which is acceptable to both parties.

13.78 Under the system which applied before 11 May 2001, there was some scope for further negotiation even after the completion notice had been issued. Since the notice invited the taxpayer to make his own amendments to his return, it was always open to the taxpayer to put in a figure which was lower than the inspector's recommendation. The inspector then had to decide whether to make a counter-assessment under the old *s 28A(4)*. Instead, it was always an option for the inspector to re-open negotiations and seek a compromise whereby the taxpayer accepted the counter-amendment when issued. The new streamlined completion procedure introduced by the *Finance Act 2001* seems to have reduced the scope for such post-notice negotiations.

Summary of points concerning completion of the enquiry

13.79

(a)   Under *s 28A(1)* all enquiries under self-assessment must be completed either by the formal issue of a closure notice, although in some cases an enquiry will be ended by a contract settlement.

(b)   A closure notice is issued in all other circumstances and whether or not additional tax has arisen from the inspector's enquiries. If additional tax does arise then the inspector must set out the reasons why, in his opinion more tax is payable, and make the appropriate amendment to the taxpayer's self-assessment.

(c)   The closure notice should include a statement by the inspector reflecting all the matters that have been the subject of enquiry therefore it must include coverage of matters that have not yielded additional tax as well as matters that have.

(d)   By this time all negotiation should have been completed and the taxpayer and his agent should be fully aware of the additional tax that will be stated in the notice.

Error or mistake relief — TMA 1970, s 33

13.80 This section is covered here because there is an interface with the self-assessment provisions with respect to amendments to the self-assessment and because enquiry work, by its very nature, sometimes unearths circumstances giving rise to the need for a claim. Moreover, an error or mistake relief claim can open a pandora's box because a claim enables the Revenue to review tax years other than those connected with the claim so creating the environment for a discovery followed by an investigation.

If a self-assessment return has been submitted then this determines the self-assessment for that year. However, the taxpayer then has twelve months from the filing date to make an amendment to the self-assessment unless the case is already under enquiry (see 13.56). For a 2000/01 return the filing date is 31 January 2002 so the amendment must be made on or before 31 January 2003.

The subject of an amendment may take a number of forms but an error or mistake in the return is certainly one class of adjustment that is covered by the amendment provisions therefore a taxpayer amendment may be made within the time limit for amendments.

Once the time limit is passed then the only way to amend an error or mistake is via *TMA 1970, s 33*. The time limit is five years after 31 January next following the end of the year of assessment to which the return relates. [*s 33(1)*]. Thus for a claim concerning the 2000/01 self-assessment, the time limit is 31 January 2007.

The expression 'error or mistake' covers:

(a)   errors of omission such as the non-deduction of an admissible expense; and
(b)   errors of commission, such as computational or arithmetical errors ; and
(c)   errors arising from a misunderstanding of the law; as well as
(d)   erroneous statements of fact.

It will be noted that any one who had deliberately set out to evade tax might be tempted to make a 'protective' error or mistake relief claim if he feared discovery before or during an aspect or full enquiry in respect of (b), (c) and/or (d) above. This is why the section enables the inspector to 'have regard to all the relevant circumstances of the case' and to take into consideration matters relevant to chargeable periods other than that to which the claim relates. [*s 33(3)*].

The expression 'all the relevant circumstances' is considered to include even years out of date for assessment under normal time limits, as well as other sources which have escaped a charge to tax for one reason or another.

For a genuine claim to succeed there must be:

(a)   an excessive assessment; and
(b)   tax charged under it which has been paid; and
(c)   an error or mistake in a return; and
(d)   a causal link between the error or mistake and the excessive assessment; and
(e)   the claim must be made within the time limit.

It should be noted that the Revenue is prepared to give relief by way of discharge of tax providing that the only reason preventing relief being given is that tax on an assessment is unpaid but in normal circumstances the relief must be given by way of tax in the form of a repayment (with a repayment supplement payable from the date of payment of tax for the later year) or credit against a later tax bill.

This is because *s 33* does not affect the original assessment if it has become final and conclusive, therefore it cannot be reopened simply to give effect to the claim. It also means that the time limit for the Revenue to enquire into the return for the earlier year is not extended.

Chapter 14

Enquiries in Practice

Graham Greenman Trading as G G Frames: a case history

14.1 Graham Greenman is an engineer working from a unit on an industrial estate near Dudley in the West Midlands trading as G G Frames. He makes anything that can be made out of metal from industrial hoppers, heavy duty storage racks through to spiral staircases but about 50% of his turnover is in the fabrication of metal frames for industrial and agricultural buildings. He only makes things to order for trade customers and farmers.

There are two full-time employees on the production side and he draws on a pool of sub-contractors who are brought in to do the heavier fabrications, such as industrial and agricultural building frames. His wife sometimes helps him out. She has been known to help with office secretarial work on occasions but she has two junior school age children to look after as well.

Graham hates paperwork. The office space in his industrial unit is limited and is often used to store fabricated components ready for on site construction. His accountant does his VAT, PAYE and self-assessment returns. All copy sales and purchase invoices, indeed any piece of paper that comes across the office threshold is quickly read and shoved in a desk drawer, to await the disinterested attention of his part-time bookkeeper. He keeps an old exercise book to record cash income and expenditure but there is not much of that.

Graham lives a short drive away from the business premises. The business has expanded in recent years so the business office accommodation is too small. All the engineering blue prints and drawings are now done at home.

He plays golf and has a sixth share in a horse that normally runs at local racecourses.

His self-assessment return for the year to 30 September 2000 is reproduced in Appendix A

The accountant, Stan Lee, has been dealing with Graham's accounts for years. His staff always struggle with Graham's books because the prime records are usually untidy and Graham's bookkeeper is a dab hand with the tippex. There is always an imbalance on cash account and sometimes Graham 'discovers' copy sales invoices, purchase invoices and the like that have 'slipped out of the back of his desk drawer onto the floor under his desk' after the quarterly VAT return has been sent in.

The self-assessment return was taken in on the filing date (31 January 2002) because, as usual, Graham had left it to the last minute to send information to Stan.

Commencement of the enquiry

14.2 Stan barely had time to breathe a sigh of relief that the filing date rush was over for another year when Graham telephoned to say he had received the following letter from Ian Overturn, an inspector from Merry Hill tax district:

'Thank you for your tax return for the year ending 5 April 2001. I am writing to tell you that I intend to make some enquiries into this return.

I enclose a copy of our Code of Practice. It explains how we make enquiries and how we keep our promise of fair treatment under the Revenue's Service Commitment to you.

When you have read the leaflet, please contact me if you require further information.'

Graham asked what this was all about. Stan told him not to worry and reminded him that he had sent Graham a letter several years ago explaining the new system of self-assessment and that this was probably a routine thing. Stan said he had not yet received Overturn's letter yet but he would contact Graham soon.

Stan was not happy. Why had Overturn written so quickly after receiving the return? Graham's records were always in a mess. The inspector was bound to find something. Stan reminded himself that he had spoken to Graham on a number of occasions about keeping better records so Graham only had himself to blame but he could do without another enquiry. Merry Hill district seemed to have gone potty recently. He already had four on the go.

When the letter arrived Stan breathed a sigh of relief. Overturn wanted an analysis of motoring expenses and repair expenses together with any invoices for more than £500 for motoring and £1,250 for repairs. He had also asked that the add back for private mileage (15%) should be reviewed and for further details of a bad debt for £18,000 owed by a firm making components for the large motor manufacturers in the area. Roddick Engineering Limited had gone bust almost immediately that Rover's troubles started but not before they had commissioned G G Frames to design and install specialised storage racking for their warehouse.

Stan concluded that it must be an aspect enquiry. Full books and records had not been requested. Inspectors always asked for all the books and records if it was a full enquiry.

He had been given 30 days to supply the information so he could relax. He telephoned Graham to give him the news. Graham did not sound so happy. He kept asking why they were asking these questions. He had always given Stan what he had asked for. Stan was paid to keep the Revenue away. Why were they so interested in what he had spent on repairs and how could you prove to anyone what your private mileage was anyway.

Stan said he would need to discuss matters with Graham but Graham said he was very busy at the moment and could not make it for at least two weeks. That suited Stan fine.

A week later, Stan looked at the repairs and motoring invoices spread out on his desk with idle interest. The roof of the industrial unit had been extensively repaired so that explained quite a sharp blip in the normal level of repairs. There was nothing out of the ordinary in this because the unit was 15 years old and flat roofs needed repairing sooner or later. The motoring side seemed OK. Most of the petrol had been purchased via a business credit card. A 20,000 miles service had been carried out on the Range Rover. His staff seemed to have analysed it all correctly.

A day before the meeting was due to take place Graham telephoned to say that he had just been asked to tender for a big job and he had to go away for a few days so could they put off the meeting until the following week. Stan could only see him the following Friday but there was no panic. The repairs expenditure was easily explained and the bad debt had been incurred by one of his other clients who had gone bust so he knew all about that. As for private mileage he would just add 5%. That would keep the inspector happy. However, he would exceed the 30 day deadline by a couple of days. He did not think Overturn would be too worried.

The Friday meeting went well. Graham had won the order that had taken up so much of his time recently and Stan's fees were paid without a murmur. Stan had already drafted the letter analysing the motoring costs and the repair costs from his working papers and gathered together the relevant invoices. Graham said there was nothing particularly noteworthy about the repairs or motoring expenses. He conceded that he had done more private mileage in recent years so an increase in the ratio to 20% was 'about right'. He complained about the bad debt but was philosophical. The owner of the car components firm was a personal friend. They went on golfing holidays together.

The selection for full enquiry

14.3 Ian Overturn read Stan's reply to his *s 9A* enquiry letter with his usual equanimity and a wry smile as he checked the 'potential enquiry' folder in Greenman's file for the third time.

The report from TIDO (Tax Information Distribution Office) of the settlement that Customs had made with Greenman over the evasion of £350 duty on the 'importation' of a Rolex watch in June 2000 puzzled him. Why had Greenman got a Jersey resident to buy a Rolex watch duty free in Stratford-on-Avon for £3,500 and then flown over to Jersey to pick it up so that he could re-import it, only to save £350? The flight from Birmingham airport must have cost £200.

He had no problem carrying out an aspect enquiry simply because the case had been starred out for review because it was on the potential enquiry list but was it enough to develop the case into a full enquiry? He had nothing else to go on but this was indicative of a devious mind of a higher order than simply bringing in a few extra bottles of spirits and it involved Jersey so there was always a possibility of some offshore interest.

The roof repairs invoice interested him. He could understand why the premises might need roof repairs because it was a flat roof and they were more vulnerable than pitched roofs but, at £9,500, the cost looked high. He thought he might have a chance of arguing that there was an improvement element in the cost which could be capitalized but that was clutching at straws.

Then something struck him about the invoice — it was a photocopy — at least it looked like a photocopy. It was hard to tell but there was a faint black line just under the description that made it look like the original description had been covered over with something like a sticky label. The typing also looked wrong. Everybody used printers these days, not typewriters, so why had the description been typed in?

Ian had a word with his investigations casework manager. Was it worth opening up? The discussion that followed covered possible ways of checking the invoice and possible reasons why it would have a false description. Three alternatives were open to them to check the matter:

1. Could they interest the VAT office in a control visit to the roofing company simply to check out their invoice? They had certainly done this before when someone had tipped them off about a civil engineer putting through false purchase invoices for crane hire — unlikely — the invoice was over six months old and the officer would probably have no real reason to delve backwards. However, if this were a false invoice of some description then there was a VAT problem for Greenman so that might interest them.
2. What about a routine PAYE audit of the roofing company — there was bound to be some PAYE/NIC or construction industry scheme failure but the auditor would have no remit to ask for sales invoices. Nevertheless that might be a way in. They could try and get a view of the sales invoices whilst they were there or simply ask openly to check the invoices generally once they gained the company's confidence. This was a bit of a long shot but having a go would lose nothing. The Schedule E compliance inspector and PAYE auditor were happy to comply though it might take a month or so.
3. Given that the invoice was from a roofing company, if Greenman wanted to falsify it why would he do so? Probably because he had has his own house re-roofed. Why not drive round and see what could be seen from the road?

They both concluded that the case was worth converting to a full enquiry.

The quest for information

14.4 Ian sat down straight away to compose his next letter.

'Dear Mr Lee

203

MR G GREENMAN TRADING AS G G FRAMES

Thank you for your letter dated 11 March and the enclosures therein.

I refer to my letter to Mr Greenman dated 7 February giving notice that I intended to enquire into his 2000/01 return. I should now be pleased to receive the following items/information:

1. All invoices, receipts and papers in support of the accounts entries.

2. Bank and building society statements of all accounts, business and private operated by Mr and Mrs Greenman, singly or jointly and on behalf of their children in the period 1 October 1999 to 30 September 2000.

3. Details of any estimates used in preparing the accounts.

4. A copy of the cash account and say the amount of any balancing figure and how it was treated.

5. How the income/sales figure in the accounts was arrived at.

6. An analysis of drawings, which provides a breakdown of cash and cheque drawings.

7. A copy of the capital allowances claim with a breakdown of what each item relates to.

8. Full details for any payments made for which no receipt is held, including the name of the recipient of the payment.

9. A breakdown of the capital introduced, with details of the date of introduction and source of funds introduced.

10. A breakdown of the interest charges and what they relate to.

11. A breakdown of motoring costs and how the private use was determined.

12. A breakdown of how the depreciation figure as per the return was calculated.

13. A breakdown of administration costs.

14. A breakdown of what the repairs relate to.

15. A breakdown of legal and professional costs.

16. A breakdown of other expenses as per the return.

17. A breakdown of creditors and accruals as in the balance sheet in the return.

18. Details of closing work in progress.

19. A breakdown of loans and overdrawn bank accounts as in the balance sheet in the return and copies of the loan agreements for all loans.

20. A breakdown of other liabilities in the balance sheet in the return.

21. A breakdown of plant, machinery and motor vehicles as in the balance sheet in the return.

I trust that my request will not present you with any great difficulties. Should you find yourself facing any problems, or do not anticipate being able to supply this information within 30 days of the date of this letter then please do not hesitate to contact me on the above telephone number to discuss the situation.

Yours sincerely

Ian Overturn'

Note: This is a real life *s 9A* enquiry letter from a Midlands tax district with very slight modifications. The queries concerning repairs, motor expenses, private mileage and bad debts have been retained to maintain authenticity.

When Stan received this letter he was angry. Why were they asking all these damn questions and how was he going to get the information to Overturn within 30 days. It was just not on. What was Graham going to say? Why had he not warned Graham that aspect enquiries could turn nasty? At least he would have covered himself. Now he would have to tell Graham the news and goodness knows how difficult it would be to get the information together. Stan decided to put the file to one side for a while. He had got plenty of other things to do and he did not want the hassle with Graham.

Two weeks later the file was still sitting on Stan's overflow desk staring at him like a wet fish with a cold eye. He was going to have to pick it up soon. One thing was certain — there was no way he would be able to comply within the 30 days so he may as well phone the inspector now.

Overturn was not in a good mood when he answered Stan's call but as soon as he realised which case it was about he lightened up.

The previous week he had driven round to Greenman's house and despite getting a good view of three sides of the roof there was not a new tile to be seen, but nestling under the trees at the bottom of the garden was a prefabricated building and at least it had a flat roof! In fact he had seen Graham Greenman sitting at a big drawing board near the window busily working away! He estimated the building was about 20 feet long by 10 feet wide.

Though in a good mood, Overturn was not in a benevolent one. Stan's request for an explanation of why Overturn had suddenly landed him with a 20 question letter simply met with the bland reply that this was a normal enquiry under self-assessment and nothing more. Stan got an equally annoying brush off when he asked why the private bank account statements, including the children's accounts, had been called for. Overturn said it was simple. It was his duty to satisfy himself that the return as a whole was correct and he had decided in this instance that he should review the private statements. After all, there was nothing to stop Mr Greenman putting business receipts in any bank account he liked, so he would not be doing his job properly if he confined his attentions to the business account.

Stan's request for more time again fell on deaf ears. Overturn pointed out that virtually all the information he wanted was probably in Stan's working papers so what was the problem? Overturn said he would be happy to be supplied with Stan's working papers so as to extract the information himself if he felt that this would speed things up. Stan did not think that was necessary but his protestations about the need to meet Graham and review the books and records also met with little sympathy. The inspector warned Stan that he would have to consider a *TMA 1970, s 19A* notice if information was not forthcoming.

Stan finally got hold of Graham several days later after he had left three messages on Graham's mobile. It transpired that Graham was in Portugal for a week on a golfing holiday with Les Roddick of Roddick Engineering Limited. Stan was not impressed, especially as he wanted Graham to get hold of all the private statements.

In answer to the inevitable question as to why they wanted the private bank statements Stan said the inspector had a right to ask so there was not much he could do about it. After a tirade from Graham about inspectors having nothing better to do but make other people's lives a misery he said he would not be back until the weekend and asked Stan to phone Joan, Graham's wife, for the information.

Stan knew full well he would get another earful from Joan when he asked for the bank statements, but he resolved to blame everything on the inspector. Joan brought the statements in herself. It was an hour before Stan could prise them from her and guide her to the door.

Pressure of work simply got in Stan's way. Overturn did not take much satisfaction from signing the *s 19A* notice because what he really wanted to do was get on with the case and Stan was equally depressed since he had been sent a copy of Graham's notice so he expected an irate call that morning. Moreover, this was the first *s 19A* notice he had ever received.

'INLAND REVENUE   **Date** *19 April 2002*

NOTICE REQUIRING PRODUCTION OF ACCOUNTS, BOOKS AND OTHER INFORMATION

Name

Graham Greenman trading as G G Frames.

Address

The Paddocks

Blacksmith's Green

Boltington

Reference 693/ENQ41281/049458/IO. **National Insurance no.** YH 87 04 68 QZ.

Income Tax Year 2000/01

(Taxes Management Act 1970, s 19A)

I wrote to your agent Mr S Lee on 18 March 2002 to ask for documents and information for the purposes of the enquiry into your 2000/01 tax return. To date I have not received the items listed below. I am now giving you notice that you are required by law to produce the documents and provide the information listed below within 30 days of the date you receive this notice.

If you do not, you may be liable to a penalty.

Documents

List of documents etc. requested in my letter to Mr S Lee dated 18 March 2002 and still outstanding.

Information

List of information requested in my letter to Mr S Lee dated 18 March 2002 and still outstanding.

Ian Overturn
Inspector

You have the right to appeal against this notice within 30 days after the notice was given to you. Your appeal must be in writing and state the grounds on which you are appealing.

Your appeal will be referred to the independent Appeal Commissioners who will decide whether the requirements set out in this notice were reasonable.

Normally appeals are heard by the local General Commissioners. You can elect for any hearing to be before the Commissioners for the area in which you live, in which your business premises are situated or in which your place of employment is located. You have the right to choose which area when you appeal.

Alternatively, in most cases, you can elect for hearing by the Special Commissioners, a full-time body which normally sits in London although they do visit other places occasionally. If you want the Special Commissioners to hear your appeal you must say so when you appeal.

If you wish to know more about appeal procedures now, please ask for leaflet IR37 Appeals.

The accountant's review

14.5 Stan finally got to grips with his working papers. As Overturn had observed — it was really a question of pulling information out of his files.

Cash account

14.6 The cash account was predictably a weak link. Graham had spent more cash by nearly £1,500 than they could trace through the bank plus the small amount of cash sales. Payments to the sub-contractors were sometimes in cash but that was not unusual. There had been some scrap sales in cash so this angle was covered since this was probably the first question Overturn would ask.

He had covered the imbalance with assumed additional sales rather than assuming that Graham had introduced cash from his own resources, which was the way acceptable to the Revenue.

Drawings

14.7 There was all the usual stuff in drawings. A lot of straightforward private expenditure had gone through as cheque payments but there were no cash drawings. There was a monthly transfer of £1,500 to the private account. Stan looked at the private bank statements. He could see the transfer in and regular payments out each month, including standing orders for mortgage, gas and electricity.

The private bank and building society statements

14.8 Stan did not ask to see his clients' private bank statements as a rule so he looked at the transactions with some interest. Apart from the regular transfers from the business account and the standing order payments there was not much else to note although he was surprised that the balance tended to fluctuate around the £6,000 mark. This seemed a little high for a current account but not extraordinarily high.

Legal and professional

14.9 Stan recognised most of the names in the list in his working papers and saw no problems in what expenses had been added back in the tax computation but there was one unfamiliar name — Carlton, Kitchen & Co of

Derby — £600. He asked one of his staff to look up the invoice. It was a firm of solicitors he had never heard of before but the work done seemed to be about some private matter. The description on the invoice was, it said: 'advice and legal services re Paddocks'. It had not been added back in the computation! Stan cursed under his breath. He rang Graham to check. Graham said that the invoice concerned a dispute with a neighbour. Stan decided he would have to make an amendment.

Work in progress

14.10 In the cold light of day Stan knew this was really a guess estimate by Graham. He had not really bothered with this in the past but Graham's business had done well over the past few years and the end of year figure did not really reflect this. It might be a coincidence that they were just a bit slack at the year end but Stan knew he could not count on it so he got the sales invoices out for the first three months of the following year and worked back from there.

The other queries

14.11 Following a general review of his working papers, Stan was confident that there was nothing worth worrying about concerning the other questions posed by the inspector so he asked one of his audit clerks to go through the rest and pull out the required information.

The letter and business records were delivered to Overturn ten days in to the 30 days imposed by the *s 19A* notice period. Stan informed the inspector about the failure to adjust for the private legal expenses of £600. He pointed out that this was a genuine oversight on his part and asked for it to be treated as an amendment to the return.

The Inspector's review

14.12 As soon as the information was in his hands Overturn could not resist the temptation to delve immediately into the books and records. This was a time honoured tradition amongst all inspectors who, like him, enjoyed investigations work. This was the first opportunity to look at what actually happened rather than have the information filter through the taxpayer and his agent. He wanted to get a good feel for the business and spot the interesting stuff straight away. If he did not see anything interesting the temptation would be to put everything away and forget about it for a while.

Many inspectors, Overturn included, had a knack of picking out unusual or questionable matters from books and records. This came from long experience at looking through sometimes hundreds of sets of records and sharing the experience of other inspectors. It sometimes made up for the lack of understanding of how the accountant had processed the information in producing the accounts.

There was an almost innate checklist in his mind as he flicked through the paperwork:

- purchase invoices that looked 'funny', the description of work done on the invoice and whether it was non committal or indicated a private expense, the delivery address and whether it was a private house, whether there was a VAT registration number and if so was it a valid number, where there was a sequence of invoices from the same person, were the invoice numbers properly sequential and how far apart were they in relation to the date on the invoice — the list was endless;

- unusual purchases, such as large items of stock or plant and equipment purchased near the year end, cheque book stub descriptions or lack of them, private expenditure that may not have been adjusted for, credit card expenditure that might show unusual place names abroad;

- sales invoices and the description on them, what was the main type of work and the pattern of issuing invoices.

He got the roof repair invoice from his file and compared it with the others — were there any other invoices that looked like photocopies? He struck a blank here but the invoice that Stan had noted as an unadjusted private expense looked quite interesting. The description of work done on the invoice was not well described, unlike the detailed bills he had seen before from solicitors.

That evening he put the name 'Carlton, Kitchen & Co' into the search facility that he used on the Internet. Up came a web site address, which then yielded that the firm was associated with others in Jersey, the Isle of Man and several other places well known to Overturn as tax havens. Further descriptions on the screen showed that this was no ordinary firm of solicitors but one which specialised in trust work, company formation and associated legal services. Overturn resolved to give the books and records a good going over as soon as he could carve out a day from his schedule.

Several weeks later Overturn finally got a day free to go through the books and records.

Purchase invoices

14.13 He first went through every purchase invoice individually and thoroughly. He starred out the following matters to discuss with Greenman:

Sub-contractors The invoices lacked much description, he could not tell which jobs they had worked on. The cashbook yielded that some payments had been made in cash and there were a number of occasions when they had clearly been paid overnight expenses. Were these sub-contractors in reality employees who should be subject to PAYE/NIC?

Additionally they had done a lot of work near to the year-end — was this reflected in the work in progress valuation? Greenman's schedule showed labour costs on several jobs at the year-end but these appeared to relate to his full-time workers.

He would ask about non-accounts records, such as job sheets. This also took his thoughts to other non-accounts records — what about Greenman's drawings and detailed costing schedules?

Repairs   The roof repair invoice needed detailed discussion.

Legal expenses   The payment to Carlton, Kitchen & Co needed detailed discussion.

Raw materials   There had been a large purchase of metal sections in July. He had difficulty trying to relate the purchase to work described in sales invoices about that time, mainly because he did not understand some of the technical terms, but the situation looked wrong. Was there more work in progress at the year-end than was in the return? Had this purchase been used on a job that had not gone through the books?

Sales invoices

14.14 *Bad debt*   Overturn had checked the Roddick Engineering file. There was no doubt that the firm was in trouble. It had called in the Receiver but that was not all that caught his eye. The company had been investigated a few years ago. Les Roddick, the owner, had been found to have set up a company registered in Panama but operated from Jersey by a firm called Brelbay Financial Services Limited. Overturn resolved to ask about this bad debt in detail.

Cash account

14.15 *Imbalance on cash account*   Apart from the fact that, in Overturn's eyes, any imbalance was intrinsically wrong and indicative of bad record keeping at the very least, reviewing this matter had got him looking at the private bank and building society accounts. There appeared to be a lack of private cash availability.

Overturn had a working rule about cash when reviewing bank accounts and the like. First decide what would be the likely cash requirements of the taxpayer and his family based on all available knowledge such as private household expenditure from the business bank account, and then assume that at least this amount of cash would be held as a balance on a monthly basis. If the answer was, say, £160, then schedule out all available information on private cash withdrawals from the business and finally assume that all round sum withdrawals (i.e. exact no-pence amounts ending zero or five) from the private bank and building society accounts up to, say, £400 were cashed cheques. This would then enable a private cash flow computation to be done that could be tested in discussion with the taxpayer. On this basis his calculations showed that Greenman was always short of cash.

Private bank and building society statements

14.16 Overturn could find no evidence of money being taken out of any of the accounts or the business drawings account to fund the purchase of a Rolex watch for £3,500. He thought he was on to a winner here.

The interview

14.17 Overturn telephoned Stan to set up a meeting with Graham Greenman. He said he was happy to have the meeting at his office or Stan's but would prefer it at the business premises simply because he could then see what work was done and how it was done so that would enable him to ask, as he put it, 'less stupid questions'. It would also mean that the interview would take less time.

Stan explained the problem regarding the office accommodation but said he would talk to Greenman. Graham said he had nothing to hide and would be happy to have the meeting at his business premises but he had a lot on at the moment. Between all three of them it transpired that the only available time was six weeks hence.

Overturn's note of interview was as follows:

G GREENMAN TRADING AS G G FRAMES

NOTE OF MEETING HELD ON MONDAY 8 JULY 2002

Persons present:	G Greenman	G G Frames
	S Lee	Lee & Co
	I Overturn	Inland Revenue Merry Hill

The meeting took place at the premises of G G Frames commencing at 10.15 a.m.

Greenman showed Overturn around the premises and explained that they made heavy metal fittings for industrial use such as storage racks and the like. They also made frames for small buildings mainly on industrial and agricultural premises. The premises were fitted out with an overhead gantry type crane with a 10 tonnes loading limit, various machines for cutting and bending metal. There was also a storage area for large gas bottles plus heavy welding equipment.

Overturn reminded Greenman that he had written to him in February stating that he intended to enquire into his 2000/01 return. He asked Greenman whether he had read Code of Practice 11, the leaflet that accompanied the letter. Greenman said he had done so. Overturn said that since his initial enquiries he had reviewed the business books and records and now wished to ask Greenman various questions to clarify certain points.

Overturn asked Greenman whether there was any matter that he wished to draw to Overturn's attention before he started. Greenman said there was nothing.

Private use of the business Range Rover

The inspector then asked Greenman to describe his non business usage of the Range Rover. What were the main journeys, was it used on holiday, did he have any hobbies that might require extensive use such as fishing etc? Greenman said that apart from driving the vehicle to work from home — a matter of a couple of miles — he hardly ever used it privately. His wife had a car and used that to ferry the children around etc. He said he had discussed the private mileage with Mr Lee who had convinced him that it was about 20%, but as far as he was concerned he doubted whether he did more than 10%. Overturn asked if he was saying that the private usage element in the tax computation should be 10%. Lee said he had discussed this with his client who had agreed it would be about 20%. He reminded Greenman that he used it when he went playing golf.

After further discussion 20% was agreed to be the private motor usage proportion. Overturn pointed out that the tax return had included a 15% adjustment so there would be additional tax to pay but he did not propose to scale it backwards.

Overturn then asked Greenman how keen a golfer he was. Greenman said he was a member of a local golf club and played on average once a week. Overturn asked whether he took his clubs with him on holiday. Greenman said he did. Overturn asked what courses he had played whilst on holiday to which Greenman listed courses in Scotland and Ireland. Overturn asked whether he had had any holidays on the continent. Greenman said he had been to France, Spain and Portugal. He confirmed that he had also taken his clubs on these occasions and asked why the inspector was so interested. Overturn explained that it was both in the Revenue's interests and his own that Overturn get a good idea of a personal lifestyle. Greenman could not think why it was in his interests. Overturn said that it meant he did not jump to conclusions about what people spent their money on. He asked whether Greenman had been anywhere else overseas apart from France, Spain and Portugal. Greenman said no, he had not.

Overturn asked if he was sure about this. Overturn said he had information that led him to believe that Greenman had been elsewhere. Greenman said he was sure but then added had he had been to Italy but that was years ago when the children were small. Overturn asked whether he had been anywhere else. Greenman asked what he meant. Overturn said again that he had information that lead him to believe that Greenman had been outside the UK to another place that Greenman had not yet listed. Lee asked what was the nature of the information. Overturn said he was not at liberty to say. Lee said in that case how did he expect Mr Greenman to answer. He again pressed Overturn for the reason why he had asked the question. Overturn then asked Greenman whether he had been to the Isle of Man. Greenman said categorically not. He then said now he realised what Overturn was getting at. He said that he had been to Jersey on a brief visit but that was not on the continent. Overturn asked if he had been anywhere else that was not on the continent. Greenman said not.

Overturn asked what was the reason for the visit. Greenman said he obviously knew so why ask. Overturn asked Greenman to give more information for the record.

At this point Lee asked Greenman if he preferred to stop the meeting for a discussion. Greenman said he yes, he would. Overturn agreed to wait in his car.

After about ten minutes the meeting reconvened. Lee said that Greenman had been involved in a Customs investigation concerning a Rolex watch. He had got friendly with someone from Jersey who originally lived in Wolverhampton and who had been in the Midlands on holiday. As a result he had given this person £3,500 to buy the watch duty-free. He then flew out to Jersey for a few day's holiday with this person, pick up the watch and return to the UK. He had been stopped at Birmingham Airport on the way back in because he was wearing the watch. Customs had matched up the serial number to a list of exported items that they got from UK firms who had permission to sell items duty free to genuine overseas tourists.

Overturn asked where he had got the money from to purchase the watch. Greenman said he had borrowed it from his father and had still not paid the money back. Overturn asked whether this could be proved. Greenman said he was positive. Customs had asked about this because they suspected him of doing this on a regular basis but had finally been satisfied it was a 'one off'. His father was relatively wealthy and had given a statement to Customs plus proof of the fact that he had got the money from his building society savings.

Overturn confirmed that he had known about this matter. He said he would contact Customs for further details about the source of the money to purchase the watch. Greenman assured Overturn that what he was saying was absolutely true.

Cash

Overturn said that he was disturbed by the fact that Greenman did not keep adequate records from which Lee could prepare a cash account when producing the annual accounts. Greenman said as far as he was concerned his records were OK, he had never had any complaints from Lee. Lee said he did not think that a small imbalance on cash account was a major concern. Overturn pointed out that £1,420 cash imbalance was a little more than 'small' as far as he was concerned. He asked whether Greenman was aware that under self-assessment everyone had a duty to keep adequate business records. Greenman said that he had a business to run and a few pounds here or there was not worth chasing. Overturn accepted Lee's point that virtually every business in the land probably could not account for 100% of its cash. He asked Greenman how he dealt with cash in the business, did he cash cheques and if so how many times a year and how much for, what did he spend the cash on, did he have a cash float for business entertaining etc.

In answer to these and other questions Greenman said that a scrap dealer had a skip parked in his yard and whenever they filled it up he called the dealer to collect it. This happened about four or five times a year. He was usually paid about £250 a time but sometimes he haggled a bit when he thought the scrap was worth more so overall he probably got about £1,500 a year from this. He used the money for all the odd cash expenses and to pay entertaining expenses. He said that he probably paid more out of his own pocket on entertaining than he got repaid by the business. He did not bother keeping any records because it was useless trying to get receipts so he did not ask.

Overturn asked Lee whether he was aware of the scrap sales. Lee said he was and if Overturn looked at the cash account detail he would see cash receipts from scrap. Overturn referred to the schedule and apologized for asking the question but pointed out that this figure was inevitably an estimate. Why should he believe it was only £1,500 a year? It could be £3,000 for all he knew. Greenman said no way was it that much and whatever it was he spent it on business expenses such as entertaining. Overturn pointed out that entertaining expenses were not allowable, therefore if the scrap sales were understated then profits were understated.

Overturn then asked where he got the cash from to pay the sub-contractors. Greenman said he also cashed business cheques occasionally so he always had about £600 with him. They were always asking for subs to cover them until the end of the week. Overturn asked whether he kept a note of what he gave them. Greenman said no but he could remember. Overturn asked whether he was certain that all the cash he had given them had been recorded as payment for services. Greenman said he was certain. Overturn asked him how he could be certain about this when he did not appear to know how much cash he had got from the scrap metal or how much he had spent on other things. Greenman said he just was. Overturn said that clearly some cash receipts had not been recorded that were taxable bearing in mind that entertainment expenditure was not allowable but he did not want to dwell on that at the moment.

He then asked about Greenman's private household expenditure. Greenman was asked what his family spent cash on. Did he get a regular cash drawing from the business? What pocket money did he give his two children for example? Greenman asked why the inspector should ask these questions. Overturn said he had already established that the business cash was not well controlled so Greenman may have used untaxed cash from the business for private expenditure. Greenman said definitely not. Overturn asked him how he knew this. Did he keep his business cash in a separate pocket from his private cash? Greenman said of course he did not but he just knew that he did not use business cash for private expenses. Overturn asked from where he got his private cash. Greenman said that his wife usually gave him £30 or so a week. Overturn asked him what cash he had on him at that moment. Greenman asked Overturn what cash he had on him. Overturn consulted his wallet and turned out his pockets and counted out £3.37. Greenman then counted out £46.49.

Overturn gave Greenman the private bank statements and asked him to point to debits in his private bank statements that he knew were cash. Greenman pointed out the following:

12 October 1999 — £125;

21 October 1999 — £125;

21 November 1999 — £150;

22 December 1999 — £75;

18 February 2000 — £50;

6 March 2000 — £50;

20 April 2000 — £100;

12 May 2000 — £40;

29 May 2000 — £150;

4 July 2000 — £70;

7 August 2000 — £90.

Overturn did not think this was much cash to live on especially as the Greenman's had two children of junior school age. Where did Mrs Greenman get the £30 a week to give him and what did she do for cash? Greenman said he didn't know — all she did was give him some cash, he had no idea where she got the cash from apart from the bank. Lee asked which supermarket Mrs Greenman used. Greenman said it was Tesco. Lee asked if she was likely to get some cash from them when she did her weekly shop. Greenman did not know that you could get cash like this. Both Lee and Overturn confirmed this. Greenman said that was where she got the cash then.

Overturn concluded by saying he was very unhappy about the cash position. He asked Lee if he would prepare a schedule of private cash availability and usage for the year. Lee agreed and said it would not be difficult so long as Mrs Greenman had kept the Tesco receipts.

Legal expenses

Overturn showed Greenman an invoice from a firm of solicitors called Carlton, Kitchen & Co. He told Lee that he appreciated his wish to make an amendment to the return but any amendment could not take effect until the enquiry was completed. In any event, he would take the amendment into account and no doubt everything would come out in the wash. Overturn asked Greenman what work had been done by this firm. He said it was not very clear to him from the description on the invoice. Greenman replied that he had had a dispute with a neighbour about a tree that had fallen over his fence in a storm. He had asked for compensation but the neighbour said the fence would have blown over anyway. The matter had been sorted out.

Overturn asked why he had used a firm of solicitors in Derby — was there any particular reason for this? Greenman replied that one of his friends had recommended them. Overturn asked which friend. Greenman did not think that was any of the inspector's business and refused to answer. Overturn thought this was a straightforward question — why was Greenman refusing to answer such a simple question? Lee interjected at this point. He could not see the relevance of the question and suggested that the answer would not advance matters one jot. He asked Overturn to desist. Overturn agreed.

Overturn then asked which neighbour had been in dispute with Greenman. Greenman again did not think he had a right to ask such a question. Lee pointed out that this was a private expense, it was only a small amount which admittedly should have been added back in the tax computation but he thought the question was not relevant.

Repairs

Overturn asked about the roof repair bill. What precisely had been done? Greenman asked what he meant — the roof had been repaired, what else was there to say? Overturn asked which roof? Greenman said the roof to Unit D. Overturn said you mean this unit. Greenman said no, this was Unit E. This was a repair to Unit D next door. Overturn asked what he was doing repairing Unit D and what did he use it for? Greenman said he had done a deal with the landlord — if he repaired Unit D he would get a cheap rent over the ten-year lease. Overturn asked Lee if he knew anything about this. Lee said it was the first he had heard about it. Overturn pointed out that this sounded like a premium and he would have to look into it. He asked Greenman what he used Unit D for. Greenman said nothing much at the moment but that he was expanding all the time and he expected to use it for storing raw materials and finished items pending delivery sooner rather than later. Overturn asked why he had not been shown around that morning. Greenman said there was nothing to see. Overturn said it was about time for a 'natural break' so he suggested that Greenman show him around.

Overturn established that the roof had indeed been repaired but observed that there were numerous stacks of metal tubing, metal brackets and other metal fittings plus about 100 sheets of 8'x 4' 10 ply plywood stacked in one part of the unit. He asked what these were for and whether Lee knew anything about them. Lee said he knew nothing about them. Greenman said they were surplus from the Roddick Engineering job that had 'gone wrong'. Overturn asked whether they were in the work in progress or stock lists. Greenman said they were not. Overturn asked why not. Greenman said because they had already been sold to Roddicks and erected on their site so they could not be in stock or WIP could they? Overturn said they were not at Roddicks but at G G Frames. Greenman said Roddicks could not afford to pay when the bad news about Rover was announced so he had contacted Les Roddick who said he could take the fittings back.

Overturn established that the work had been done in September 2000 mainly by the self-employed sub-contractors. They then had to dismantle everything they had erected. This event had occurred just before the year end. He then asked Greenman why he had not told Lee about it. As far as Greenman was concerned the fittings were now junk. They were designed to Roddick's specifications and no-one else would want them. Overturn asked why then did he bother to get them back, especially as he had to pay men to dismantle them. He asked Greenman how much it had cost to dismantle the fittings. Greenman estimated £450. Lee accepted that this was a matter for further discussion in due course.

On returning to the office Overturn then raised the question of the sub-contractors again. He expressed concern that they appeared to be employed by Greenman not self-employed. They did not seem to have any independent say in what they were doing. They had the same working hours as the employees and used the same tools. They were subject to the same supervision as the other workers. Lee said that they could and did provide substitutes. He said that he had asked Greenman about this and found that if the self-employed people were ill, or went on holiday during the time that Greenman wanted them, they would get someone to fill their place. Overturn did not think that this amounted to the provision of a substitute but he was no expert on this so would ask the appropriate officer in his district to look at the matter.

Raw materials and work in progress

Overturn asked various questions about the purchase and usage of raw materials and the finished goods. He suggested that the stock was undervalued and pointed to the Roddick materials as an example. Lee disagreed. Lee said he appreciated that he had not been told about the Roddick situation but pointed out that, notwithstanding that Greenman had extra storage space in the form of Unit D, there was nothing stored in it just now and that was probably indicative of the fact that Greenman did not need the space just yet for normal work. Therefore it was far more likely that whatever was stored in Unit E was the sum total of stock and work in progress. Greenman said this was the case. Because a lot of his work was in the manufacture of components of much larger jobs, and because he had not had much space in the past for storage anyway, he only bought in materials at the last minute and then shipped off the prefabricated items to the site as soon as possible when they were finished. Overturn asked if unbilled but finished work off site was included in the valuations. Lee said it was. He always asked that question. Overturn asked again about the Roddick work. It was ascertained that the work had been billed before the year-end.

Other matters

Overturn asked Greenman to describe the process of getting a job underway from the first telephone call to starting the manufacturing process. Greenman said that he first had to go and look at the site and discuss the specifications with the customer and measure up. Occasionally he had to get load bearing calculations done if the job involved storing heavy weights but most of the time he did these himself. He sometimes had to work from architect's plans. After this he then designed the fabrication by producing detailed engineering drawings. In answer to further questions, Overturn ascertained that Greenman kept a bound note book with detailed notes of discussions with his customers and his detailed measurements.

He said that he started doing this some years ago after having several disputes with customers about what they had asked for being different from what he had produced. Greenman produced all the engineering drawings at home. Greenman said he had a small shed in the garden which he used for this purpose. He had built it years ago. It was sited in such a position that he could get the north light, which was best for drawing in natural light. Overturn asked Lee what expense had been charged in the accounts for this office. Lee said Greenman had decided not to claim any — there was only a small amount of electricity for heat and light. Greenman confirmed this — he did not want the hassle of arguing how much.

Overturn asked if Lee saw this notebook when he did the accounts. Lee said he did not. He did not think it was necessary. Overturn asked if he could see the notebook. Greenman asked what for. Overturn said it would be a help in understanding the accounts. Greenman said it was at home. Overturn said that this was no problem, as he had to pass Greenman's house to get back to the office. He said he had more or less finished the interview and therefore asked Greenman if they could meet at his house so he could review the notebook. This was agreed.

The meeting then adjourned to Greenman's house. Overturn was shown to a prefabricated office building where he reviewed the notebook. Following discussion about various jobs, which Overturn ascertained had been properly reflected in the business accounts, Overturn noted that there was a large damp patch down one wall of the office. Overturn asked about this and was told that the roof had started leaking some time ago but it was OK now. Overturn asked about the cost of the repair. Greenman said he had done the repair himself using some of the roofing felt that had been left over from re-roofing Unit D.

Overturn then asked that since they were now at Mr Greenman's home would it be possible to see whether Mrs Greenman had kept any Tesco receipts so as to check on the cash position. Greenman then asked Mrs Greenman to find any old Tesco receipts. After about five minutes she returned with receipts covering the last six weeks. She said that she tended to collect them in her purse until it got full up then she would have a clear out. Overturn was able to ascertain that Mrs Greenman regularly got an extra £40 to £75 in cash from the checkout till when she paid for the main shopping. On this basis it was agreed between Lee and Overturn that they should discuss the matter of an add back for cash once Overturn had had a chance to review matters and contact Customs & Excise regarding the Rolex watch.

Greenman and Lee were thanked for their cooperation. It was agreed that Lee and Overturn would meet to discuss the various matters that had arisen from the interview.

The aftermath

14.18 When Overturn had gone Stan remarked that it had been a heavy meeting. Graham agreed. He said he did not know about 'Overturn' — he felt as though he had been turned over! Stan asked him why he had not told Overturn about his part interest in the racehorse. Graham said Overturn had not asked about it. Lee pointed out that Overturn had asked about Graham's hobbies. Graham said wryly — horse racing was not a hobby of his — it was a religion!

Overturn was very thoughtful on the way back to the office. He relished his work but never felt that he had ever done a really good job. He thought the Customs investigation would open the case up but he was sure Greenman was telling the truth when he said that his father had lent him the money. Still, he had got a good adjustment out of the Roddick Engineering work, and he thought he would get something out of the Unit D roofing conundrum. He would have to check that one in his instruction books. He would also get a cash adjustment out of it, so he felt reasonably happy.

It was several weeks later before Stan and Overturn met. The following matters were resolved.

Cash

14.19 Overturn said he was prepared to accept an add back of £4,000 to include money spent on entertaining expenditure that would not be allowable as an expense if it had been reflected in the books. He also pointed out that the position regarding the self-employed workers was unsatisfactory. He considered that they had received more than they would declare as taxable. Stan considered that the figure was far too high but he had to admit that Mr Greenman's record of cash transactions was inadequate. After some discussion, a figure of £2,750 was agreed. Overturn said that he probably should scale this back to earlier years but that might mean he would have to do a full investigation of those years. He did not want to do this as the other matters requiring adjustment were all in the year under review, but asked Stan to bear that in mind.

Overturn ensured that Stan understood this would be a contract settlement therefore there would be some penalty to pay on the tax.

The Roddick stock

14.20 As far as Overturn was concerned there should be an adjustment of £18,000 on the basis that he was denying the bad debt. There was no bad debt. Mr Greenman had effectively taken the goods back. Clearly Mr Greenman thought the stock was valuable to him because he had got it back and it had cost him at least £450 to do so.

Stan agreed it must have some value but there was clearly a loss here as well. What about the profit he had lost on the deal? After some discussion, Overturn suggested that the stock should be valued at £10,800 as there was a 25% mark up to knock off and a percentage reduction from that figure on the grounds that Greenman would have to find a buyer for it when he usually made to customer order. Stan disagreed. He said that Mr Greenman would be very lucky to find a buyer but he accepted that he could recycle most of the materials. On that basis, he suggested a value of £5,000. Further discussion took place after which Overturn agreed to accept a figure of £7,500 as the stock value. Overturn said that the total adjustment was therefore £15,000 being a reduction in the bad debt figure of £7,500 and an increase in end of year stock of £7,500. Stan said Overturn was incorrect.

He politely pointed out that there was no longer a bad debt because there was no longer a sale so gross sales had fallen on the one hand and the bad debt had disappeared on the other hand leaving the increase in stock value as the adjustment to profits. Overturn thought about this but could not accept it — a sale was a sale — so what Mr Greenman had to do was to reduce his claim against Roddicks from £18,000 to £10,500. He would accept a bad debt write off of £10,500 so increasing the adjusted profits by £7,500 and of course there was the increased stock figure. Stan again explained the bookkeeping to Overturn who reluctantly agreed that Stan was probably right.

Unit D roofing

14.21 Overturn said he had looked at his instruction books for guidance in this matter. Under *ICTA 1988, s 34(2)* the value of this work (not necessarily the cost price) was undoubtedly a premium on renting the Unit, but since the landlord would have got an allowance for the repair had he carried it out, then it was exempt to him, but the question was whether anything would be allowable to Greenman, and if so, how much.

Consequently, Overturn said, according to the instructions, they needed to estimate the increased value in the premises at the beginning of the lease of the landlord's interest in the reversion. For the purposes of finalising the matter Overturn said he wished to agree a figure now that would be allowable to Mr Greenman even though he would need the name of the landlord so that he could pass information to the appropriate tax district to negotiate with him and so the amount may be different once it had been agreed with the landlord.

As the cost was £9,500 and there would be up to ten years' wear and tear before the lease reverted to the landlord, he suggested that the value of the premium would be, say, £4,000.

Stan said he was not happy about this. As far as he was concerned the requirement to do roof repairs merely imposed an extra revenue cost on Mr Greenman so the whole of the expense was allowable. Stan said that had the roof been normal repair of an asset owned by Mr Greenman it would have been an allowable expense. After further discussion Overturn accepted this position.

Summary of adjustments

14.22 The following adjustments to the tax computation were finally agreed:

			£
1.	Unadjusted private expenditure		600
2.	Adjustment to private motoring proportion (including capital allowances adjusted)		650
3.	Adjustment for additional cash income		2,750
4.	Increase in end of year stock		7,500
		TOTAL	11,500

Penalty negotiations and settlement

14.23 Overturn considered that there should be a penalty of 30% of £4,600 (being the tax liability at 40%) on additional profits of £11,500. Stan asked how he had got to this figure. Overturn said that he had allowed the following amounts in mitigation:

1.	Quality of disclosure	5%	(maximum 20%)
2.	Cooperation	35%	(maximum 40%)
3.	Size and gravity	30%	(maximum 40%)

Overturn said he had allowed only 5% for disclosure because the only matters that had been brought to light before he commenced the detailed enquiry were the private mileage adjustment and the unadjusted private expense. He felt that Mr Greenman should have disclosed the cash problem and as far as he was concerned the Roddick stock had been hidden from Stan Lee.

As regards cooperation he had had to issue a *TMA 1970, s 19A* notice and Lee had still been late in complying with that. Stan took issue here. He had not been late — he had provided the information within ten days leaving 20 days still to go on the notice. Overturn conceded this but said he still had to wait a long time for the information. Stan pressed home this point. He said he had carried out a 'time audit' on this case and by coincidence both he and Overturn had taken exactly the same number of days to deal with issues when the ball was in their court as the other one. On that basis he felt that Overturn should call it quits and give the full mitigation. On reflection Overturn agreed to this.

On size and gravity Overturn said the amounts involved were quite high but the roof repair matter was one that he accepted was a one off and, for that matter, so was the bad debt issue, except that in his opinion Mr Greenman had clearly hidden this from Lee.

Stan said he was not prepared to comment either way on that matter but in the order of things he thought Overturn was being harsh. After some discussion, Overturn agreed that the mitigation for size and gravity should be 32.5% so long as Mr Greenman agreed to pay the settlement figure within 30 days of the issue of the letter of acceptance. This was agreed and therefore, overall, the penalty would be 22.5%, i.e. £1,035.

Interest on the outstanding tax came to £368 so the offer figure came to £6,003. Overturn therefore suggested a 'rounding up' to £6,050. Stan thought there should be a 'rounding down' to £6,000. He asked Overturn to recommend a figure of £6,000. Overturn said that Stan had finally ground him down so he agreed to this so long as he could get the offer cheque with the offer, although this would have to be treated as a payment on account until the offer was accepted.

The offer with the cheque payment was made formally and accepted several weeks later.

A couple of weeks after Overturn had forgotten the case and was getting to grips with the next one, his telephone rang. It was the PAYE auditor in the district. He had finally got round to doing an audit on the roofing company. They had simply left him and his assistant in the board room with instructions to the wages clerk to give them anything they wanted so they had asked for the sales invoices. He had tracked down the one for the roofing work done for G G Frames. Sure enough the description on the copy invoice did not tally with the invoice Overturn had given him. In fact two jobs had been described on the roofing company's invoice. Some work had been done at Greenman's industrial unit but there had also been £3,000 for re-roofing some stables at somewhere called 'The Paddocks'. Overturn thanked him for the information, smiled to himself, and looked up the telephone number for Special Compliance Office. . .

Appendix A – Self-Assessment Forms

GRAHAM GREENMAN T/A G G FRAMES ACCOUNTS FOR Y.E. 30 SEPTEMBER 2000

Trading, Profit & Loss Accounts				Balance Sheet			
sales		629628		Fixed assets			
op. stk/wip	34390			P&M		32097	
carriage	6361			Motor		13044	45141
sub contract	22608						
direct wages	42076			Current Assets			
materials	409339			stock & wip		35309	
	514774			Trade debtors		43640	
cl.stk/wip	35309	479465		prepayments		3675	
		150163		Business resrve accoı		4313	
bank int rec		270		High Interest			
		150433		business account		6752	
bookkeeper	3290			Bank account		21807	
telephone	905			Cash in hand		327	
postage etc	379					115823	
advt	2033			Current liabilities			
motor	6288			VAT		2365	
repairs	17176			trade creditors		39659	
entertaining	1759			Bank Loan		12678	
sundry	451			Accrued expenses		1544	
legal & professional	6470					56246	
bad debts	18000						104718
rent	9200						
rates	1668						
ins	2600			Financed by			
motor ins	380						
light heat	2209	72808		Capital account			
		77625					
				Balance brot fwd		94078	
Bank loan int	254						
bank charges	1319	1573		Net Profit		52050	
		76052				146128	
Deprn				Drawings		41410	104718
PI & M	18574						
Motor	4348	22922			Capital allowances		
		53130		Plant & Machinery			
loss on motor		1080		w.d.v. brot fwd		49241	
Net Profit		52050		w.d.a. this year 25%		12355	12355
				w.d.v to carry fwd.		36886	

Tangible fixed asset schedule

	P&M	Motor	Total	Car #2			
at 1 Oct 99	74295	17600	91895	cost		17392	
addns		17392	17392	max w.d.a.		3000	
disposals		-17600	-17600	w.d.a. net of 15% pte.			2550
at 30 Sep 2000	74295	17392	91687	w.d.v to carry fwd.		14392	
Depn				Car #1			
at 1 Oct 99	23624	4400	28024	w.d.v. brot fwd		14600	
charge for year	18574	4348	22922	sold for		12120	
eliminated on disposals	0	-4400	-4400	balancing allowance		2480	
	42198	4348	46546	less 15% pte use		-372	
				net balancing allowance			2108
Net Book Value							
at 30 Sep 2000	32097	13044	45141	Total capital allowances			17013

224

	for the year ended
Tax Return	**5 April 2001**

UTR
Tax reference
Employer reference

Date 6/4/2001

Inland Revenue office address

Officer in Charge

MERRY HILL 2
CAPSTAN HOUSE
THE WATERFRONT
BRIERLEY HILL
WEST MIDLANDS DY5 1YA

Issue address

MR G GREENMAN
THE PADDOCKS
BLACKSMITH'S GREEN
BOLTINGTON
WEST MIDLANDS

Telephone

For
Reference

 Please read this page first

The green arrows and instructions will guide you through your Tax Return.

This Notice requires you by law to send me a Tax Return for the year from 6 April 2000 to 5 April 2001. Give details of all your income and capital gains using:

- this form and any supplementary Pages you need, **OR**
- other Inland Revenue approved forms, **OR**
- our Self Assessment (SA) by Internet Service, **OR**
- our Electronic Lodgement Service (ELS).

Make sure your Tax Return, and any documents I ask for, reach me by:

- the later of **30 September 2001** and **2 months after the date this notice was given** if you want me to calculate your tax, **OR**
- the later of **31 January 2002** and **3 months after the date this notice was given, at the latest**, or you will be liable to an automatic penalty of £100.

Make sure your payment of any tax you owe reaches me by 31 January 2002, or you will have to pay interest and perhaps a surcharge.

Any Tax Return may be checked. Please remember that there are penalties for supplying false information.

Your Tax Return

I have sent you pages 1 to 8 of your Tax Return:

- page 2 tells you about supplementary Pages for some types of income and gains. For example, there are Pages for employment, and for self-employment income
- pages 3 and 4 are for details of other income, for example, pensions and savings
- page 5 is for claiming reliefs
- page 6 is for claiming allowances
- pages 7 and 8 are for other information.

I have included any supplementary Pages I think you need after page 8. You are responsible for making sure you have the right ones. Use page 2 to check.

Also, unless I know you have a tax adviser, I have sent you:

- a Tax Return Guide to help you fill in your Tax Return (read pages 2 to 5 of the Guide before you start), and
- a Tax Calculation Guide to help you if you are calculating your own tax.

If you do want them, call our Orderline or download them from our website; see Step 1 on page 2 for details.

If you need help:

- refer to the Tax Return Guide, **OR**
- ring the number above - most questions can be answered by telephone, **OR**
- when the office is closed, phone our Helpline on 0845 9000 444 for general advice, **OR**
- if you do not want to explain your question on the phone, call in at an Inland Revenue Enquiry Centre - look under 'Inland Revenue' in the phone book.

SA100

TAX RETURN: PAGE 1

Please turn over

App A *Self-Assessment Forms*

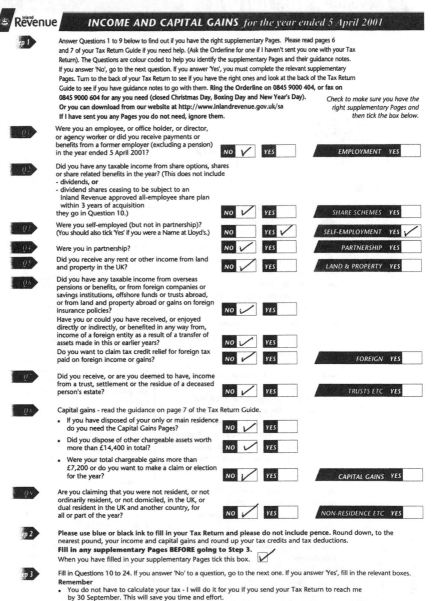

INCOME AND CAPITAL GAINS *for the year ended 5 April 2001*

Step 1

Answer Questions 1 to 9 below to find out if you have the right supplementary Pages. Please read pages 6 and 7 of your Tax Return Guide if you need help. (Ask the Orderline for one if I haven't sent you one with your Tax Return). The Questions are colour coded to help you identify the supplementary Pages and their guidance notes. If you answer 'No', go to the next question. If you answer 'Yes', you must complete the relevant supplementary Pages. Turn to the back of your Tax Return to see if you have the right ones and look at the back of the Tax Return Guide to see if you have guidance notes to go with them. **Ring the Orderline on 0845 9000 404, or fax on 0845 9000 604 for any you need** (closed Christmas Day, Boxing Day and New Year's Day). **Or you can download from our website at http://www.inlandrevenue.gov.uk/sa** If I have sent you any Pages you do not need, ignore them.

Check to make sure you have the right supplementary Pages and then tick the box below.

Q1 Were you an employee, or office holder, or director, or agency worker or did you receive payments or benefits from a former employer (excluding a pension) in the year ended 5 April 2001?   NO ✓   YES ☐   EMPLOYMENT YES ☐

Q2 Did you have any taxable income from share options, shares or share related benefits in the year? (This does not include
- dividends, **or**
- dividend shares ceasing to be subject to an Inland Revenue approved all-employee share plan within 3 years of acquisition they go in Question 10.)   NO ✓   YES ☐   SHARE SCHEMES YES ☐

Q3 Were you self-employed (but not in partnership)? (You should also tick 'Yes' if you were a Name at Lloyd's.)   NO ☐   YES ✓   SELF-EMPLOYMENT YES ✓

Q4 Were you in partnership?   NO ✓   YES ☐   PARTNERSHIP YES ☐

Q5 Did you receive any rent or other income from land and property in the UK?   NO ✓   YES ☐   LAND & PROPERTY YES ☐

Q6 Did you have any taxable income from overseas pensions or benefits, or from foreign companies or savings institutions, offshore funds or trusts abroad, or from land and property abroad or gains on foreign insurance policies?   NO ✓   YES ☐

Have you or could you have received, or enjoyed directly or indirectly, or benefited in any way from, income of a foreign entity as a result of a transfer of assets made in this or earlier years?   NO ✓   YES ☐

Do you want to claim tax credit relief for foreign tax paid on foreign income or gains?   NO ✓   YES ☐   FOREIGN YES ☐

Q7 Did you receive, or are you deemed to have, income from a trust, settlement or the residue of a deceased person's estate?   NO ✓   YES ☐   TRUSTS ETC YES ☐

Q8 Capital gains - read the guidance on page 7 of the Tax Return Guide.
- If you have disposed of your only or main residence do you need the Capital Gains Pages?   NO ✓   YES ☐
- Did you dispose of other chargeable assets worth more than £14,400 in total?   NO ✓   YES ☐
- Were your total chargeable gains more than £7,200 or do you want to make a claim or election for the year?   NO ✓   YES ☐   CAPITAL GAINS YES ☐

Q9 Are you claiming that you were not resident, or not ordinarily resident, or not domiciled, in the UK, or dual resident in the UK and another country, for all or part of the year?   NO ✓   YES ☐   NON-RESIDENCE ETC YES ☐

Step 2

Please use blue or black ink to fill in your Tax Return and please do not include pence. Round down, to the nearest pound, your income and capital gains and round up your tax credits and tax deductions.
Fill in any supplementary Pages BEFORE going to Step 3.
When you have filled in your supplementary Pages tick this box. ✓

Step 3

Fill in Questions 10 to 24. If you answer 'No' to a question, go to the next one. If you answer 'Yes', fill in the relevant boxes.
Remember
- You do not have to calculate your tax - I will do it for you if you send your Tax Return to reach me by 30 September. This will save you time and effort.
- The Tax Calculation Guide will help you if you decide to calculate the tax yourself.
- You do not have to wait until 30 September 2001, or 31 January 2002, to send me your Tax Return.

INCOME *for the year ended 5 April 2001*

Q 10 ▶ **Did you receive any income from UK savings and investments?** NO ☐ YES ✓ | If yes, fill in boxes 10.1 to 10.26 as appropriate. Include only your share from any joint savings and investments.

■ *Interest*

● Interest from UK banks, building societies and deposit takers

- where **no tax** has been deducted

Taxable amount

10.1 £ ☐

	Amount **after** tax deducted	Tax deducted	Gross amount **before** tax
- where **tax has** been deducted	**10.2** £ 168	**10.3** £ 42	**10.4** £ 210

● Interest distributions from UK authorised unit trusts and open-ended investment companies (dividend distributions go below)

Amount after tax deducted	Tax deducted	Gross amount before tax
10.5 £	**10.6** £	**10.7** £

● National Savings (other than FIRST Option Bonds and Fixed Rate Savings Bonds and the first £70 of interest from a National Savings Ordinary Account)

Taxable amount

10.8 £

● National Savings FIRST Option and Fixed Rate Savings Bonds

Amount after tax deducted	Tax deducted	Gross amount before tax
10.9 £	**10.10** £	**10.11** £

● Other income from UK savings and investments (except dividends)

Amount after tax deducted	Tax deducted	Gross amount before tax
10.12 £	**10.13** £	**10.14** £

■ *Dividends*

● Dividends and other qualifying distributions from UK companies

Dividend/distribution	Tax credit	Dividend/distribution plus credit
10.15 £	**10.16** £	**10.17** £

● Dividend distributions from UK authorised unit trusts and open-ended investment companies

Dividend/distribution	Tax credit	Dividend/distribution plus credit
10.18 £	**10.19** £	**10.20** £

● Scrip dividends from UK companies

Dividend	Notional tax	Dividend plus notional tax
10.21 £	**10.22** £	**10.23** £

● Non-qualifying distributions and loans written off

	Notional tax	Taxable amount
10.24 £	**10.25** £	**10.26** £

App A   *Self-Assessment Forms*

INCOME *for the year ended 5 April 2001, continued*

Q11 **Did you receive a taxable UK pension, retirement annuity or Social Security benefit?**
Read the notes on pages 12 to 14 of the Tax Return Guide.

NO ✓   YES

If yes, fill in boxes 11.1 to 11.13 as appropriate.

■ *State pensions and benefits*

Taxable amount for 2000-2001

- State Retirement Pension *(enter the **total** of your entitlements for the year)*   **11.1** £

- Widow's Pension   **11.2** £

- Widowed Mother's Allowance   **11.3** £

- Industrial Death Benefit Pension   **11.4** £

- Jobseeker's Allowance   **11.5** £

- Invalid Care Allowance   **11.6** £

- Statutory Sick Pay and Statutory Maternity Pay paid by the Department of Social Security   **11.7** £

	Tax deducted	Gross amount before tax
• Taxable Incapacity Benefit	**11.8** £	**11.9** £

■ *Other pensions and retirement annuities*

	Amount after tax deducted	Tax deducted	Gross amount before tax
• Pensions (other than State pensions) and retirement annuities	**11.10** £	**11.11** £	**11.12** £

- Deduction
  - see the note for box 11.13 on page 14 of your Tax Return Guide

Amount of deduction

11.13 £

Q12 **Did you receive any gains on UK life policies or refunds of surplus funds from AVCs?**

NO ✓   YES

If yes, fill in boxes 12.1 to 12.12 as appropriate.

	Number of years		Amount of gain(s)
• Gains on UK annuities and friendly societies' life insurance policies where no tax is treated as paid	**12.1**		**12.2** £

	Number of years	Tax treated as paid	Amount of gain(s)
• Gains on UK life insurance policies etc. on which tax is treated as paid - *read pages 14 and 15 of the Tax Return Guide*	**12.3**	**12.4** £	**12.5** £

	Number of years	Tax deducted	Amount of gain(s)
• Gains on life insurance policies in ISAs that have been made void	**12.6**	**12.7** £	**12.8** £

Amount

• Corresponding deficiency relief   **12.9** £

	Amount received	Notional tax	Amount plus notional tax
• Refunds of surplus funds from additional voluntary contributions	**12.10** £	**12.11** £	**12.12** £

Q13 **Did you receive any other taxable income which you have not already entered elsewhere in your Tax Return?**
Make sure you fill in any supplementary Pages before answering Question 13.

NO ✓   YES

If yes, fill in boxes 13.1 to 13.6 as appropriate.

	Amount after tax deducted	Tax deducted	Amount before tax
• Other taxable income *(read page 17 of your Tax Return Guide if you made losses)*	**13.1** £	**13.2** £	**13.3** £

Losses brought forward	Earlier years' losses used in 2000-2001
13.4 £	**13.5** £

2000-2001 losses carried forward

13.6 £

RELIEFS *for the year ended 5 April 2001*

Q 14 **Do you want to claim relief for pension contributions?**
Do not include contributions deducted from your pay by your employer to their pension scheme or associated AVC scheme, because tax relief is given automatically. But do include your contributions to personal pension schemes and Free-Standing AVC schemes.

NO ✓   YES

If yes, fill in boxes 14.1 to 14.17 as appropriate.

■ *Retirement annuity contracts*

Qualifying payments made in 2000-2001 **14.1** £	2000-2001 payments used in an earlier year **14.2** £	Relief claimed box 14.1 *minus* (boxes 14.2 and 14.3, but not 14.4)
2000-2001 payments now to be carried back **14.3** £	Payments brought back from 2001-2002 **14.4** £	**14.5** £

■ *Self-employed contributions to personal pension plans*

Qualifying payments made in 2000-2001 **14.6** £	2000-2001 payments used in an earlier year **14.7** £	Relief claimed box 14.6 *minus* (boxes 14.7 and 14.8, but not 14.9)
2000-2001 payments now to be carried back **14.8** £	Payments brought back from 2001-2002 **14.9** £	**14.10** £

■ *Employee contributions to personal pension plans* (include your gross contribution - see the note on box 14.11 in your Tax Return Guide)

Qualifying payments made in 2000-2001 **14.11** £	2000-2001 payments used in an earlier year **14.12** £	Relief claimed box 14.11 *minus* (boxes 14.12 and 14.13, but not 14.14)
2000-2001 payments now to be carried back **14.13** £	Payments brought back from 2001-2002 **14.14** £	**14.15** £

■ *Contributions to other pension schemes and Free-Standing AVC schemes*

● Amount of contributions to employer's schemes **not deducted** at source from pay   **14.16** £

● Gross amount of Free-Standing Additional Voluntary Contributions paid in 2000-2001   **14.17** £

Q 15 **Do you want to claim any of the following reliefs?**
If you have made any Gift Aid payments or other annual payments, after basic rate tax, answer 'Yes' to Question 15 and fill in boxes 15.6 and 15.9, as appropriate.

NO ✓   YES

If yes, fill in boxes 15.1 to 15.12, as appropriate.

● Payments you made to a non-UK training provider for NVQ/SVQ training undertaken outside the UK (read the box 15.1 note on page 20 of your Tax Return Guide)
Amount of payment **15.1** £

● Interest eligible for relief on qualifying loans
Amount of payment **15.2** £

● Maintenance or alimony payments you have made under a court order, Child Support Agency assessment or legally binding order or agreement (see page 21 of your Tax Return Guide)
Amount claimed up to £2,000 **15.3** £

● Subscriptions for Venture Capital Trust shares (up to £100,000)
Amount on which relief is claimed **15.4** £

● Subscriptions under the Enterprise Investment Scheme (up to £150,000)
Amount on which relief is claimed **15.5** £

● Gift Aid and payments under charitable covenants
Amount on which relief is claimed **15.6** £

● Gifts of qualifying investments to charities
Amount of relief claimed **15.7** £

● Post-cessation expenses, pre-incorporation losses brought forward and losses on relevant discounted securities, etc. (see page 22 of your Tax Return Guide)
Amount of payment **15.8** £

● Annuities
Amount on which relief is claimed **15.9** £

● Payments to a trade union or friendly society for death benefits
Half amount of payment **15.10** £

● Payment to your employer's compulsory widow's, widower's or orphan's benefit scheme (available in some circumstances – first read the notes on page 23 of your Tax Return Guide)
Relief claimed **15.11** £

● Relief claimed on a qualifying distribution on the **redemption** of bonus shares or securities.
Relief claimed **15.12** £

ALLOWANCES *for the year ended 5 April 2001*

Q 16 You get your personal allowance of £4,385 automatically. **If you were born before 6 April 1936, enter your date of birth in box 22.6** - you may get a higher age-related personal allowance.

Do you want to claim any of the following allowances?

NO ✓   YES

If yes, please read pages 23 to 25 of your Tax Return Guide and then fill in boxes 16.1 to 16.18 as appropriate.

Date of registration (if first year of claim)

Local authority (or other register)

■ *Blind person's allowance*   16.1 / /   16.2

■ *Married couple's allowance* - *In 2000-2001 married couple's allowance can only be claimed if either you, or your husband or wife, were born before 6 April 1935. So you can only claim the allowance in 2000-2001 if either of you had reached 65 years of age before 6 April 2000. Further guidance is given beginning on page 23 of your Tax Return Guide.*

If **both** you and your husband or wife were born after 5 April 1935 you cannot claim; **do not** complete boxes 16.3 to 16.13.

If you can claim fill in boxes 16.3 and 16.4 if you are a married man or if you are a married woman and you are claiming half or all of the married couple's allowance.

- Enter your date of birth (if born before 6 April 1935)   16.3 / /

- Enter your spouse's date of birth (**if** born before 6 April 1935 **and** if older than you)   16.4 / /

Then, if you are a married man fill in boxes 16.5 to 16.9. If you are a married woman fill in boxes 16.10 to 16.13.

. . . .

- Wife's full name   16.5
  - Date of marriage (if after 5 April 2000)   16.6 / /

- Tick box 16.7 if you or your wife have allocated half the allowance to her   16.7

- Tick box 16.8 if you and your wife have allocated all the allowance to her   16.8

- Enter in box 16.9 the date of birth of any previous wife with whom you lived at any time during 2000-2001. *Read 'Special rules if you are a man who married in the year ended 5 April 2001' on page 25 before completing box 16.9.*   16.9 / /

. . . .

- Tick box 16.10 if you or your husband have allocated half the allowance to you   16.10

- Tick box 16.11 if you and your husband have allocated all the allowance to you   16.11

- Husband's full name   16.12
  - Date of marriage (if after 5 April 2000)   16.13 / /

■ *Widow's bereavement allowance* - *see page 25 of your Tax Return Guide before completing box 16.14.*

- Date of your husband's death   16.14 / /

■ *Transfer of surplus allowances* - *see page 25 of your Tax Return Guide before you fill in boxes 16.15 to 16.18.*

- Tick box 16.15 if you want your spouse to have your unused allowances   16.15

- Tick box 16.16 if you want to have your spouse's unused allowances   16.16

Please give details in the 'Additional information' box, box 23.6, on page 8 - see page 25 of your Tax Return Guide for what is needed.

If you want to calculate your tax, enter the amount of the surplus allowance you can have.

- Blind person's **surplus** allowance   16.17 £

- Married couple's **surplus** allowance   16.18 £

Q17 **Are you liable to make Student Loan Repayments for 2000-2001 on an Income Contingent Student Loan?** *Read the note on page 25 of your Tax Return Guide.*

NO ✓   YES

If yes, and you are calculating your tax enter in box 18.2A the amount you work out is repayable in 2000-2001.

OTHER INFORMATION *for the year ended 5 April 2001*

Q 18 **Do you want to calculate your tax and any Student Loan Repayment?**   NO ✓   YES   *If yes, do it now and then fill in boxes 18.1 to 18.8. Your Tax Calculation Guide will help.*

- Unpaid tax for earlier years **included in your tax code for 2000-2001**   18.1 £
- Tax due for 2000-2001 included in your tax code for a later year   18.2 £
- Student Loan Repayment due   18.2A £
- Total tax, Class 4 NIC and Student Loan Repayment due for 2000-2001 **before** you made any payments on account *(put the amount in brackets if an overpayment)*   18.3 £
- Tax due for earlier years   18.4 £
- Tick box 18.5 if you have calculated tax overpaid for earlier years and enter the amount in the 'Additional information' box, box 23.6 on page 8.   18.5
- Your first payment on account for 2001-2002 *(include the pence)*   18.6 £
  Tick box 18.7 if you are making a claim to reduce your 2001-2002 payments on account and say why in the 'Additional information' box, box 23.6, on page 8   18.7
- Tick box 18.8 if you are reclaiming any 2001-2002 tax now and enter the amount in the 'Additional information' box, box 23.6 on page 8.   18.8

Q 19 **Do you want to claim a repayment if you have paid too much tax?** *(If you tick 'No' or the tax you have overpaid is below £10, I will use the amount you are owed to reduce your next tax bill.)*   NO   YES ✓   *If yes, fill in boxes 19.1A to 19.12 as appropriate.*

Should the repayment be sent:
- direct to your bank or building society account?
  Tick box 19.1A and fill in boxes 19.3 to 19.7   19.1A
- by cheque to you at your home address?
  Tick box 19.1B   19.1B ✓
or
- to a nominee? *Tick box 19.2, fill in boxes 19.3 to 19.11, as appropriate, and box 19.12*   19.2

Fill in boxes 19.3 to 19.7 if the repayment is to be sent to your own, or your nominees' bank or building society account

Name of bank or building society   19.3

Branch sort code   19.4   –   –

Account number   19.5

Name of account holder   19.6

Building society ref.   19.7

- If your nominee is your agent, *tick box 19.8*   19.8

Agent's reference for you (if your nominee is your agent)   19.9

Name of your nominee/agent

I authorise   19.10

Nominee/ agent address   19.11

Postcode

to receive on my behalf the amount due

This authority must be signed by you. A photocopy of your signature will not do.   19.12

Signature

Q 20 **Have you already had any 2000-2001 tax refunded or set off by your Inland Revenue office or the Benefits Agency (in Northern Ireland, the Social Security Agency)?** *Read the notes on page 26 of your Tax Return Guide*   NO ✓   YES   *If yes, enter the amount of the refund in box 20.1.*

20.1 £

Q 21 **Are your name or address on the front of the Tax Return wrong?**   NO ✓   YES   *If yes, please make any corrections on the front of the form.*

Q 22 **Please give other personal details in boxes 22.1 to 22.7.** *This information helps us to be more efficient and effective and may support claims you have made elsewhere in your Tax Return*

Please give a daytime telephone number if convenient. It is often simpler to phone if we need to ask you about your Tax Return.

Your telephone number   22.1 RING STAN LEE

or, if you prefer, your agent's telephone number   22.2

and their name and address   22.3

Postcode

Enter your first two forenames   22.4 GRAHAM

Say if you are single, married, widowed, divorced or separated   22.5 MARRIED

Enter your date of birth   22.6 20/09/46

Enter your National Insurance number (if known)   22.7 YH 8 7 0 4 6 8 Q2

OTHER INFORMATION *for the year ended 5 April 2001, continued*

> *Q 23* Please tick boxes 23.1 to 23.5 if they apply. Provide any additional information in box 23.6 below.

Tick box 23.1 if you expect to receive a new pension or new Social Security benefit in 2001-2002.

`23.1`

Tick box 23.2 if you do **not** want any tax you owe for 2000-2001 collected through your tax code.

`23.2`

Tick box 23.3 if this Tax Return contains figures that are provisional because you do not yet have final figures. Page 26 of your Tax Return Guide explains the circumstances in which Tax Returns containing provisional figures may be accepted and tells you what you must enter in box 23.6 below.

`23.3`

Tick box 23.4 if you are claiming relief now for 2001-2002 trading, or certain capital, losses. Enter in box 23.6 the amount and year.

`23.4`

Tick box 23.5 if you are claiming:

- to have post-cessation or other business receipts taxed as income of an earlier year. Enter in box 23.6 the amount and year
- backwards or forwards spreading of literary or artistic income. Enter in box 23.6 details of any amounts spread back to last year and, if appropriate, the year before.

`23.5`

23.6 *Additional information*

> *Q 24* **Declaration**

I have filled in and am sending back to you the following pages:

	Tick			Tick			Tick
1 TO 8 OF THIS FORM	✓						
EMPLOYMENT		PARTNERSHIP			TRUSTS, ETC		
SHARE SCHEMES		LAND & PROPERTY			CAPITAL GAINS		
SELF-EMPLOYMENT	✓	FOREIGN			NON-RESIDENCE, ETC		

➤ Before you send your completed Tax Return back to your Inland Revenue office, you must sign the statement below. If you give false information or conceal any part of your income or chargeable gains, you may be liable to financial penalties and/or you may be prosecuted.

24.1 The information I have given in this Tax Return is correct and complete to the best of my knowledge and belief.

Graham Greenman

Signature   Date 25/1/2002

If you are signing for someone else please read the notes on page 27 of the Tax Return Guide, and:

- state the capacity in which you are signing (for example, as executor or receiver)

`24.2`

- give the name of the person you are signing for and **your** name and address in box 23.6 above.

Income for the year ended 5 April 2001

Inland **Revenue**

SELF-EMPLOYMENT

Name

Fill in these boxes first

GRAHAM GREENMAN

Tax reference

693/049458

If you want help, look up the box numbers in the Notes

Business details

Name of business

3.1 G G FRAMES

Description of business

3.2

Address of business

3.3 UNIT E
BLACKBRIDGE INDUSTRIAL ESTATE
DIBDALE LANE
LOWER GONNAL
WEST MIDLANDS Postcode

Accounting period - read the Notes, page SEN2 before filling in these boxes

Start 3.4 01/10/99

End 3.5 30/09/00

- Tick box 3.6 if details in boxes 3.1 or 3.3 have changed since your last Tax Return **3.6**

- Date of commencement if after 5 April 1998 **3.7** / /

- Date of cessation if before 6 April 2001 **3.8** / /

- Tick box 3.9 if the special arrangements for certain trades apply - *read the Notes, pages SEN10 and SEN11* **3.9**

- Tick box 3.10 if you entered details for all relevant accounting periods on last year's Tax Return and boxes 3.14 to 3.73 and 3.99 to 3.115 will be blank *(read Step 3 on page SEN2)* **3.10**

- Tick box 3.11 if your accounts do not cover the period from the last accounting date (explain why in the 'Additional information' box, box 3.116) **3.11**

- Tick box 3.12 if your accounting date has changed (only if this is a permanent change and you want it to count for tax) **3.12**

- Tick box 3.13 if this is the second or further change (explain in box 3.116 on Page SE4 why you have not used the same date as last year) **3.13**

Capital allowances - summary

	Capital allowances	Balancing charges
- Cars (Separate calculations must be made for each car costing more than £12,000 and for cars used partly for private motoring.)	3.14 £4658	3.15 £
- Other business plant and machinery	3.16 £12355	3.17 £
- Agricultural or Industrial Buildings Allowance (A separate calculation must be made for each block of expenditure.)	3.18 £	3.19 £
- Other capital allowances claimed (Separate calculations must be made.)	3.20 £	3.21 £
	total of column above	total of column above
Total capital allowances/balancing charges	3.22 £17013	3.23 £

Income and expenses - annual turnover below £15,000

*If your annual turnover is £15,000 or more, **ignore** boxes 3.24 to 3.26. Instead fill in Page SE2*

*If your annual turnover is below £15,000, **fill in** boxes 3.24 to 3.26 instead of Page SE2. Read the Notes, page SEN2.*

- Turnover, other business receipts and goods etc. taken for personal use (and balancing charges from box 3.23) **3.24** £

- Expenses allowable for tax (including capital allowances from box 3.22) **3.25** £

box 3.24 minus box 3.25

Net profit (put figure in brackets if a loss) **3.26** £

You must now fill in Page SE3

SA103

BMSD 12/2000net

TAX RETURN ▦ SELF-EMPLOYMENT: PAGE SE1

App A *Self-Assessment Forms*

You must fill in this Page if your annual turnover is £15,000 or more - read the Notes, page SEN2

If you were registered for VAT, do the figures in boxes 3.29 to 3.64, include VAT? **3.27** ☐ or exclude VAT? **3.28** ✓

Sales/business income (turnover)

3.29 £ 629628

Disallowable expenses included in boxes 3.46 to 3.63

Total expenses

- Cost of sales — **3.30** £ — **3.46** £ 408420
- Construction industry subcontractor costs — **3.31** £ — **3.47** £
- Other direct costs — **3.32** £ — **3.48** £ 71045

box 3.29 minus (boxes 3.46 + 3.47 + 3.48)

Gross profit/(loss) **3.49** £ 150163

Other income/profits **3.50** £ 270

- Employee costs — **3.33** £ — **3.51** £ 3290
- Premises costs — **3.34** £ — **3.52** £ 15677
- Repairs — **3.35** £ — **3.53** £ 17176
- General administrative expenses — **3.36** £ — **3.54** £ 1735
- Motor expenses — **3.37** £ 1000 — **3.55** £ 6668
- Travel and subsistence — **3.38** £ — **3.56** £ ⟋
- Advertising, promotion and entertainment — **3.39** £ 1759 — **3.57** £ 3792
- Legal and professional costs — **3.40** £ — **3.58** £ 6470
- Bad debts — **3.41** £ — **3.59** £ 18000
- Interest — **3.42** £ — **3.60** £ 254
- Other finance charges — **3.43** £ — **3.61** £ 1319
- Depreciation and loss/(profit) on sale — **3.44** £ 24002 — **3.62** £ 24002
- Other expenses — **3.45** £ — **3.63** £

Put the total of boxes 3.30 to 3.45 in **box 3.66 below**

Total expenses

total of boxes 3.51 to 3.63

3.64 £ 98383

boxes 3.49 + 3.50 minus 3.64

Net profit/(loss) **3.65** £ 52050

boxes 3.30 to 3.45

- Disallowable expenses — **3.66** £ 26761
- Goods etc. taken for personal use and other adjustments (apart from disallowable expenses) that increase profits — **3.67** £
- Balancing charges (from box 3.23) — **3.68** £

boxes 3.66 + 3.67 + 3.68

Total additions to net profit (deduct from net loss) **3.69** £ 26761

- Capital allowances (from box 3.22) — **3.70** £ 17013
- Deductions from net profit (add to net loss) — **3.71** £ 270

boxes 3.70 + 3.71

3.72 £ 17283

boxes 3.65 + 3.69 minus 3.72

Net business profit for tax purposes (put figure in brackets if a loss) **3.73** £ 61528

BMSD 12/2000net   TAX RETURN ▣ SELF-EMPLOYMENT: PAGE SE2   *Now fill in Page SE3* ▶

234

▶ You **must** fill in boxes 3.74 and 3.75 and **all other boxes** that apply to you, on this Page

Adjustments to arrive at taxable profit or loss

Basis period begins **3.74** 01/10/99 and ends **3.75** 30/09/00

Profit or loss of this account for tax purposes (box 3.26 or 3.73) **3.76** £ 61528

Adjustment to arrive at profit or loss for this basis period **3.77** £

- Overlap profit brought forward **3.78** £ 18766 • Deduct overlap relief used this year **3.79** £

- Overlap profit carried forward **3.80** £ 18766

Adjustment for farmers' averaging (*see Notes, page SEN8, if you made a loss for 2000-2001*) **3.81** £

Adjustment on change of basis **3.82** £

Net profit for 2000-2001 (if you made a loss, enter '0') **3.83** £ 61528

Allowable loss for 2000-2001 (if you made a profit, enter '0') **3.84** £

- Loss offset against other income for 2000-2001 **3.85** £

- Loss to carry back **3.86** £

- Loss to carry forward
  (that is allowable loss not claimed in any other way) **3.87** £

- Losses brought forward from earlier years **3.88** £

- Losses brought forward from earlier years used this year **3.89** £

box 3.83 *minus* box 3.89
Taxable profit after losses brought forward **3.90** £ 61528

- Any other business income (for example, Business Start-up Allowance received in 2000-2001) **3.91** £

box 3.90 + box 3.91
Total taxable profits from this business **3.92** £ 61528

- Tick box 3.93 if the figure in box 3.92 is provisional **3.93**

Class 4 National Insurance contributions

- Tick box 3.94 if exception or deferment applies **3.94**

- Adjustments to profit chargeable to Class 4 National Insurance contributions **3.95** £

Class 4 National Insurance contributions due **3.96** £ 1108.20

Subcontractors in the construction industry

- Deductions made by contractors on account of tax (you must send your CIS25s to us) **3.97** £

Tax deducted from trading income

- Any tax deducted (excluding deductions made by contractors on account of tax) from trading income **3.98** £

App A *Self-Assessment Forms*

Summary of balance sheet

> *Leave these boxes blank if you do not have a balance sheet*

Assets
- Plant, machinery and motor vehicles — 3.99 £ 45141
- Other fixed assets (premises, goodwill, investments etc.) — 3.100 £
- Stock and work-in-progress — 3.101 £ 35309
- Debtors/prepayments/other current assets — 3.102 £ 47315
- Bank/building society balances — 3.103 £ 32872
- Cash in hand — 3.104 £ 327

total of boxes 3.99 to 3.104
3.105 £160964

Liabilities
- Trade creditors/accruals — 3.106 £41203
- Loans and overdrawn bank accounts — 3.107 £12678
- Other liabilities — 3.108 £ 2365

total of boxes 3.106 to 3.108
3.109 £56246

Net business assets (put the figure in brackets if you had net business liabilities)

box 3.105 minus 3.109
3.110 £104718

Represented by

Capital Account
- Balance at start of period* — 3.111 £94078
- Net profit/(loss)* — 3.112 £52050
- Capital introduced — 3.113 £
- Drawings — 3.114 £41410

total of boxes 3.111 to 3.113
minus box 3.114
3.115 £104718

- Balance at end of period*

*If the Capital Account is overdrawn, or the business made a net loss, enter the figure in brackets.

3.116 | *Additional information*

Now fill in any other supplementary Pages that apply to you.
Otherwise, go back to Page 2 of your Tax Return and finish filling it in.

IR Code of Practice 11

Enquiries into tax returns by local Tax Offices

This Code of Practice tells you how our local Tax Offices will carry out enquiries into Self Assessment tax returns issued from April 1997 onwards. There are separate Codes of Practice for other cases dealt with by our specialist offices, such as where we suspect serious fraud.

This Code of Practice promises you fair treatment under the law and in accordance with the Taxpayer's Charter, which is reproduced at the bottom of this page. It explains the rules we will follow and your rights and responsibilities in particular situations.

We want you to pay the right amount of tax: no more, no less. We will do everything we reasonably can to help you make sure this happens.

Please let us know at any time if you need information about how to complete your tax return.

We also want you to feel confident other taxpayers are paying what they should and that we operate the tax system fairly.

To help achieve these aims, we enquire into some tax returns to check that they are right, or if we need further information to understand the figures. We want to make sure you do not pay too much tax or too little. Either way, we will tell you if we find something wrong. We do not set targets for the amount of additional tax our staff should collect.

To discourage tax evasion and ensure the whole system is operating fairly, we will select some returns for enquiry at random. We can then check if anything is wrong which may not be apparent on the face of the return.

At any time after you have sent in your return, you should tell us at once about anything in it which is wrong or which should have been in it but has been omitted. You may amend your self assessment at any time up to 12 months following the filing date (the filing date is normally 31 January following the tax year to which the return relates). You cannot make an amendment to your self assessment in the following circumstances

- when the return is under enquiry, but you should still tell us at once about any changes needed and we will take these into account at the end of the enquiry
- after 12 months following the filing date, but you should always tell us about any changes needed and we will then discuss with you how we can settle matters.

What we do when we receive your return

- We use the figures that you provide to establish the tax you should pay or, subject to certain checks, that we should repay to you.
- If we find any obvious mistakes, for example in the arithmetic, we may

correct them without making enquiries. If we do so we will send you details of the corrected figures. If you disagree with what we have done, you can ask us to reverse or amend any changes we have made.

- We carry out a comprehensive programme of checks. We look at information in your return and we also compare it with information from other sources.

- Following these checks, if we think there is a risk your return may be incorrect, or if we think something requires fuller explanation, we start enquiries.

- We also enquire into some returns at random.

- If we make enquiries into a return under Self Assessment it does not imply that we think it is incorrect, so when we ask questions or seek information we will not give reasons for making the enquiries. The initial request may, however, identify particular areas on which the enquiries will focus.

- If your return shows that you have paid too much tax, we will normally repay the excess to you. But if we have started enquiries into your return before the repayment is made, we will usually hold it back until we are sure the return is correct. However if it is clear from the facts that some repayment will be due whatever the outcome of our enquiries, we will repay that amount pending final settlement of your tax liability.

How an enquiry is conducted

Starting enquiries

- We will tell you in writing that we intend to start enquiries.

- We will tell you what your rights and responsibilities are.

- We will, at the same time, try to tell you the information we require. Exceptionally, we may not be able to do this, but we will always explain why and say when we expect to be able to do so.

- We normally have 12 months from the filing date for your return in which to tell you that we intend to start enquiries. We may have longer if you send in your return late. We will always have at least 12 months to enquire into any amendment that you make to your return.

- At the end of that period, if we have not begun enquiries, your return will normally become final. We can make an assessment after that period only if we discover an error which we could not reasonably have been expected to be aware of from the information provided in or with your return. In that case, we can make an assessment at any time up to 31 January five years after the end of the tax year. If we discover that your return was incorrect because of fraudulent or negligent conduct, we can make an assessment at any time up to 31 January twenty years after the end of the tax year.

Professional representation

- You can choose to be professionally represented, for example, by an accountant. You may exercise that right at any time.

- You may change or stop using a professional adviser at any time.

- We will deal with any professional adviser you have appointed unless you ask us not to. If there is little progress in settling matters, we will tell you and may then deal with you direct (or with any other professional adviser you may then appoint).

- You should make sure your professional adviser has all the facts. You will always be personally responsible for your own tax affairs and for the accuracy of all information supplied to us, even if you have a professional adviser.

Providing information

- We will ask questions and explain what further information we need as clearly and simply as possible.
- We may limit our enquiries to one or more specific aspects of your return. These may range from requests for clarification of particular entries, to detailed consideration of whether those entries have been treated correctly for tax purposes. They may involve a check of the records on which the particular entries were based.
- We may decide to conduct an extensive examination which considers all aspects of your tax affairs. Enquiries of this type will typically involve an in depth review of the records on which your return was based including, if you are self-employed, your business records.
- We will ask only for information which is relevant to the entries in your tax return.
- If we ask to see the records on which your return was based you should be able to provide these quickly and easily, as they should already be in your or your professional adviser's possession. If we decide we need other information, we will explain our request fully.
- We will take up as little of your time as possible by trying to ask early on in our enquiries for everything we need to know. We will try to avoid asking for information in a piecemeal way, but this is not always possible as one question may lead to another. It may help if you tell us about any special features of your personal financial affairs or your business which you think may be relevant to any questions we have asked.
- We will give you a reasonable amount of time to provide any information we need. You should tell us if you think we have not given you enough time to provide information and say how much more time you need, and why. We will let you have more time if this seems reasonable. If we cannot agree, we will tell you why.
- You should respond as promptly as you can when we ask for information. This will help to keep down your time and costs, and ours.
- You should tell us straightaway if you have difficulty obtaining the information we have asked for and we will discuss with you how you might obtain it. You should also tell us if you think it is not relevant to our enquiries. We will consider your reasons carefully and if we think we still need the information we will tell you why.
- If you do not provide the information we have asked for and we have to use our statutory powers to obtain it from you we will

  - explain our statutory powers to you
  - advise you of any penalties that might arise if you do not comply and

- tell you about your rights of appeal to independent Appeal Commissioners.

- If you are in business you can ask us to examine your records at your business premises. We will do so if possible. Sometimes we may wish to suggest this ourselves. This will save you sending them to us and can often be more convenient for everyone.

- We will always try to return your records as soon as possible. If you need them in the meantime, you may ask for the return of any records which we hold. You should tell us what you need, and when you expect to be able to return them. We will then

  - send them to you if we can. You should take care of these records so that you are able to return them to us complete and undamaged; or
  - if we need to keep them, we will give you copies. We will do this free of charge, and within seven days of receiving your request if possible.

- You should not let our enquiries into one year's return delay submission of a return for any other year. You may be unable to provide final figures because you think these might be affected in some way by the enquiries which are under way. If so, include your best estimates in the return and indicate which figures may be affected by the outcome of the existing enquiries.

- The information you provide should be correct to the best of your knowledge. If you provide information you know to be false, you could be liable to prosecution.

- You have the right to ask us why we are continuing our enquiries, if you believe that you have provided all the information and explanations necessary to check your return and that we have had adequate time to consider the information and explanations. We will reconsider the matter to see whether we can agree or explain what further information we need for checking your return.

- If you think we have no grounds for continuing our enquiry, you may ask the Appeal Commissioners to consider whether the enquiry should be closed. For example, you may believe that you have provided all the information reasonably required to determine the accuracy or completeness of the return, or that the enquiry is being prolonged unnecessarily by us.

Meetings

- We may ask to meet you to discuss those aspects of your financial affairs of which only you have first hand knowledge.

- You can ask your professional adviser, if you have one, to attend any meeting we have with you.

- You are not obliged to come to any meeting, but we will expect you to provide promptly any information we consider essential to our enquiries. Meetings allow you to clarify and explain any points you think we may not have understood, and allow you to ask questions as well. If we consider that correspondence will not be an adequate substitute for a meeting, we will make this clear to you.

- You should tell us if it is difficult for you to come to our offices. We may be able to meet you at a different location.

- You should ensure the answers you give us at meetings are correct. If you are not sure about an answer you should say so. Similarly, if afterwards you realise something you said at a meeting may have been wrong, you should tell us straightaway.
- You and your professional adviser should bring any documents which you think may help you answer questions or support points you might wish to raise about your return, or your business for the period under enquiry.
- We will make a written record of any meeting we have with you and you can ask for a copy. We may ask you to sign a copy of our notes to show that they record the substance of what was said. You have the right to comment on these notes and to tell us about anything with which you do not agree. You do not have to sign them or comment on them, but a signed record could be useful if we cannot reach agreement and have to ask the Appeal Commissioners to resolve matters.

If we find nothing wrong

- If we find nothing wrong, we will tell you and let you know that our enquiries have finished.

If we find something wrong

Paying tax during our enquiries

- We will ask you to make a payment on account towards any additional tax we think may be due from you, but until your self assessment is amended, you do not have to pay anything additional on account if you do not think you should. However, making a payment on account will help reduce any interest charges if, at the end of our enquiries, we find you do owe additional tax. If it turns out that you have paid too much, we will repay with interest any tax you have overpaid.
- We may make a provisional amendment to your self assessment before the end of our enquiries. We may do this if we think that additional tax is due and that it might not be paid if we did not act promptly. We may also make assessments for earlier years. You have a right to appeal against any such assessments or amendments and may ask to postpone payment of any of the tax. If we cannot reach agreement, you may ask the Appeal Commissioners to decide how much tax you should pay at this stage of our enquiries.

Revised figures

- We will try to agree with you any changes needed to your own figures.
- We will only suggest changes we consider to be reasonable in the light of all the information we have.
- When our enquiries are completed, we will tell you in writing and set out any adjustments we think are necessary.
- We will always explain how we arrived at the figures we put forward. If you do not understand them you should let us know.

- We will invite you, if you agree with our figures, to amend your self assessment. You will have 30 days to do so. If you do not do so within 30 days, we will amend your self assessment.
- We may make an assessment for earlier years if necessary.

Appeal hearings

- You can appeal to independent Appeal Commissioners against any amendment we make to your self assessment or against any other assessment we make that you do not think is correct. You will have 30 days to do so.
- You can find out how to make an appeal by reading the notes with the amendment or assessment, or by asking us to explain the process to you. Or you can ask us for our leaflet IR37 'Appeals against tax' which tells you more about appeals and the Commissioners.
- We will try, wherever possible, to reach agreement with you about your tax without a formal hearing of any appeal.
- If agreement cannot be reached, you have the right to ask for any appeals to be heard by the Commissioners. We will arrange for this to be done or, if you prefer, you can contact the Clerk to the Commissioners yourself. We will give you the Clerk's address if you ask for it.
- If the appeal hearing has been arranged at your request and we think we will need more time to conclude our enquiries, we will ask the Commissioners to adjourn the hearing to a later date.
- We may ask the Commissioners to hear your appeal if there is little or no progress being made towards settling it by agreement.
- If the appeal hearing has been arranged at our request and you need more time to provide information, you may ask the Commissioners to adjourn the hearing to a later date. It will be up to them to decide whether to do so.
- We will tell you if we intend to ask the Commissioners to settle your appeal. We will explain the figures we propose to put forward at least 14 days before the date fixed for the hearing, unless there are exceptional circumstances. The figures we put forward may differ from those we suggested to you during our negotiations.
- You have the right to put your case to the Commissioners and to tell them the figures you believe to be correct.
- You can choose whether or not to have your case presented for you by a professional representative or by any other person, providing the Commissioners do not object.
- After listening to both parties and considering all the evidence, the Commissioners will decide whether the amendment or assessment should remain unchanged, be increased or be reduced.
- You may ask us, or, if you prefer, the Clerk to the Commissioners if there is anything about the appeal hearing procedure which you do not understand or feel you need to know.

Interest, surcharge and penalties

- Interest will be payable whenever amounts due are paid late. A surcharge (a fixed percentage of any tax unpaid at a specific date), or penalties, or both may also be due but surcharge and penalties cannot both be imposed on the same tax.

- We can seek penalties for incorrect returns only if an error was due to negligent or fraudulent conduct.
- When calculating any penalty, we will take into account the extent to which you disclosed voluntarily anything that was wrong, your help in concluding our enquiries and the seriousness of your errors or omissions. The way we work out penalties is set out in our leaflet IR73 'Inland Revenue enquiries: how settlements are negotiated'.
- You should tell us about any matters you think are relevant when we are working out the penalty to be charged.
- We will seek an agreed settlement on the amounts of tax, interest, surcharge and penalties due from you. If we cannot reach agreement, we may determine formally the penalty we consider appropriate.
- You have the right to appeal against any penalty determination, and can ask for the appeal to be heard by the Appeal Commissioners.
- We will also, where necessary, determine the amount of surcharge that may be due. You have the right to appeal against surcharge on the grounds that you had a reasonable excuse for not paying the tax on time.
- If you do not understand how we have calculated interest, surcharge or penalties, or why they are due, you should ask us, or your professional adviser, or read our leaflet IR73.

At the end of our enquiries

- When our enquiries have shown something is wrong we will
- explain what it is
- tell you how to get things right for the future
- make suggestions about improvements to your business or personal records if they do not meet legal requirements or we consider they are inadequate. If you are professionally represented, we may recommend that you seek advice from your professional adviser.
- If you are still unsure about the records you need to keep in future, or the amount of detail required, ask your professional adviser or us to help you. You may also ask for our leaflets SA/BK3 'Self Assessment – A guide to keeping records for the self employed' and SA/BK4 'Self Assessment – A general guide to keeping records'.
- If our enquiries show that your return was incorrect we may ask you to sign a Certificate of Disclosure, confirming that you have now declared all your taxable income and gains. We will not do so if our enquiries have shown your return was correct or overstated your taxable income or gains. We will take a very serious view if you sign a Certificate of Disclosure you know to be false, so you should consider it carefully before signing.
- If your return was incorrect because it overstated your taxable income or gains, we will repay any tax you have overpaid plus appropriate interest.

Your rights under the Taxpayer's Charter

During our enquiries

- We will always be courteous, fair and professional.

243

- We will deal promptly with letters from you or your professional adviser – normally within our 28 day target for replies. If we cannot reply quickly, for instance because of the amount or complexity of the material you have sent us, we will let you know the reason for the delay.

Keeping you informed

- Although we will not give reasons for making enquiries, we will explain your legal rights and the reasons for any actions we take as our enquiries proceed. We will tell you, for example, why we
    - think we need a meeting with you
    - are not satisfied with any explanation you may have given
    - are amending your self assessment
    - need to use our statutory powers to obtain information or documents
    - are reviewing your returns for earlier years
    - are making assessments for earlier years.

- You can ask us at any time to explain your rights, or tell you why we have taken a particular action, or explain what you are obliged to do under the law. You may ask for these explanations even if we have already given them to your professional adviser.
- You can also ask for any of our information leaflets, some of which are listed on the inside front cover. These have been written to help you.

Confidentiality

- You have the right to the same high degree of confidentiality which all taxpayers receive.
- We may ask you to discuss your personal tax affairs in front of other people such as your business partners, and your spouse or domestic partner. This may help speed up our enquiries, and help to reduce costs all round. But we will ask for your agreement beforehand. You do not have to discuss your personal tax affairs in front of other people. If there are matters you do not wish to discuss with others present, tell us.
- Only in the limited circumstances allowed by law (such as at Appeal Commissioners' hearings) will we give information to people you have not authorised.

Your costs

- We know that dealing with our questions may cost you time and money, so we will only ask for information we reasonably require to check that your return is correct.
- We will end our enquiries as soon as possible. That is, when we are confident your return is correct, or that all errors or omissions involving more than a trivial amount of tax have been identified and put right.
- Our leaflet Code of Practice 1 'Mistakes by the Inland Revenue' explains the circumstances in which we will give financial redress for mistakes we make.

Complaints

If you believe

- we have not followed our Code of Practice
- you have been denied your rights in some respect
- we have made a mistake
- you have been treated badly in some other way during our enquiries

you can ask for your case to be reviewed by the person in charge of the office in which the enquiry was carried out. We will give you the name of the Officer in Charge if you ask for it.

If you are still not satisfied you can ask the Controller who has overall responsibility for that office to examine your complaint. Our leaflet IR120 'You and the Inland Revenue' tells you how to do that. It is available from any Tax Enquiry Centre or Tax Office.

If the Controller does not settle your complaint to your satisfaction you can ask the Adjudicator to look into it and recommend appropriate action. The Adjudicator, whose services are free, is an impartial referee whose recommendations are independent. The address is

The Adjudicator's Office
Haymarket House
28 Haymarket
London SW1Y 4SP.

Tel: 020 7 930 2292
Fax: 020 7 930 2298

Finally, you can ask a Member of Parliament to refer a complaint to the independent Parliamentary Commissioner for Administration, commonly known as the 'Ombudsman'. Further information is available from

The Parliamentary Commissioner for Administration
Church House
Great Smith Street
London SW1P 3BW.
Tel: 020 7 276 2130

Suggestions

We set high standards for the way we carry out our enquiries and are constantly looking for ways to improve those standards.

If you would like to suggest any changes to the way we do things or if you have any comments about this Code of Practice, please write to us at this address

Inland Revenue
Compliance Division Strategy and Standards
5th Floor
South West Wing
Bush House
Strand
London WC2B 4RD.

The Taxpayer's Charter

You are entitled to expect the Inland Revenue

To be fair

- By settling your tax affairs impartially
- By expecting you to pay only what is due under the law
- By treating everyone with equal fairness

To help you

- To get your tax affairs right
- To understand your rights and obligations
- By providing clear leaflets and forms
- By giving you information and assistance at our enquiry offices
- By being courteous at all times

To provide an efficient service

- By settling your tax affairs promptly and accurately
- By keeping your private affairs strictly confidential
- By using the information you give us only as allowed by the law
- By keeping to a minimum your costs of complying with the law
- By keeping our costs down

To be accountable for what we do

- By setting standards for ourselves and publishing how well we live up to them

If you are not satisfied

- We will tell you exactly how to complain
- You can ask for your tax affairs to be looked at again
- You can appeal to an independent tribunal
- Your MP can refer your complaint to the Ombudsman

In return, we need you

- To be honest
- To give us accurate information
- To pay your tax on time

These notes are for guidance only and reflect the tax position at the time of writing. They do not affect your right of appeal about your own tax.

Issued by the Corporate Communications Office of the Inland Revenue

July 1996.

Inland Revenue: Help Sheets

1: Individual self-assessment

TAX RETURN — Individuals		**1 to 8**
TAX RETURN GUIDE		**1 to 30**

- IR310   War Widow's and dependant's pensions
- IR320   Gains on UK life insurance policies
- IR325   Other income
- IR330   Pension payments
- IR340   Interest eligible for relief on qualifying loans
- IR341   Enterprise Investment Scheme–Income Tax Relief
- IR342   Charitable giving

EMPLOYMENT Pages	**E1 and E2**
Notes on EMPLOYMENT	**EN1 to EN8**

- IR201   Vouchers, credit cards and tokens
- IR202   Living accommodation
- IR203   Car benefits and car fuel benefits
- IR204   Lump sums and compensation payments
- IR205   Foreign Earnings Deduction: Seafarers
- IR206   Capital allowances for employees and office holders
- IR207   Non-taxable payments or benefits for employees
- IR208   Payslips and coding notices
- IR210   Assets provided for private use
- IR211   Employment — residence and domicile issues
- IR212   Tax equalisation
- IR213   Payments in kind — assets transferred

MINISTERS OF RELIGION Pages	**M1 and M2**
Note on MINISTERS OF RELIGION	**MN1 to MN7**

- IR214   Service rights connected with job related living accommodation

SHARE SCHEMES Pages	**S1 to S4**
Notes on SHARE SCHEMES	**SN1 to SN8**

- IR216   Shares as benefits
- IR217   Shares acquired: post-acquisition charges
- IR218   Shares acquired: operation of Pay as You Earn (PAYE)
- IR219   Shares acquired, from your employment

SELF-EMPLOYMENT Pages	**SE1 to SE4**
Notes on SELF-EMPLOYMENT	**SEN1 to SEN11**

- IR220   More than one business
- IR222   How to calculate your taxable profits

- IR223   Rent a Room for traders
- IR224   Farmers and market gardeners
- IR227   Losses
- IR229   Information from your accounts
- IR231   Doctor's expenses
- IR232   Farm stock valuation
- IR233   The 'true and fair view' for professions and the adjustment on withdrawal of cash basis

LLOYDS Pages	**LU1 to LU4**
Notes on LLOYDS	**LUN1 to LUN14**

PARTNERSHIP Pages (Short Version)	**P1 and P2**
Notes on PARTNERSHIP (Short)	**PN1 to PN4**
PARTNERSHIP Pages (Full Version)	**P1 to P4**
Notes on PARTNERSHIP (Full)	**PN1 to PN6**

LAND AND PROPERTY Pages	**L1 and L2**
Notes on LAND AND PROPERTY	**LN1 to LN8**

- IR250   Capital allowances and balancing charges in a rental business
- IR251   Agricultural land and 'land managed as one estate'

FOREIGN Pages	**F1 to F5**
Notes on FOREIGN	**FN1 to FN26**

- IR260   Overlap
- IR261   Tax credit relief: capital gains
- IR321   Gains on foreign life insurance policies

TRUSTS ETC Pages	**T1 and T2**
Notes on TRUSTS ETC	**TN1 and TN3**

- IR270   Trusts and settlements - income treated as the settlors'

CAPITAL GAINS Pages	**CG1 and CG8**
Notes on CAPITAL GAINS	**CGN1 to CGN20**

- IR278   Temporary Non-residents and Capital Gains Tax
- IR279   Taper relief
- IR279   — Update
- IR280   Rebasing — assets held at 31 March 1982
- IR281   Husband and wife, divorce and separation
- IR282   Death, personal representatives and legatees
- IR283   Private residence relief
- IR284   Shares and Capital Gains Tax
- IR285   Share reorganisations, company takeovers and Capital Gains Tax
- IR286   Negligible value claims and Income Tax losses for new shares you have subscribed for in unlisted trading companies
- IR287   Employee share schemes and Capital Gains Tax
- IR288   Partnerships and Capital Gains Tax
- IR289   Retirement relief and Capital Gains Tax
- IR290   Business asset roll-over relief
- IR292   Land and leases, the valuation of land and Capital Gains Tax

- IR293   Chattels and Capital Gains Tax
- IR294   Trusts and Capital Gains Tax
- IR295   Relief for gifts and similar transactions
- IR296   Debts and Capital Gains Tax
- IR297   Enterprise Investment Scheme and Capital Gains Tax
- IR298   Venture Capital Trusts and Capital Gains Tax
- IR299   Non-resident trusts and Capital Gains Tax
- IR301   Calculation of the increase in tax charge on capital gains from non-resident, dual resident and immigrating trusts

NON-RESIDENCE ETC Pages   **NR1 and NR2**
Notes on NON-RESIDENCE ETC   **NRN1 to NRN12**
- IR300   Non-residents and investment income
- IR302   Dual residents
- IR303   Non-resident entertainers and sports persons
- IR304   Non-residents relief under double taxation agreements

TAX CALCULATION GUIDE

2:   Partnership forms
PARTNERSHIP TAX RETURN   **1 to 8**
          Partnership Statement (full)
          Trading pages
PARTNERSHIP TAX RETURN GUIDE   **1 to 17**
- IR380   Partnerships: foreign aspects

PARTNERSHIP LAND AND PROPERTY Pages   **PL1 and PL2**
Notes on PARTNERSHIP LAND AND PROPERTY   **PLN1 to PLN7**
PARTNERSHIP FOREIGN pages   **PF1 to PF4**
Notes on PARTNERSHIP FOREIGN   **PFN1 to PFN7**
PARTNERSHIP CHARGEABLE ASSETS   **PA1 and PA2**
Notes on PARTNERSHIP CHARGEABLE ASSETS   **PAN1 to PAN4**
PARTNERSHIP SAVINGS pages   **PS1 and PS2**
Notes on PARTNERSHIP SAVINGS   **PSN1 to PSN6**

3:   Trust and Estate forms
TRUST AND ESTATE TAX RETURN   **1 to 12**
TRUST AND ESTATE TAX RETURN GUIDE   **1 to 27**
- IR391   Trusts & Estate Tax Return

TRUST AND ESTATE TRADE pages   **TT1 to TT4**
Notes on TRUST AND ESTATE TRADE   **TTN1 to TTN7**
TRUST AND ESTATE LLOYDS pages   **TLU1 to TLU4**
Notes on TRUST AND ESTATE LLOYDS   **TLUN 1 to TLUN 12**
TRUST AND ESTATE PARTNERSHIP pages   **TP1 and TP2**
Notes on TRUST AND ESTATE PARTNERSHIP   **TPN1 to TPN5**
TRUST AND ESTATE LAND AND PROPERTY pages   **TL1 and TL2**
Notes on TRUST AND ESTATE LAND AND
PROPERTY   **TLN1 to TLN7**
TRUST AND ESTATE FOREIGN pages   **TF1 to TF5**

Notes on TRUST AND ESTATE FOREIGN pages   **TFN1 to TFN22**

- IR390   Trust and estates of deceased persons:
  tax credit relief for capital gains

TRUST AND ESTATE CAPITAL GAINS pages   **TC1 to TC8**
Notes on TRUST AND ESTATE CAPITAL GAINS   **TCN1 to TCN20**
TRUST AND ESTATE NON-RESIDENCE pages   **TNR1 and TNR2**
Notes on TRUST AND ESTATE NON-RESIDENCE   **TNRN1 to TNRN4**
TRUST AND ESTATE CHARITIES pages   **TCH1 and TCH2**
Notes on TRUST AND ESTATE CHARITIES   **TCHN1 and TCHN2**
TAX CALCULATION GUIDE FOR TRUSTS AND ESTATES

Transitional Provisions

Existing businesses

C.1   Businesses already trading on 5 April 1994 were on a preceding year basis until the fiscal year 1995/96. To facilitate the move to current year basis of assessment, the year 1996/97 was a transitional year. The year 1997/98 was the first year of assessment to which the current year basis fully applied.

The fiscal year 1996/97

C.2   The Revenue had clearly given much thought to the problem of the transitional year. The basic simple concept was that the preceding year basis period and the current year basis period for the year 1996/97 should be aggregated, with 50% of the profits being assessable. [*FA 1994, 20 Sch 2*].

Overlap relief on transition

C.3   However, if a business had used the closing year rules under the preceding year basis, and had an accounting date other than 5 April, then more than twelve months of accounts would have dropped out of assessment. For example, a business making up its accounts to 30 April in each year and having an initial accounting period of twelve months would have had assessments of:

Year 1 — 1 May to 5 April following
Year 2 — Year ended 30 April
Year 3 — Year ended 30 April

Thus, the first set of accounts would effectively have been assessed for two years eleven months giving an overlap of 23 months. The simple transitional rules would have given a reduction of that period of twelve months, but would not give credit for the remaining overlapped opening assessments.

C.4   To give relief for this additional period, the transitional provisions relating to overlap profits and periods were brought into play. Insofar as the assessable profits for the year 1997/98 related to a period falling before 6 April 1997, then the profit for that earlier period, before deduction of capital allowances, was transitional overlap profit and the number of days before 6 April 1997 was the overlap period. [*FA 1994, 20 Sch 2(4)(4A)*].

Example of transitional year without change of accounting date

C.5 Laura Moore has been in business for many years, making up her accounts to 30 June in each year.

Her adjusted profits are:	*Before CAs*	*Capital Allowances*	*After CAs*
	£	£	£
Year ended 30.6.94	10,000	500	9,500
Year ended 30.6.95	14,000 ⎫	600	
Year ended 30.6.96	16,500 ⎭		
Year ended 30.6.97	19,000	750	18,250

Her assessments are:

	£		£
1995/96	10,000 − 500 =		9,500
1996/97			
365/731 × (14,000 + 16,500)	15,229 − 600 =		14,629
1997/98			18,250

Overlap profits are:

279/365 × 19,000 = £14,524
based upon an overlap period of 1 July 1996 to 5 April 1997 = 279 days.

The capital allowance basis periods are:

1995/96 1.7.93 to 30.6.94
1996/97 1.7.94 to 30.6.96

The capital allowances for 1997/98 are based on the period of account 1 July 1996 to 30 June 1997.

Although additions and disposals are taken into the 1996/97 basis period for the two years ended 30 June 1996, only one year's allowances are available under the old provisions. The technical basis period will be the period 1 July 1995 to 30 June 1996, together with a gap period. Such a gap period is then added to the later basis period. [*CAA 1990, s 160(3)(b)* old provisions]. For 1997/98 the profits are those after capital allowances, with the allowances for the year ended 30 June 1997 being treated as trading expenses.

Change of accounting date in the transitional period

C.6 To enable businesses to use the simpler fiscal year basis, it was permissible to change the accounting date during the transitional period. The number of days between the last day of the preceding year basis period for the fiscal year 1995/96 to the new accounting date was calculated. The profits then assessable for 1996/97 were:

$$\text{Aggregate profits for the period} \times \frac{365}{\text{Total number of days in the period}}$$

253

C.7   Transitional Provisions

Because the new rules for capital allowances did not come into force until 1997/98, the profits were taken for all of the above periods before deducting capital allowances. The long basis period in the transitional year only gave rise to one year's writing-down allowances.

Example of transitional year with change of accounting date

C.7   If preferred, it was possible to prepare accounts to 5 April 1997 (or any other date). Where the accounting date was changed, the period of time between the end of the basis period for 1995/96 and 5 April 1997 (or the chosen date) is averaged, with 365 days of that period was used as the basis of assessment.

Example

C.8   Maurice Norton has been in business for many years, making up accounts to 30 June. He decides to change his accounting date to 5 April.

His adjusted profits are:

	£
Before capital allowances:	
Year ended 30.6.94	10,000
Year ended 30.6.95	14,000
Year ended 30.6.96	16,500
Period ended 5.4.97	13,950
After capital allowances:	
Year ended 5.4.98	18,250

His assessments are:

1995/96	10,000
1996/97	
365/1010 × (14,000 + 16,500 + 13,950)	16,063
1997/98	18,250

There is no overlap profits or overlap period.

The capital allowances basis periods are:

1995/96 1.7.93 to 30.6.94
1996/97 1.7.94 to 5.4.97

The capital allowances for 1997/98 are based on the period of account 6 April 1997 to 5 April 1998.

In this instance the additions and disposals of the period 1 July 1994 to 5 April 1997 are taken into the capital allowance computation for 1996/97. Again, it should be noted that the profits for the year ended 5 April 1998 will be net of capital allowances. Technically there is no reference to a basis period for 1997/98 but to the period of accounts of the year ended 5 April 1998.

Businesses not on PY basis for 1995/96

C.9   If a business was on an actual basis for 1995/96, then the basis period for 1996/97 was actual. Current year basis of assessment applied for 1997/98.

This could occur because of a partnership change without a continuation basis election. This is illustrated at paragraph 7.19 above. The same provision would apply to a new business that commenced before 6 April 1994 and which elected for an actual basis to apply to the second and third years of assessment under *ICTA 1988, s 62*.

Example

Maurice Jones commenced his trade on 1 May 1993, making up his accounts to 30 April each year. He has elected for actual basis to apply for 1994/95 and 1995/96.

His adjusted profits before capital allowances are:

	£
Year ended 30.4.94	27,375
Year ended 30.4.95	21,900
Year ended 30.4.96	15,372
Year ended 30.4.97	22,265

His capital allowances are:

Year of Assessment	Basis Period	£
1993/94	1.5.93 to 5.4.94	950
1994/95	6.4.94 to 5.4.95	1,310
1995/96	6.4.95 to 5.4.96	1,420
1996/97	6.4.96 to 5.4.97	1,200

For 1997/98 the period of account is the year ended 30 April 1997, thus giving an entitlement to one full year's writing-down allowances, but additions and disposals will only be included for the period 6 April 1997 to 30 April 1997. His capital allowances deductible from profits for that period are £1,095.

His assessments are:

		£	£
1993/94	1 May 1993 to 5 April 1994		
	Schedule D, Case I	25,500	
	340/365 × £27,375		
	Less capital allowances	950	24,550

1994/95	6 April 1994 to 5 April 1995			
	Schedule D, Case I			
	25/365 × £27,375	1,875		
	340/365 × £21,900	20,400	22,275	
	Less capital allowances		1,310	20,965

1995/96	6 April 1995 to 5 April 1996			
	Schedule D, Case I			
	25/365 × £21,900	1,500		
	341/366 × £15,372	14,322	15,822	
	Less capital allowances		1,420	14,402

1996/97	6 April 1996 to 5 April 1997			
	Schedule D, Case I			
	25/366 × £15,372	1,050		
	340/365 × £22,265	20,740	21,790	
	Less capital allowances		1,200	20,590

1997/98	Year ended 30 April 1997			
	Profits before capital			
	allowances		22,265	
	Less capital allowances		1,095	21,170

Overlap relief is available for 340 days, i.e. for the period 1 May 1996 to 5 April 1997, being 340/365 × £22,265 = £20,740.

Cessation of existing businesses

C.10   Under the transitional rules, if an existing business ceases to trade in the fiscal year 1997/98 the normal transitional rules applied for 1996/97 and the assessment for 1997/98 was the profits from the accounting date ending in 1996/97 to the date of cessation in 1997/98. [*ICTA 1988, s 63(b)*]. Transitional rules enable the Revenue to elect that the new rules were disapplied. [*FA 1994, 20 Sch 3(2)*]. If the Revenue took this option then the old rules were deemed to apply for 1995/96 and 1996/97, i.e. the assessment was based originally on the preceding year basis with the Revenue having the option to increase both the penultimate and pre-penultimate assessments to actual. The assessment for 1997/98 was then on the actual basis as under the old rules. The Revenue would normally only apply those provisions when profits were rising such that the actual basis would apply for the 1995/96, 1996/97 and 1997/98 assessments. [Inland Revenue SAT 1, 6.39].

If a business that had commenced before 6 April 1994 ceases in the fiscal year 1998/99 then the new rules, with transitional relief, applied. However, the Revenue had the option to elect for the 1996/97 assessment to be based upon the actual profits of the year ending 5 April 1997, rather than the assessable amount computed under transitional provisions. Overlap profit relief was then granted against the final assessment. [*FA 1994, 20 Sch 3(3)*].

Example of cessation in 1998/99

C.11 By comparison, if Laura Moore had ceased on 30 June 1998, with final profits of £24,000, her asessments would have been:

	£	£	£	CAs
1995/96			10,000	– 500
1996/97 transitional profits as above		15,229		
Revenue option to revise to actual				
86/365 × £16,500	3,887			
279/365 × £19,000	14,524	18,411		
Revenue opt for higher assessment			18,411	– 600
1997/98 year ended 30 June 1997			18,250	
1998/99 year ended 30 June 1998		24,000		
Less overlap profits		14,524	9,476	

Initially, the 1996/97 assessment will be based upon the transitional profits of £15,229. The Revenue have the option to increase the assessment to actual. Although, in law, interest would be charged on the increased tax liability from 31 January 1998 to the actual date of payment, the Revenue have announced that they will not charge that interest in normal circumstances.

The capital allowance basis periods will be:

1995/96	1.7.93 to 30.6.94
1996/97	1.7.94 to 30.6.96

For 1997/98 and subsequent periods, the allowances are deducted as trading expenses of the relevant period.

Her assessments will therefore be:

		£
1995/96	10,000 – 500 =	9,500
1996/97	18,411 – 600 =	17,811
1997/98		18,250
1998/99 (net of overlap relief)		9,476

Example of cessation in 1997/98

C.12 Assume that Laura Moore ceased trading on 30 June 1997, with adjusted profits for the year ended 30 June 1997 of £18,250.

Her assessments would then be:

	Without Election		With Revenue Election	
			Actual	Original
	£	£	£	£
1997/98	18,250			
Less overlap profits	14,524	3,726		
Actual				
(86/365 × £18,250)			4,300	
1996/97		15,229		
Actual (as above)			18.411	14,000
1995/96		10,000		10,000
Actual				
280/366 × £16,500 = 12,622				
86/365 × £14,000 = 3,298			15,920	

As the assessable profits under the old provisions on an actual basis are higher than under the new provisions, the Revenue would elect for the old rules to apply. The resulting assessments would therefore be:

1995/96	£15,920 – £500 = £15,420
1996/97	£18,411 – £600 = £17,811
1997/98	£4,300

In the above example it has been assumed that the quantum of capital allowances remain constant even though the basis periods change. For example with cessation on 30 June 1997 the basis periods would have become.

| 1995/96 | 1.7.93 to 5.4.96 |
| 1996/97 | 6.4.96 to 5.4.97 |

after an election for the actual 'old' basis by the Revenue.

The 1997/98 capital allowances would be based on the balancing adjustment on cessation and deducted from the profits to arrive at the adjusted profits for taxation.

By concession, the Revenue will not charge interest on the increased tax liability in 1996/97 from 31 January 1998 until 30 days after the issue of the revised demand.

Change of partner before 5 April 1997

C.13   For existing businesses that ceased after 6 April 1994 but before 5 April 1997, continuation elections were available and the old rules then applied. If the partners did not sign a continuation election under *ICTA 1988, s 113(2)*, then there was a deemed cessation, with the result that the old rules applied to the previous partnership and the new rules applied to the new partnership.

In the circumstances where profits were declining, so that there was no revision to actual basis on the application of the old cessation rules, then no continuation election would be made, thus using the new rules at an earlier stage. The comparison was with the period of dropout applicable under cessation rules compared with the period of dropout under transitional rules. Whichever average profit was higher would be allowed to drop out of account.

The transitional period

C.14 For partnerships trading before 6 April 1994 and still trading after 5 April 1997, the normal transitional rules apply. Therefore, in 1996/97, the profits of the accounts on the preceding year basis for that year, plus the profits for the current year basis for that year, are aggregated, and 365/731 of that figure was taken as the assessable amount. For 1997/98, the current year basis applied and the profits after capital allowances of the accounting period ending in that year formed the basis of assessment.

The transitional overlap relief was calculated for the period of time before 5 April 1997 included in the 1997/98 assessment, based upon the adjusted profits before capital allowances. That overlap relief was divided between the partners for use by them when they leave the partnership. Just as the assessable profits of the partnership for 1997/98 were divided between the partners in their profit-sharing ratio for the period of account, so the overlap profit relief was divided between the partners in accordance with their profit-sharing ratio for the period of overlap.

Transitional overlap relief was also calculated for all other sources of untaxed income as though it were the income of a second deemed trade.

Example

C.15 The Peter partnership has traded for many years, making up its accounts to 31 December in each year.

Its adjusted profits (before capital allowances) are:

	Profits £	Capital allowances £
Year ended 31.12.95	30,100 ⎱	2,500
Year ended 31.12.96	43,000 ⎰	
Year ended 31.12.97	50,000	2,000

The partners, Peter and Paul, share profits in the ratio 60%:40% until 31 March 1997, when profit shares become equal.

The assessable profits are:

		£	£
1996/97	Year ended 31.12.95	30,100	
	Year ended 31.12.96	43,000	
	365/731 × 73,100		36,500
Less capital allowances 1996/97			
(Basis period 1.1.95 to 31.12.96)			2,500
			34,000

	Divided	
Peter – 60%	20,400	
Paul – 40%	13,600	

1997/98	Year ended 31.12.97	50,000
	Less capital allowances	2,000
		48,000

	Divided	*Total*	*Peter*	*Paul*
		£	£	£
1.1.97 to 31.3.97	60:40	11,836	7,102	4,734
1.4.97 to 31.12.97	50:50	36,164	18,082	18,082
		48,000	25,184	22,816

Overlap profits are computed as follows:

Profits before capital allowances for year ended 31.12.97 = £50,000

	Total	*Peter*	*Paul*
	£	£	£
90/365 × £50,000 to 31.3.97	12,329	7,397	4,932
5/365 × £50,000 to 5.4.97	685	343	342
	13,014	7,740	5,274

Partnerships assessed on an actual basis in 1995/96

C.16 If an existing partnership has had a change of personnel before 5 April 1994 and has not made an *ICTA 1988, s 113(2)* election for the continuation basis, then *ICTA 1988, s 61(4)* applies so that the actual basis was used for the first four years of assessment. If the partnership change occurred during 1993/94, then actual basis applied for that year and the three following years. There was no transitional year in 1996/97. The new rules were then applied for 1997/98, with overlap profit relief being calculated in the normal way.

Example

C.17 The Rudge partnership has a change of partners on 30 September 1993 and no election was made for continuation basis to apply.

The adjusted profits before capital allowances are:

	£
Year ended 30.9.94	27,375
Year ended 30.9.95	29,200
Year ended 30.9.96	28,548
Year ended 30.9.97	36,500

Capital allowances are:

	£
1993/94 year ended 5.4.94	2,250
1994/95 year ended 5.4.95	3,310
1995/96 year ended 5.4.96	3,120
1996/97 year ended 5.4.97	2,640

For the accounting period to 30 September 1997, the new rules applied, so that additions and sales for the period from 6 April 1997 to 30 September 1997 were taken into account, together with the carried forward amount at 5 April 1997. One full year's writing down allowance applied.

Where there is an overlap of two periods of account the common period is deemed to fall in the first period of account only. [*CAA 1990, s 160(3)(a)*].

Assume that the computed capital allowances for 1997/98 amount to £2,920.

Actual basis will apply because of *ICTA 1988, s 61(4)* (old rules).

	£

1993/94
$187/365 \times 27,375$ $14,025 - 2,250 = 11,775$

1994/95
$178/365 \times 27,375 = 13,350$
$187/365 \times 29,200 = \underline{14,960}$ $28,310 - 3,310 = 25,000$

1995/96
$178/365 \times 29,200 = 14,240$
$188/366 \times 28,548 = \underline{14,664}$ $28,904 - 3,120 = 25,784$

1996/97
$178/366 \times 28,548 = 13,884$
$187/365 \times 36,500 = \underline{18,700}$ $32,584 - 2,640 = 29,944$

Under the new rules the current year basis applies:

	£

1997/98
Year ended 30.9.97 $(36,500 - 2,920)$ 33,580

With overlap profits of
$187/365 \times 36,500$ 18,700

The overlap profits will be divided between the partners in their profit-sharing ratio of the period 1 October 1996 to 5 April 1997.

C.18 If the partnership change occurred before 6 April 1993, then the normal transitional rules applied with the taxpayer having the option to revise the fifth and sixth year of assessment to actual. Should the transitional year be the sixth year, the assessments would have been as for the Rudge partnership above, i.e. actual basis until 1996/97 and current year basis thereafter. The same would effectively happen if 1996/97 is the fifth year and an election has been made under *ICTA 1988, s 62* for actual basis.

Farmer's averaging

C.19 The calculation of transitional overlap relief in 1997/98 was made before the farmers' averaging provisions were applied. This was because the overlap legislation referred to the profits before capital allowances arising in the basis period, and then to the proportion of those profits that related to the period prior to 6 April 1997. By comparison, the legislation in *ICTA 1988, s 96* referred to the averaging of profits after capital allowances relating to the year of assessment. *ICTA 1988, s 60(2)* refers to the basis period which is normally the twelve months ending after the previous accounting date. [*section 62(3)(b)*]. Accordingly, the profits before capital allowances for the accounting year crossing 5 April 1997 are apportioned to give transitional overlap relief carried forward in box 3.80. The farmers' averaging adjustment is then entered in box 3.81.

Where the average is to be applied to the years 1996/97 and 1997/98, or any later years, averaging is under the new rules, i.e. after capital allowances.

In the case of partnerships, the averaging up to and including 1995/96 and 1996/97 was made by reference to the partnership. Thereafter, i.e. for averaging for 1996/97 and 1997/98 or subsequent years, the claim and calculation is made by the individual partner. For partnerships commencing or deemed to have commenced on or after 6 April 1994, all claims are on an individual basis.

Anti-avoidance

C.20 The anti-avoidance provisions applied when profits were artificially moved from the period before averaging into the transitional averaging period, or if profits were moved backwards into a period of account that formed the basis of the transitional overlap relief.

The Inland Revenue applied the anti-avoidance legislation in the following circumstances:

(a) any change or modification of an existing accounting policy (e.g. a change in the basis of valuation of trading stock), but excluding any change of accounting date which brings the end of the basis period for 1996/97 closer to 5 April 1997 [*FA 1995, 22 Sch 14(2)*];

(b) any change of business practice, i.e. any change in an established practice of a trade as to:

    (i)   the obtaining of goods or services;

    (ii) the incurring of business expenses;

    (iii) the supply of goods or services;

    (iv) the invoicing of customers or clients;

    (v) the collection of debts; or

(vi) the obtaining or making of payments in advance or payments on account [*FA 1995, 22 Sch 14(3)*];

(c) any self-cancelling transaction, including an agreement for the sale or transfer of trading stock or work in progress or the acquisition or grant of an option which is subsequently exercised to buy back or re-acquire trading stock or work in progress [*FA 1995, 22 Sch 15, 16*];

(d) any transaction with a connected person [*FA 1995, 22 Sch 15*].

The anti-avoidance provisions did not apply where:

(a) the transaction was entered into solely for bona fide commercial reasons. The obtaining of a tax advantage is specifically stated not to be a bona fide commercial reason;

(b) the main benefit from the transaction that could reasonably be expected was not a tax advantage;

(c) the profits moved fall within the de minimis exemptions [*FA 1995, 22 Sch*], that is:

(i) where the average annual turnover for the relevant period is less than £50,000; or, for a partnership, £50,000 multiplied by the number of partners; or

(ii) where the amount of profits artificially moved into the relevant period is less than £10,000; or, for a partnership, £7,500 multiplied by the number of partners (up to 20) plus £1,000 per partner (above 20).

If profits were artificially moved into the transitional period, then the 1996/97 assessment was calculated in the normal manner. The assessment was then increased by 1.25 × the complementary percentage of the profits identified as being moved. The complementary percentage was [1 − (365/the number of days in the transitional period)] expressed as a percentage. The effect of the above was to impose an automatic penalty equal to 25% of the tax saving that the taxpayer sought to achieve by shifting profits.

In the same way, if profits were moved into the transitional overlap period, the 1997/98 assessment was based upon the profits as returned by the taxpayer, but the overlap profit relief was reduced by 1.25 × the increase in the overlap profit resulting from profits having been moved into that base period. Again, there was an automatic 25% penalty.

Where the remittance basis applied, any increase in remittances during the transitional period was not the subject of anti-avoidance legislation. [Inland Revenue booklet SAT 1, 10.5].

In addition to the above anti-avoidance rules, the provisions also applied to movements of income under Schedule D, Cases III to V (other than interest or profits from an overseas business) and to interest paid by individual partners on the refinancing of partnership borrowing.

The purpose of the anti-avoidance legislation penalty was to ensure that taxpayers did not gamble on making such transactions on the assumption that they could not be worse off. If the anti-avoidance provisions were triggered there was an automatic increase in the amount payable.

The tax return enabled taxpayers to correct any such transactions after accounts had been prepared, but before the tax return was filed, without penalty.

Losses — fiscal year basis in practice

C.21 Under the previous legislation, relief for trading losses was technically given on an actual basis. In practice, the strict basis was not always used and instead loss relief was given on a basis equivalent to a current year basis. That is, relief was given for the loss of the accounts ending in the fiscal year as opposed to apportioning losses over fiscal years. However, the strict basis always applied to the opening and closing years of a business and where the taxpayer had elected for that basis. A further complication was that capital allowances were dealt with separately, adding to the number of options for relief.

The old rules continued to apply to businesses trading on 5 April 1994 for the years of assessment up to and including 1995/96. Special rules applied for the year 1996/97. Relief in that year was against total income for 1996/97 or 1995/96. The time limit for claims in that year is twelve months after 31 January following the end of the fiscal year, i.e. 31 January 1999. To ensure that full relief was given for losses, they were treated as nil in the transitional calculation, but granted in full in the loss relief claim. If the loss was included in the normal transitional calculation, then one half or more of those losses could be effectively lost. The new rules applied to businesses that commenced on or after 6 April 1994 from that time, and to existing businesses from 1997/98.

Care was needed if a loss arose in the transitional period and the accounting date was changed. It was first necessary to compute the profit or loss for the 'relevant period' and for 'the twelve months to the new accounting date in 1996/97'. The 'relevant period' was the time from the end of the period assessed in 1995/96 to the commencement of the twelve months to the new accounting date in 1996/97. A loss for either period was treated as 'nil'. However, it may be that, because of apportionment, one or both periods show profits which were then included in the transitional relief assessment. (See Inland Revenue Help Sheet IR230 for further details). The normal rule was that, if a set of accounts showed an adjusted loss in the transitional period, one should not change the accounting date.

Loss relief in 1996/97

C.22 Because loss relief under the previous rules was given on a fiscal year basis, whereas assessments were calculated on a preceding year basis, there was not normally a duplication of losses in opening year aggregation. Accordingly, loss relief is not included in the calculation of the transitional year assessment. Trading losses available for 1996/97 were relieved in full against the taxpayer's general income for that year or the year preceding (1995/96), with any unused losses being available for carry forward against subsequent profits of the same trade.

It would appear that the transitional assessment was calculated by reference to the profits of the transitional period and that any *section 385* loss relief brought forward was deducted from the resultant assessable profits. In the same way, losses arising during the basis period for the transitional year were not restricted, but are available for carry forward in full under *section 385*.

Example

C.23   John Smith, who has made up his accounts to 31 December for many years, has the following adjusted profits and capital allowances. He is single and has other income of £5,000 per year. (Fiscal year basis of loss claim does not apply.)

	Profit before capital allowances	*Capital allowances*
	£	£
Year ended 31.12.94	7,000	1,450
31.12.95	2,100 }	
31.12.96	(10,000) }	600
31.12.97	6,000	450

Assessments with claim for *section 380* loss relief:
1995/96

Schedule D, Case I profits	7,000	
Less capital allowances	1,450	5,550
Other income		5,000
		10,550
Less section 380 loss (see below)		4,552
		5,998
Less personal allowance		3,525
		2,473

1996/97	Year ended 31.12.95	2,100	
	Year ended 31.12.96	NIL	

	365/731 × 2,100	1,048
Less capital allowances		600
		448
Other income		5,000
		5,448
Less section 380 loss (see below)		5,448
		NIL

Section 380 loss relief:

Loss year ended 31 December 1996		10,000

Available:

Year of loss (1996/97)	5,448	
Year preceding (1995/96)	4,552	10,000

Section 380 relief could have been claimed for the preceding year only. This would give a better result:

		£
Loss available in 1995/96 — £10,000		
1996/97 as above		5,448
Less personal allowances		3,765
		1,683

	£	£
1995/96 — as above		10,550
Less section 380 relief		10,000
		550
Less personal allowance		550
		NIL

The amount on which tax is payable is therefore reduced from £2,473 in 1995/96 to £1,683 in 1996/97.

Alternatively, relief could be claimed under *section 385* giving assessable amounts of:

1996/97 — Schedule D, Case I (as above)		448
Other income		5,000
		5,448
Less personal allowance		3,765
		1,683
1997/98 — Schedule D Case I	5,550	
Less loss b/f	10,000	
Loss c/f under *section 385*	4,450	NIL
Other income		5,000
Less personal allowance (say)		4,045
		955

This would leave £4,450 relievable against Schedule D, Case I profits after capital allowances of the year ended 31 December 1998 and subsequent years, which may be the best possible alternative dependant upon the total taxable income of 1998/99 and the tax rates in each year.

C.24   A loss in the transitional period, accompanied by a change of accounting date, can result in the loss being used in aggregation rather than in a separate loss claim.

Example

Joseph has the following adjusted profits and no claims for capital allowances:

	£
Year ended 30.4.95 profit	28,000
Year ended 30.4.96 loss	(12,000)
Period ended 31.3.97 profit	14,000

His profits of the relevant period are:

Year ended 30.4.95	28,000
Period ended 31.3.96	
11/12 × (12,000)	(11,000)
	17,000

His profits of the 12 months to 31.3.97:

Period ended 30.4.96	
1/12 × (12,000)	(1,000)
Period ended 31.3.97	14,000
	13,000

As both periods are profits the assessable amount will be:

1996/97
365/1066 × (17,000 + 13,000) =   10,272

By comparison, if Joseph had not changed his accounting date and his profits for the year to 30 April 1997 were £16,000, his assessments would be:

1996/97
365/731 × (28,000 + nil)   =   13,980

(with a loss relief claim available based upon £12,000 in 1996/97 and/or 1995/96)

1997/98   16,000

(with overlap relief of 340/365 = £14,905 to carry forward).

Schedule D, Case III

C.25   The basis of assessment under Schedule D, Case III has changed from the preceding year basis (in most instances) to an actual basis on all occasions. [*ICTA 1988, s 64*]. As with trading income, the provisions apply to new sources from 6 April 1994. In the case of existing sources, the old rules apply if the source ceased before 6 April 1998. [*FA 1994, 20 Sch 5*].

C.26   In the case of continuing sources, i.e. where the income arose before 6 April 1994 and continues beyond 5 April 1998, then:

(a)   the old rules apply for 1994/95 and 1995/96 (preceding year basis);

(b)   for 1996/97, the assessment will be one half of the interest received in 1995/96 and 1996/97 [*FA 1994, 20 Sch 4(2)*]; and

(c)   for 1997/98 and subsequent years, the income actually arising in the fiscal year forms the basis of assessment.

It must be remembered that if the old rules apply and there is a cessation, then the Revenue had the option to revise the penultimate assessment to actual.

Example of a continuing source

C.27   Henry Ing has received bank deposit interest for many years. His interest received is:

		£
Year ended	5 April 1995	1,800
	5 April 1996	1,750
	5 April 1997	1,650
	5 April 1998	1,500

His income assessable under Schedule D, Case III is:

		£
1995/96 (preceding year basis)		1,800
1996/97 (transitional year)		
Year ended 5.4.96	1,750	
Year ended 5.4.97	1,650	
	50% × 3,400	1,700
1997/98 (actual)		1,500

Example of a source closing before 5 April 1998

C.28   Henry closes his deposit account on 31 December 1997, with interest for that part year of £1,500.

His assessable Schedule D, Case III income would be:

	£
1995/96 (preceding year basis)	1,800
1996/97 (preceding year basis)	1,750
(with Revenue option to revise	
to actual — £1,650)	
1997/98 (actual)	1,500

(The transitional year (1996/97) only applies if the source continues beyond 5 April 1998.)

C.29   Summary of transitional basis of assessment

If source arises before 6 April 1994 and continues beyond 5 April 1998	Actual basis applies for 1997/98 onwards
	Transitional rules applied for 1996/97, that is one half of the income arising in 1995/96 and 1996/97
	Preceding year basis applied up to and including 1995/96. If 1995/96 was on actual basis, then actual basis will apply throughout.

If source commences after 5 April 1994   Actual basis applies throughout

If source ceases before 6 April 1998   Preceding year basis rules apply
and had commenced before 6 April 1994   throughout

Schedule D, Cases IV, V and VI

C.30   Where Schedule D, Case IV or V income arose, the rules for Schedule D, Case III above applied, unless the source was a foreign trade in which case the rules for Schedule D, Case I above applied.

In cases where Schedule D, Case VI income was being assessed on a preceding year basis, transitional provisions will applied for 1996/97 by taking 50% of the total of the income that would have been assessed for that year on the preceding year basis and the income assessable on the current year basis.

Index